Palgrave Studies in Democracy, Innovation, and Entrepreneurship for Growth

Series Editor
Elias G. Carayannis, The George Washington University, Washington, DC, USA

The central theme of this series is to explore why some areas grow and others stagnate, and to measure the effects and implications in a trans-disciplinary context that takes both historical evolution and geographical location into account. In other words, when, how and why does the nature and dynamics of a political regime inform and shape the drivers of growth and especially innovation and entrepreneurship? In this socio-economic and socio-technical context, how could we best achieve growth, financially and environmentally?

This series aims to address such issues as:

- How does technological advance occur, and what are the strategic processes and institutions involved?
- How are new businesses created? To what extent is intellectual property protected?
- Which cultural characteristics serve to promote or impede innovation? In what ways is wealth distributed or concentrated?

These are among the key questions framing policy and strategic decision-making at firm, industry, national, and regional levels.

A primary feature of the series is to consider the dynamics of innovation and entrepreneurship in the context of globalization, with particular respect to emerging markets, such as China, India, Russia, and Latin America. (For example, what are the implications of China's rapid transition from providing low-cost manufacturing and services to becoming an innovation powerhouse? How do the perspectives of history and geography explain this phenomenon?)

Contributions from researchers in a wide variety of fields will connect and relate the relationships and inter-dependencies among (1) Innovation, (2) Political Regime, and (3) Economic and Social Development. We will consider whether innovation is demonstrated differently across sectors (e.g., health, education, technology) and disciplines (e.g., social sciences, physical sciences), with an emphasis on discovering emerging patterns, factors, triggers, catalysts, and accelerators to innovation, and their impact on future research, practice, and policy.

This series will delve into what are the sustainable and sufficient growth mechanisms for the foreseeable future for developed, knowledge-based economies and societies (such as the EU and the US) in the context of multiple, concurrent and inter-connected "tipping-point" effects with short (MENA) as well as long (China, India) term effects from a geo-strategic, geo-economic, geo-political and geo-technological set of perspectives.

This conceptualization lies at the heart of the series, and offers to explore the correlation between democracy, innovation and growth.

More information about this series at
https://link.springer.com/bookseries/14635

Rajagopal · Ramesh Behl
Editors

Managing Disruptions in Business

Causes, Conflicts, and Control

palgrave
macmillan

Editors
Rajagopal
Tecnologico de Monterrey
EGADE Business School
Mexico City, Distrito Federal, Mexico

Ramesh Behl
International Management Institute
Bhubaneswar, Odisha, India

ISSN 2662-3641 ISSN 2662-365X (electronic)
Palgrave Studies in Democracy, Innovation, and Entrepreneurship for Growth
ISBN 978-3-030-79708-9 ISBN 978-3-030-79709-6 (eBook)
https://doi.org/10.1007/978-3-030-79709-6

This Palgrave Macmillan imprint is published by the registered company Springer Nature Switzerland AG
The registered company address is: Gewerbestrasse 11, 6330 Cham, Switzerland

Preface

Disruption in business is a recurring phenomenon evidenced when innovations spur in the society and economy. Companies often invest in resources to build distinctive capabilities to overpower the disruptive innovations in market. The theory of disruptive innovation has significantly influenced the industry and business circles as a powerful tool for estimating the success of business agglomerations within industries and predicting the risk and business growth of companies. The classic model of disruption emphasizes the penetration of a cheap, innovative substitute to a high-end product or service, then gradually move up the customer chain with gradual improvement in its quality to overpower the competition and lead the market. Disruption in market is driven by psychodynamics in its early stages, which succumbs to an entropy at the end of its lifecycle.

A disruptive innovation is a technology, product, or process that creeps up from the bottom line in an existing business and threatens to displace it. Gradually, it evolves to the point where it displaces the conventional business players. Disruptions have moved from business operations to administration processes over time. Digital management, Internet of Things, and Industry 4.0 revolution support various types of disruptions in business and management processes. Some customer-centric companies are experimenting to harnesses the collective wisdom of the organization to measure the potential of a particular innovation to damage an incumbent's business. The disruptions, thus, need to be viewed from the point of view of both positive and negative perspectives. However, in dynamic business scenarios that exist today, the organizational model changes along with the customer expectations and preferences. However, defensive playbook for confronting disruptive innovation often falls short. Indeed, disruption has greater effect on the less known, but vital, foundations such as the design cube comprising design-to-market, design-to-value, and design-to-system. Therefore, disruption in business and management threatens the architecture of the survival of a company in a way that alters the overall operations and philosophy of business.

Existing and long-standing businesses usually consider innovation as a threat to be met with defensive measures. Disruptive technology-led business models have driven down many companies because of their temporary surge in the market and left the story behind the industry. Disruptive innovation is, therefore, considered by most businesses as a destructive tool at face value. Nevertheless, in broad sense, disruption is regarded as a change agent within the market, industry, and company, that ensures the net effect of total market growth over time. The counter arguments on disruption offer a powerful growth avenue for frugal innovations and discovering new markets for the existing companies, incumbents, and start-ups. Disruption in business and management slow the process down, but may emerge as radical innovation and thrust its consequences heavily on the established market. During the initial phase, disruptive products serve as a strong instrument to acquire new customers and to build an organization that is capable of standing as a new competitor within the industry. Studies analyzing the effects of disruption in business and management suggest that customer focus holds the key determinant to co-evolve with radical innovations.

Most companies run by deep, experienced management teams dominate almost every industry and develop a shield against disruptive innovation. How do upstarts create disruption? Is disruption a management process of evolving companies? This book intends to document the experience of firms, management process, and business systems that have faced disruption and succeeded of slack markets. Deliberation in the book aims at discussing the causes and effects and challenges associated with the disruptions in business and management. Portraying disruption-resistant business designs, and customer value propositions across the industries are some of the comprehensive objectives of this international academic meet.

Most firms trying to gain competitive advantage build their marketing strategies based on product improvements as innovations to attract consumers and the society. The return on innovation investment concept correlates directly with organic growth, and links innovation-spending with financial performance in ways that can lead decision-makers to generate higher, more reliable returns on innovation and research and development. Various schools of thought during the classical, neo-classical, and modern eras have contributed theories in support of learning organizations. Theory of disruption is a relatively new knowledge pool as compared to the schools of thought of twentieth century. The relationship between business models, value chains, and business ecosystems affects the business growth and performance. It explores new information-intensive business system in the production and services segments. The thematic discussion also focuses on the connection between technology and governance disruption, often enabling the latter in context of the former, or the latter offering prospects for the innovative entrepreneurs and investors to develop new business models.

Competitive advantage is built by the companies in an increasingly interconnected global economy. International firms collaborating with local enterprises often innovate their business models. Firms tend to develop design-to-market and collaborative business models (with stakeholders) for implementation through a set of activities to transform the existing businesses based on a socio-economic model. Besides, discussions also encompass sustainable development business modeling as the emerging global trend. Focusing on the affective reactions as behavioral responses to business disruptions caused by technology and innovation invasions, articles in this theme elaborate the strategy-as-practice perspective. Fast track innovations with prolonged technology lifecycle in high-velocity markets imply business considerations to manage frequent, unforeseen, potentially threatening, and disruptive incidents. Chronological evidence shows the evolution of several innovations in the governance models and planning instruments. The implementation of market-oriented planning innovations faces the major challenge of sustained lifecycle and managing value disruptions among the customers. Market-oriented innovations reinforce social, cultural, and geographical integration to overcome the disruptive market tendencies.

Business analytics demands an increased collaboration across organizations on issues relating to information selection and screening the datasets, and to warn managers about the data intricacies and risks, and teams about the information oversights. The software tools that a company considers as a part of business analytics span across various areas, including analytics, data integration, querying and reporting, and managing information technology projects. Manufacturing and operations systems including marketing, logistics, and inventory systems have been discussed in the articles in this theme. Over the years of government patronage in developing countries, the small and medium enterprises have spread their business across various economic sectors. These enterprises have built their sector-specific portfolios in customer-centric industries and business-to-business industries. The sectoral industries span across agribusiness, health care, education, and housing in the developing countries. The government policies and public infrastructure have set new trends in services in the emerging markets. Disruption in management is a complex phenomenon for emerging companies. However, disruption is a continuous process in business and marketing. To disrupt or not to disrupt, is a critical decision with the companies. Young entrepreneurial companies evaluate the trade-offs between disruption and other strategies and critically appraise the costs and benefits of emerging enterprises as a disrupter. Doing so allows them to choose a strategy for market disruptors in a given market and time, and to learn its implications as the company commercializes its idea. The concept of classic disruption entails a small enterprise targeting the overlooked customers with an innovative and modest offering and gradually moving upstream market challenge. Different types of disruptions have different degrees of impact, which affect how companies prioritize risk management efforts. As disruptions occur with different frequencies or likelihoods, they are difficult to be identified in the initial stages of intervention.

Many forces drive local enterprises to globalize by expanding their brand reach and participating in foreign markets through various modes of entry. In developed countries, domestic markets have become mature and are seeking international markets. Regional enterprises in big emerging markets are mainly the domains of large, well-resourced national enterprises. These enterprises are now open to global trade and are supported by multinational companies and business diplomacy of the countries with trade power. Focusing on the above debate, articles in this thematic section discuss investment and domestic trade environment, internationalization and cross-country trade management, and globalization and business diversity. Global economy faces significant challenges as it continues to integrate high levels of public debt in Europe and North

America that are causing the fear of a negative impact on GDP growth. Emerging markets with young and growing populations are increasingly becoming the focus of rising consumption and production, and major providers of capital, talent, and innovation. Such economic and environmental growth in the business ecosystem endorses the above-mentioned attributes of global branding and product-innovation management across markets. Besides the core discussion on branding and innovation management, this section discusses various perspectives on global pricing, global supply chain management, and global market segmentation. The market competitiveness factors in global business have been discussed in this section.

Regional innovation strategies in the context of emerging innovation policies in emerging markets have been discussed in the articles of this theme. The impact of multi-level entrepreneurial governance, role of knowledge networks, and shifts in the consumerism are critically examined in the articles of this thematic section. As the adequate knowledge transfer programs do not support most of the innovation of small and medium enterprises, the knowledge diffusion strategies have been discussed in this section. Most companies did not expect the severity of disruptions in manufacturing and supply when the COVID-19 pandemic struck. To provide quick supply, there has been steep disruptions in manufacturing and supply of health care equipment segment. The supply chains in depth, which includes identifying alternate sources of items, is changing the way of procurement function to include revenue assurance.

This book discusses business disruptions as strategic measures to dominate the design-to-market, design-to-society, and design-to-value business segments. Auditing the disruption matrix in context of innovation, competitiveness, and customer value is the major contribution of this volume, which helps managers connect with the strengths and weaknesses of the firms in market and explore diversified opportunities. Innovation audit in the companies needs to be conducted following the contemporary trends that exhibit market and consumer behaviors toward the innovative products and services. Disruptive innovations led by trends tend to transform the market and consumers' landscape. These trends include shifts from closed to transparent and open models of innovation (openness), shifts from providing only physical products to industrial product-services combination (servitization), and moving from conventional manufacturing and marketing paradigms to Industry 4.0 business philosophy (automation).

This edited volume includes 22 articles spread across 6 themes, which aim at bringing together the international forum for raising rich discussion on symbiotic themes of disruption in business and management, and their impact on global-local business imperatives. It critically analyzes the convergence of disruption in innovation and technology, business practices, public policies, political ideologies, and consumer values to strengthen competitive business practices. The anthology of selected papers in this volume enriches the knowledge and skills on contemporary business models, disruptive and radical interventions in manufacturing, services, and marketing organizations. This book discusses about developing new business models and hybrid management perspectives to match with the changing priorities of regional economic development in the developing countries. The chapters in this volume envisage developing innovative business practices to overcome disruptive trends and collective and collaborative perspectives to match with the changing priorities of businesses in the emerging markets. Interestingly, this volume has an exclusive section on case studies, which manifests the ground reality of changing managing practices in developing economies.

The chapters in the book cover varied studies on entrepreneurship, resource planning and regional development. Hence, it will serve as a managerial guide and think tank for the researchers, management students, and working managers. This book will serve as an important resource for start-up firms, market analysts and business consultants engaged in local-global business ventures.

Mexico City, Mexico — Rajagopal
Bhubaneswar, India — Ramesh Behl
June 2021

Contents

Editors and Contributors

About the Editors

Dr. Rajagopal is Professor of Marketing at EGADE Business School of Monterrey Institute of Technology and Higher Education (ITESM), Mexico City Campus and Fellow of the Royal Society for Encouragement of Arts, Manufacture and Commerce, London. He is also fellow of the Chartered Management Institute, and Fellow of Institute of Operations Management, United Kingdom. He is also Adjunct Professor at Boston University, Boston, Massachusetts. He has been listed with biography in various international directories. Dr. Rajagopal holds Post-graduate and doctoral degrees in Economics and Marketing respectively from Ravishankar University in India. His specialization is in the fields of Marketing Management. He has to his credit 65 books on marketing management and rural development themes and over 400 research contributions that include published research papers in national and international refereed journals. He is Editor-in-Chief of *International Journal of Leisure and Tourism Marketing* and *International Journal of Business Competition and Growth*. He is on the editorial board of various journals of international repute. His research contributions have been recognized by the National Council of Science and Technology (CONACyT), Government of Mexico by awarding him the highest level of National Researcher-SNI

Level- III in 2013. Dr. Rajagopal received the recognition of Distinguished Professor of EGADE Business School, Tecnologico de Monterrey in December 2020.

Prof. Ramesh Behl is the Director and Professor at International Management Institute, Bhubaneswar and a full Professor at IMI Delhi. Prof. Ramesh Behl is credited with building and transforming IMI Bhubaneswar to an institution of National importance. Prof. Behl is a United Nations fellow on Information Systems and International Operations and a SAP Certified International Consultant. His teaching expertise includes Business Analytics, Enterprise Systems and Emerging Technologies. In addition to teaching, Prof. Behl is an active researcher in the area of e-Business and Business Analytics. He has also designed and developed several software for various industry applications. Prof. Behl has over thirty-five years of teaching, research, and consulting experience; and has worked with premier institutions like Indian Institute of Foreign Trade (IIFT), New Delhi, Indian Institute of Management (IIM), Lucknow and Statesman New Delhi. He has done number of research and consulting assignments for Government and Private Organizations in the areas of Information Systems and International Trade. He has authored Twenty-three Books, Seventeen Case Studies, and number of research papers. Prof. Ramesh Behl is an International Accredited Professor of International Accreditation Organization, USA. He sits on the Board of leading Business Schools and Technology Companies. Prof. Behl has conducted corporate trainings and trained over 8000 mid and senior level executives. He has also conducted training workshops for the faculties & students at various International universities in Singapore, Indonesia, Thailand, Hong Kong, Australia, China, Germany and Korea. He has received accolades and significant recognition as a demonstration of his leadership qualities and innovations such as "Outstanding Academic Award 2010" from SAP Inc. and "Best Professor in Information Technology" as part of Asia's Best B-School Awards presented by CMO Asia at Singapore in July 2011. Professor Behl has been conferred also with the awards of "Best Professor in Information Technology Management" as part of 21st Dewang Mehta Business School Awards on 23rd October, 2013, "Rashtriya Jewels Award", and "Shining Achievers Award" in January, 2015.

Contributors

Chandresh Baid holds a Ph.D. in Strategy and Entrepreneurship from Washington State University. He has obtained a graduate degree in mechanical engineering from IIT Guwahati and completed his M.B.A. from IIM Lucknow. Prior to pursuing his Ph.D., he worked with MNCs in IT Consulting and the Software Product Development domain for more than 15 years. His research interest includes strategy, entrepreneurship, and innovation management. His current research falls under two broad streams: resource acquisition & resource orchestration by entrepreneurial firms, and entrepreneurial failures and subsequent outcomes.

Devesh Baid is an Associate Professor in accounting and finance area at International Management Institute, Bhubaneshwar. He holds Masters in Commerce, CMA, CA (Inter), FDP (IIMA), and Ph.D. (IIT Bombay) degrees to his academic credential. He has more than 17 years of teaching, training, and consulting and research experience. He has published research papers & case studies in various reputed journals and presented papers in national and international conferences. He has served as consultant with National Institute of Agricultural Marketing, Ministry of Agriculture, Government of India besides other corporates business offices. He has conducted numerous MDP programs for working executives. He is fellow member of Institute of Cost Accountants of India.

Pronobesh Banerjee is an Associate Professor of Marketing at Indian Institute of Management, Kozhikode. He was previously an Assistant Professor at Pennsylvania State University, Abington College. He received his Ph.D. from the University of Kansas. His research focuses on consumer judgment and decision making, primarily in the area of context effect, choice conflict, and choice deferral. His research has been published at Psychological Science and appeared in many media outlets. He has presented at many international conferences such as Association of Consumer Research and Society for Consumer Psychology.

Subhajit Bhattacharya is serving as an Associate Professor, Marketing Area at XIM University Bhubaneswar (previously known as Xavier University Bhubaneswar). He has obtained doctoral degree in Business Administration from the University of Burdwan, India. He has more than 14 years of experience in academics and teaches different courses in the marketing domain. Dr. Subhajit has published articles in quite a few international journals mostly indexed in ABDC, Web of Science, and SCOPUS. He has also presented papers at several national and international conferences. He is the reviewer of several leading international journals.

M. Bhuvana, Ph.D. is working as Post-Doctoral Researcher of Indian Council of Social Science Research at the School of Management Studies, Vels Institute of Science, Technology & Advanced Studies (VISTAS), Chennai. She has published several papers in *Scopus Indexed Journals* and has written and published 3 Books in the field of Human Resources, Finance, and Management. She has been received 3 awards as a Best young researcher.

Promothesh Chatterjee is an Assistant Professor of Marketing at the University of Utah. He has Ph.D. in Marketing from the University of South Carolina. His research has appeared in numerous leading journals of marketing and psychology such as the *Journal of Consumer Research*, *Psychological Science*, *Journal of Academy of Marketing Science*, and *Organizational Behavior and Human Decision Processes*. His work has been featured in a variety of media outlets such as *MSNBC*, *TIME*, *The New York Times*, and *Chicago Tribune*.

Bindu Chhabra is a Professor of Organizational Behaviour and Human Resource Management and Dean (Academic Programs & International Relations) at International Management Institute, Bhubaneswar. She holds a Ph.D. in Psychology in stress management. She has over 22 years of teaching, research, and industry experience. Her areas of research interest include leadership, emotional intelligence, stress management, personality, and work attitudes. She has published various research papers in national and international journals and has presented papers in conferences in India and abroad. Prof. Chhabra has undertaken numerous Leadership Development Programs with the organizations such as SAIL, NTPC, BHEL, EIL, Power Grid, HPCL, Ministry of Social Defense and various other Government organizations. She is the recipient of National Education Leadership Award for Best Teacher in Human Resource Management. Her paper titled "Emotional Intelligence and Occupational Stress: A Study of Indian Border Security Force Personnel" was published in a reputed journal and won the Best Paper Award.

Subhasish Das works as an Assistant Professor at GIET University, Gunupur, one of the premier University in the state of Odisha, India.

He has completed his Ph.D. in Management from CUTM University, Odisha, India. He teaches Marketing Management, Retail Management, Service Marketing, etc., and his area of research is Customer Relationship Management (CRM) and Entrepreneurship. He has a couple of research papers published in reputed journals and in edited books. In addition, he has published papers in the proceedings of national and international conferences.

Sharanika Dhal is a research scholar, pursuing her Ph.D. in Business Administration at Birla Global University, Bhubaneswar. She has obtained M.B.A. in human resources management. Her areas of research interest are competency mapping, training and development, corporate social responsibility and key issues and challenges of hospital and healthcare sectors.

Munmun Goswami is currently pursuing her doctoral studies as a full-time Research Scholar (FPM-HRM) at XLRI Jamshedpur after spending almost a decade in corporate HR. She completed her engineering (electronics and communication), then completed PGDM from IIM Ahmedabad. She has rich work experience of a decade in HR in various industries, including aviation, banking, FMCG, and tourism. Her academic area of interest lies in work and life interface and the realms of positive psychology.

Linda D. Hollebeek, Ph.D. is a Senior Associate Professor of Marketing at Montpellier Business School and Full Professor of Marketing at Tallinn University of Technology (Adj.). Her research, which centers on customer/consumer engagement, has appeared in the *Journal of the Academy of Marketing Science*, *Journal of Service Research*, *International Journal of Research in Marketing, and Tourism Management*, among others. She is the recipient of the 2020 SERVSIG Emerging Scholar Award, has been named a Clarivate Highly Cited Researcher (2020) is included on Stanford University's Top 2% of Researchers (2020), and serves as Associate Editor of the *Journal of Service Research*.

Lalatendu Kesari Jena is an Assistant Professor (Human resources) in Xavier School of Human Resource Management, Xavier University, Bhubaneswar, India. He specializes in the areas of human resource planning, performance management, learning and development, and talent assessment. He has obtained Ph.D. from IIT Kharagpur, India, on the topic "Workplace Spirituality and Human Resource Effectiveness" and is pursuing Post Doc. on "Employee Retention and Leadership Challenges" at Loyola Leadership School, Universidad Loyola, Seville, Spain.

Lakshmi Kannan is an Assistant Professor in the area of Services Marketing, International Business and Managerial Economics at Ramaiah Institute of Management Bangalore. She has industry experience of about 20 years, which includes 5 years in the exports domain and 15 years in ITES sector.

Pradeep Kautish is an Associate Professor of Marketing at Institute of Management, Nirma University, Ahmedabad, India. He has published research papers in various reputed International journals.

Arpita Khare is a researcher and academician in University of Allahabad, Allahabad, India. She has published research papers in some of the reputed International journals like *International Journal of Consumer Studies*, *Journal of Retailing and Consumer Services*, *Marketing Intelligence & Planning*, *International Review of Retail, Distribution and Consumer Research*, and *International Journal of Retail & Distribution Management* to name a few. She is included on Stanford University's Top 2% of Researchers (2020) and in the editorial board of *International Journal of Retail & Distribution Management*, *Journal of Marketing Analytics* and *International Journal of Competition Business and Growth* etc.

Rohit Vishal Kumar has obtained doctoral degree in business management from University of Calcutta on his work in psychographic segmentation. He worked with ORG-MARG, New Delhi and TNS-MODE, Kolkata and joined academics in 2001 as Lecturer. Dr. Kumar is currently serving as faculty at International Management Institute, Bhubaneswar, India. He has several publications in international journals of repute.

Ranjani Kumari is FPM Scholar in marketing area at Chandragupt Institute of Management, India. Her areas of interest include green marketing, sustainability, mindful consumption, minimalism, and consumer behavior.

Andrée Marie López-Fernández is a business professor and researcher at the Universidad Panamericana. Her research areas of interest include corporate social responsibility, marketing strategy, and consumer behavior. She holds a Doctoral Degree in Administrative Sciences from the EGADE Business School, and is a Level-I member of the Mexican National System of Researchers by CONACYT.

Swaminathan Mani is a part-time research scholar, pursuing his second Ph.D. (Psychology) with Lovely professional university in India and has over 25 years of full-time industry work experience. He obtained his first Ph.D. in management from UPES, Dehradun in India. Presently, he works as a Vice President with a leading IT firm that is part of a large conglomerate in India.

Tamara Masters is an Assistant Professor of Marketing at the University of Utah, USA. She was previously an Assistant Professor at Brigham Young University. Her research focuses on consumer judgment and decision-making, primarily in the area of Neuro-psycho-economics. Her research has been published in academic journals such as the *Journal of Consumer Research* and *Journal of Consumer Psychology* and appeared in media outlets throughout the world including *The Wall Street Journal*, *Science*, and *Times of India*. Dr. Masters presents at international conferences such as the Association of Consumer Research and Society for Judgement and Decision Making.

Manit Mishra is an Associate Professor and Dean (Research & Strategic Initiatives) at International Management Institute Bhubaneswar. He has completed his Ph.D. in Business Administration from Utkal University, Bhubaneswar, India. His teaching expertise includes Marketing Analytics, Marketing Research, and Consumer Behavior. His areas of research interest are behavioral modeling and methodological research. He has published research papers in *Psychology & Marketing*; *Journal of Retailing and Consumer Services*; *Journal of Purchasing and Supply Management*; *International Journal of Retail & Distribution Management*; and *Journal of Marketing Analytics*, besides other publications. Overall, he has four "A" category research publications (Scopus/ABDC). He is Associate Editor of the journal *Global Business Review* and has received funding for research projects from organizations such as All India Council of Technical Education and Indian Council of Social Science Research.

Mridula Mishra, Ph.D. is Professor and domain head (HR) at Mittal School of Business, Lovely Professional University, India. She has over 25 years of experience in academics and Industry. Her research focusses on leadership and psychometric testing. After her doctorate in Psychology, she specialized in SIS projective test from SIS Centre, Anchorage, Alaska, USA.

Supriti Mishra has experience spans over 29 years with a mixed bag of experience from academic, industry, and non-profit sectors. She is serving as faculty at International Management Institute, Bhubaneswar, Indian. Her areas of specialization include strategy and corporate social responsibility (CSR). She has widely published in the areas of CSR, sustainability, and corporate governance in reputed refereed journals including FT50 indexed journals. She was a Visiting Fulbright Scholar at Leonard N. Stern School of Business of New York University during the year 2009–2010. She serves in the editorial board/team of journals including *Journal of Public Affairs*, Wiley.

Pitabas Mohanty has more than twenty-five years of teaching experience in Investments and Corporate Finance. He was a Visiting Fulbright Scholar at Leonard N. Stern School of Business of New York University in the year 2009–2010. He is actively engaged in research in corporate finance and investments and has many publications in books and refereed journals to his credit.

Snigdha Mohapatra is an Assistant Professor (OB-HR) at Birla Global University, Bhubaneswar, Odisha, India. She has completed her Ph.D. in Business Administration from Utkal University, Bhubaneswar. She is M.Phil. and M.A. in Psychology; and M.B.A. in HRM. She is a Merit Certificate awardee in M.A. (Psychology). Her teaching expertise includes Behavioral Psychology. Her areas of research interest are shopper psychology, emotional intelligence, and employee engagement.

T. Praveen Kumar is an Assistant Professor at the MS Ramaiah Institute of Management and has been in academics for ten years. He is passionate about teaching, research, and learning. He has completed his Ph.D. in Corporate Social Responsibility area from Bharathiar University, Tamil Nadu. He has been interested in statistical data analysis, econometrics modeling, reengineering, and quality management. He has presented papers in IISC, IIMs, Great Lakes Institute of Management, SP Jain Institute of Management. He has published research papers in Scopus indexed and peer-reviewed journals.

Ananya Rajagopal holds a Ph.D. in Administration with focus on Entrepreneurship and Marketing Strategies from EGADE Business School, Tecnológico de Monterrey. She also holds a B.S. degree in Industrial and Systems Engineering, a B.S. degree in International Business Administration, and M.B.A. with specialization in Strategic Management.

She currently holds the position of Research Professor at Universidad Anahuac Mexico, Mexico City. She has ample experience in the financial industry in Mexico City since 2006. She has published many papers in international refereed journals of repute and chapters in edited books. Ananya Rajagopal has contributed research works in various international conferences of high standing. She is also an author of a book on entrepreneurship.

N. V. Subbarao is a research scholar pursuing the FPM program at International Management Institute, Bhubaneswar. His research area is concerned with the understanding of social media usage behavior in job search and its wider implications to the employment ecosystem. Subba Rao has +25 years of work experience via marketing, sales, and business leadership (CXO) roles from leading global companies, including P&G, Conagra Foods, Bharti Airtel, Tata Docomo, Tanla Platforms, and as an entrepreneur. He is presently working as an Entrepreneur in Residence (EIR) with a private equity firm and is associated with several angel networks. Subba Rao's research interests include social media, entrepreneurship, social cybernetics and understanding consumer—technology interactions in the evolving social media and platform space.

Raouf Ahmed Rather is a scientific researcher at Kashmir University, Jammu and Kashmir, India. His research areas are social media, customer engagement, co-creation, service innovation, customer loyalty and crises. His recent work has been published in *European Journal of Marketing*, *Journal of Travel Research*, *Journal of Travel & Tourism Marketing*, among others. He also serves as a reviewer of leading international journals.

Pável Reyes-Mercado is a Professor of Marketing and Market Research at Anahuac University Mexico where he chairs the Marketing Research Group. He has earned Ph.D. in Management Science from EGADE Business School, Tecnologico de Monterrey. Mexico. He holds membership of the National Research System under the National Council of Science and Technology, Government of Mexico. His research focuses on technology adoption and entrepreneurial marketing. He has professional experience in Alcatel, Coca Cola Femsa, and HSBC Bank. He teaches courses on marketing for financial services, marketing analytics, pricing. He is invited professor for universities in India, Ecuador, and Mexico.

Kalpana Sahoo is an Assistant Professor in the area of Organizational Behavior at Xavier School of Human Resource Management, Xavier University, Bhubaneswar, India. She has more than 15 years of teaching experience. She has published several papers in the areas of Learned Optimism, Positive Psychology, Competency Mapping, Employee Engagement, Emotional Intelligence and Personality in national and international journals.

Abhipsa Satpathy is Ph.D. scholar in Xavier School of Human Resource Management, Xavier University Bhubaneswar, India. She holds a master's degree in psychology and specializes in counselling.

Megha Sharma, Ph.D. is an Associate Professor for Organizational Behaviour and Human Resource Management (OB and HRM) at NIIS Group of Institutions, Bhubaneswar, India. She has been associated with Management Education for over a decade now. She has expertise in the areas of Organizational Behaviour, Human Resource Management, Organizational Change & Development, Leadership & Team building, Psychology for Management and Talent Management.

Sourabh Sharma is an Associate Professor for Information Systems at International Management Institute (IMI), Bhubaneshwar, India. He is an eminent Management Consultant, outstanding Professional Practitioner, Trainer, Academician and Educationist Counselor in Management, has been associated with Management Education and Industrial practitioner for over two decades now. Dr. Sharma has organized five international conferences as a convener at International management Institute, Bhubaneswar jointly organized with EGADE Business School, Mexico. Dr. Sharma also have the international participation in the conferences organized at SASS, Chengdu, China in 2017 and B&ESI, Vienna, Austria in 2019. He has expertise in the areas of Management Information System, Enterprise Resource Planning, Database Management System, Digital Marketing, Software Project Management, Data warehousing & Mining and many different Programming languages.

S. Vasantha, Ph.D. is working as a Professor in the School of Management Studies, Vels Institute of Science, Technology and Advanced Studies. She has 27 years of Teaching and 10 years of research experience. She has published about 90 research articles in *Scopus Indexed Journals*, 75 papers in other indexed journals and published 8 books.

Jyoti Verma, Ph.D. is currently serving as Assistant Professor at Chandragupt Institute of Management Patna (CIMP), India. Her research interest areas are Knowledge Management and Knowledge Sharing, Attitudes and Job Satisfaction, Talent Acquisition and Management, Strategic Leadership Innovation in Services.

Rajeev Verma is currently serving as an Assistant Professor at Chandragupt Institute of Management Patna (CIMP). He did Fellow program from the Indian institute of Management (IIM) Indore, India. He has been instrumental in conducting leading significant research consultancy projects sponsored by Government of Bihar, Indian Railways, UK Global Research Fund and ITTO Japan.

List of Figures

List of Tables

List of Exhibits

PART I

Understanding Disruption in Developing Economies

CHAPTER 1

Critical Insights on Disruption in Marketing Strategies: Some Perspectives in Latin American Countries

Rajagopal

Understanding Disruption

Disruption in marketing is not a new phenomenon. Both planned and radical innovations have disrupted the growth of products and services over time in the consumer and industrial markets. The growth of technology has affected both high-end and low-end markets, which has disrupted the market economy, operations, and performance significantly since the mid-twentieth century. The disruptive products emerged with low-cost innovations, economies of scale, high perceived use value, and low operations costs, which have transformed consumer preferences, product demand, and market performance. The disruption in markets

Rajagopal (✉)
Tecnologico de Monterrey, EGADE Business School, Mexico City, Distrito Federal, Mexico
e-mail: rajagopal@tec.mx

Rajagopal and R. Behl (eds.), *Managing Disruptions in Business*, Palgrave Studies in Democracy, Innovation, and Entrepreneurship for Growth, https://doi.org/10.1007/978-3-030-79709-6_1

has both positive (high use value, low price, ease of use, and enhanced features of products) and negative (overriding the existing businesses, polarization in market competition, and trigger imbalance in industry performance). Most disruptive products enter market as a cheap substitute (frugal innovation) to a high-end product, which tend to establish in the market by increasing in quality and inculcating the customer value over time. Frugal innovations from local and international destinations penetrate low-end consumer markets by attacking on both price and quality and rapidly grow by altering the consumer preferences in mass customer segment. Such *big bang (BB)* disruption has infiltrated the consumer electronics, fashion accessories, shoes, and consumer packaged goods, and destroyed progressing product lines through e-commerce. The market for disruptive products has grown manifold today with the support of information technology, which has stimulated customers to use free navigation applications on mobile devices preloaded on smartphones. Such applications had entered the market with the devices made by TomTom, Garmin, and Magellan. Similar applications, which provide ease of use, value to customers, and assist in quick decision-making, are in competition today and are frequently developed as low-cost experiments with existing technologies to crash launch new products in the market. However, such innovation goes out of bounds of conventional marketing practices and drives consumers to adapt to the new market ecosystem with disruptive products. However, it is debatable whether to slow the disruptive innovation down at the cost of customers and to leverage high-end products competition in the marketing. Consequently, most customer-centric and technology companies are leaving low-end markets and diversifying into the product portfolios for premier customer segments. Such business drift has caused the congestion of low-cost technology-led products in the mass market and bottom-of-the-pyramid segment, which appears to be an unhealthy business practice (Downes & Nunes, 2013).

Marketing planning and business development of consumer products in association with consumers have been the contemporary trend in the consumer products companies. The design process of consumer-centric business models integrates customers, stakeholders, and entrepreneurs in delivering values. The need for innovation is instituted in the linear path of understanding the customer by identifying the problem, need, and solutions. Marketing of customer-centric products is aimed at nurturing customer emotions and developing positive perceptions toward the products and services (Beckman & Barry, 2007). The multidimensional growth of marketing organization is best understood as the next step in the evolution from a resource-centric business model to a customer-centric, knowledge-sharing model. It is a way of managing competitive markets that are particularly well adapted to stimulating the market leadership necessary to create economic value in the complex markets (Strikwerda & Stoelhorst, 2009). Business transformation in consumer-centric companies evolves over the years in reference to values-based governance. Market segments of consumer products deliver convenience to consumers and build on price-value convergence business model. Companies tend to target consumer-centric brands to the most effective target segment, which has the push- and pull-potential to attract new customers. The process of targeting the consumers includes need-based, anthropometric measures; and community oriented and public policy centered approaches.

Disruption in market and customer desires are often synchronized. The desire to have a quality product gradually turns into a need, which paves path for the disruptive products to enter the marketplace. Therefore, the market structure often takes shape from customers' point of view, which is exploited by the low-cost technology disrupters. The disrupters tend to understand customers' needs and launching the congruent products to stimulate the need. Most of the consumer brands such as Starbucks, Amazon, and Spirit Airlines Inc (Ultra low-cost airline of the USA) to name a few have emerged to grow as disruptive brands. However, over time, the power of a disruptive brand tends to grow unless the company creates a new competitive brand of a higher quality (Christensen et al., 2005). Confrontations between disruptive innovators and strong firms in the market explore the possibilities to adapt to the radical engagements in doing business. However, most companies feel that in view of the increasing market size of the disruptive products, making small or incremental changes may not be enough to override the effects of disruptions. They need to change their operating models and business systems from manufacturing to marketing, including the customer relations management perspectives (Iansiti, 2020).

Most consumer-focused companies highlight the distinction of attributes regarding innovativeness, technology applications, use value, and current trends of the product, driving the vogue-psychodynamics in positioning the brands. As consumers are sensitive to price and promotion offers, brands positioned on these indicators generate wider psychodynamics and purchase intentions among consumers. The brand advertisements are built around user-generated contents, and celebrity and professional endorsements. Pricing is one of the critical elements in segmenting the markets for the consumer products. Customer-centric segments can be identified by analyzing price sensitivity, product attributes, customer perceptions, and tradeoffs of competitors with customers. Building right market segments assures creating the right customer value in the marketplace. Effective business models can be developed by mapping the market evolution, causes and effects of changes, and technological development of products. These factors need to be integrated and critically examined in the process of determining the product lifecycle (Baker et al., 2010). Corporate success depends on building business strategies following relevant marketing research through the existing market chaos in the existing products and consumers in the marketplace. Since adapting to an innovative idea, whether it is a new product, package, price, or promotion, poses great risk for companies. An appropriate market analytics can help companies in developing effective business plans.

Many consumer companies use traditional forecasting models to measure competitive performance and predict the market shares of new products, or the effects of marketing strategies. Interaction among consumers, comprising normative influences and word-of-mouth, is one of the key processes behind this complex market behavior (Gilbert, 2007). Product design and research and development is a cycle of continuous improvement over time, that moves through the product idea generation, product selection, product development, and launch stages involving the research process continuously. Marketing communication has four elements including credibility, understanding of an audience, a solid argument, and effective communication. Consumer socialization through peer communication in social media has become an important marketing issue through the development and increasing popularity of social media.

Disruptive Business Practices in Latin America

Industrial firms (within paper, oil, and textile industries) in Colombia and Peru began sustainability-led manufacturing and marketing operations as disruptive measures to stay ahead in competition. The sustainability-driven business practices have eventually led to spin the commercialization, and mergers and acquisition processes in the region. In the above stated industries, the disruption in energy and emissions, and Green Extraction Technology (GET) process have emerged as a strong market differentiator against the conventional businesses (Radnejad & Vredenburg, 2019). Consequently, most industrial firms have changed their conventional business model to a new strategy of growing internationally with disruptive technology, which leads the firms to move from *problem child* to *cash cow* quadrant within the *product portfolio matrix*. In the paper industry, farm-based solutions like manufacturing paper with farm-waste (maize straw, sugarcane straw, husk, and wild cactus) have emerged as disruptive innovations and market competitive solutions in terms of pricing and quality. In addition, digital solutions are transforming the forest-based bio economy (Fracaro et al., 2012). Digitalization has enabled real-time, end-to-end supply chain visibility, improved delivery accuracy as well as stock level optimization and alignment with demand planning. Consequently, the deployment of technology to protect forest resources has opened up new avenues for disruptive innovations in the paper industry (Watanabe et al., 2018).

Digitalization in businesses in Latin American countries has emerged in the past two decades of the twenty-first century as a major disruptor among the conventional business operations. Latin American and Caribbean region has seen significant growth in the digitalization metrics, such as developing broadband infrastructure for enhancing the use of artificial intelligence, remote operations, and the adoption of the Internet and social media (Katz & Callorda, 2018). Technological innovation and digitalization of business operations have proved to be major disruptors in national business settings. Such disruption has led to significant transformations in business models, incremental and frugal innovations, and customer-centric strategy in Latin America. The scale and scope of these changes have significantly altered the market competition within the region (Bianchi et al., 2019). Countries such as Argentina, Venezuela, Ecuador, Peru, and Bolivia have even lowered the economic liberalization processes to encourage local innovations as a disruptive drive to compete with the business operations of multinational companies in these countries. However, conventional businesses in the countries of Latin America are confined to niche and face the challenge of responding to increasing levels of technology and automation, which still remains a potential threat to domestic market competition (Vendrell-Herrero et al., 2017).

The previous industrial revolutions have motivated Latin American firms to engage in developing customer-centric business and following systems approach to standardize the manufacturing and supply chain process. The *Industry 4.0* revolution has driven these companies to drive their business through digitalization process, which has emerged as a principal disruptive tool in the conventional business ecosystem. The digitalization process has developed firms that are able to innovate and adapt to the new scenario with the existing tools to differentiated themselves from the rest of the market over time. The digital transformation has not only helped firms in decision-making, but also enhanced their abilities to adjust to new market realities. Among many, a major effect of digitalization process includes working through technological platforms that seek to integrate into a single portal or access point all procedures pertaining to goods import, export, and transit operations. This process has accelerated the supply chain process and given competitive lead to the firms in the marketplace toward delivering products to the end-users (ECLAC, 2020).

Gradual disruption has taken place in the services segment besides manufacturing and marketing segments. Among many services operations, financial institutions are also using disruptive technologies to grow in the competition. Microfinance institutions in Mexico have been considered as disruptive to the banking system because they can cannibalize the market share of established financial institutions (banks). Compartamos Banco,[1] a microfinance company under the parent organization Gentrea in Mexico, is a successful disruption at large scale in the banking and finance industry. Compartamos has gone for initial public offer (IPO) in April 2007, and it was valued at $1.5 billion at the then current prices. This microfinance company has become the first bank wholly dedicated to microfinance to be quoted in a major stock exchange in the country. Since then, the financial market has become intensely competitive as both large established institutions and new entrants have entered the market to cater to the same customers (Chu & Larangeira, 2019).

[1] For details on institutional profile see https://www.compartamos.com.mx/compartamos.

Marketing Matrix

External Factor Evaluation (EFE) Matrix is a combination of several macro factors within the business and economic ecosystem. It is a strategic analysis tool used to evaluate the external environment affecting the marketing strategies of the firm. The EFE analytics reveal strengths and weaknesses of marketing strategies of a firm. The EFE matrix help firms identify the key external opportunities and threats that are affecting or might affect a company by analyzing categorically the political, economic, social, technological, environmental, and legal (PESTEL) factors. In addition, the industry attractiveness and market competition matrix discussed by Michael E. Porter emphasizes the impact of effects of new entrants, substitutes, and bargaining power of customers and suppliers also affect the market performance of the firm. However, the general rule is to identify as many key external and internal factors as possible. The EFE Matrix analysis extends the strategy focus of marketing capability of firms ambidextrously toward inside-out and outside-in perspectives. Such analysis helps in developing upstream buyer–supplier relationship and building downstream buyers' marketing capabilities (Yang et al., 2019).

Internal Factor Evaluation (IFE) Matrix is built around the analysis of strengths and weaknesses. This is a strategy tool used to evaluate firm's internal environment and to reveal its strengths and weaknesses. Strengths and weaknesses are used as the key internal factors in the evaluation. This matrix is a strategic management tool for auditing or evaluating major strengths and weaknesses in functional areas of a business. The analysis of matrix elements provides a basis for identifying and evaluating relationships among those areas. The IFE matrix is used in strategy formulation (Kaplan & Norton, 1992). The IFE matrix method conceptually relates to the Balanced Scorecard method, which involves following activities:

- Assessment
- Strategy
- Objectives
- Strategy map
- Measures and target
- Strategic initiatives
- Performance analysis (weights, ranking, cumulative effect)
- Alignment
- Evaluation.

The strategic position and stock evaluation matrix has four quadrants that place a strategy as aggressive, conservative, defensive, or competitive; and this gives us information on whether a certain strategy is suitable for our organization or not. It is visually represented by two axes that create four quadrants of which, two correspond to: Internal environment: financial strength and competitive advantage, and external environment organizational stability and industry strength. The broad elements in the matrix are exhibited in Fig. 1.1.

Growth-share matrix is a business tool, which uses relative market share and industry growth rate factors to evaluate the potential of business brand portfolio and suggest further investment strategies. One of the dimensions used to evaluate business portfolio is the relative market share, which explains that higher market share yields the higher cash returns. High market growth rate means higher earnings, and sometimes profits, but it also consumes lots of cash, which is used as investment to stimulate further growth. These two dimensions are explained by Star, cash Cow, Dog, and Problem Child in the product portfolio matrix. Stars operate in high growth industries and maintain high market share. Stars are both cash generators and cash users (Star). Cash cows are the most profitable

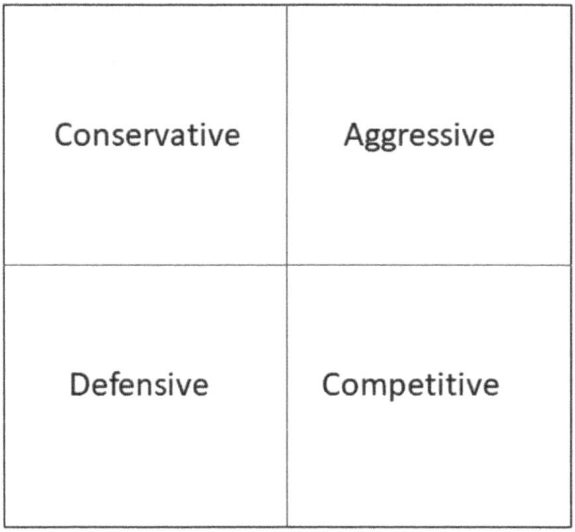

Fig. 1.1 Strategic position and evaluation matrix (*Source* Author)

brands and should be exploited to provide as much cash as possible. The revenue earned by such companies is invested into stars to support their further growth. Low market share compared to competitors and operated in a slowly growing market (Cash Cow). In general, these portfolios are not worth investing in because they generate low or negative cash returns (Dog). Some companies require much closer consideration to promote their brands in competitive and complex environments (Problem Child).

Quantitative strategic planning matrix is based on time-series analysis in business data to evaluate the performance of product portfolios in specific markets. The big data and business analytics methods support the performance analysis and decision-making for most companies in the competitive marketplace (Pérez-Chacón et al., 2020). The competitive matrix is an industry analysis tool similar to the Five Forces analysis suggested by Michael E. Porter. This matrix compares the characteristics of multiple brands within the market segment to identify their differences, strengths, and weaknesses. strategic measurement and performance evaluation tools discussed above are interrelated with the strategic marketing. The analysis of strengths, weaknesses, opportunities, and threats is associated with the industry attractiveness analysis and market competition matrix while the product portfolio matrix is related to the growth-market share analysis of a firm for specific brand portfolios. These strategic tools are affected by the internal and external factors. The balance score card suggested by Kaplan and Norton has emerged as the key tool to measure the organizational performance.

Markets for implementing brand strategies can be divided into three levels comprising premium markets, regular markets, and Bottom of the Pyramid (BoP) markets located in rural habitat in a region. Consumer behavior toward large firms in the premium markets and regular markets are generally driven by push factors including brand equity, brand personality, and brand endorsements; while brand strength is determined by the consumer pull factors like price advantage, social status, and perceived use value in the BoP market segments. The BoP marketing strategies are contemplated toward stimulating commerce which reveals that multinationals could radically improve the lives of billions of people and help create a more stable, less dangerous world. Achieving this goal does not require a multinational company to spearhead global social development initiatives for charitable purposes (Rajagopal, 2012).

Market Segmentation in Latin America

Traditionally, the companies based on demographic attributes of a market form market segments. Segmentation analysis allows the companies to understand buyer attitudes, motivations and values, patterns of usage, competitive preferences, and degree of association with the products. Current practices of market segmentation for consumer and industrial products show that most companies are relying on demographic and anthropomorphic segmentation by focusing on the cognitive dimensions of the consumers mapping their perceptions, attitudes, and behavior toward buying (Yankelovich, 1964). In the markets, where consumer preferences are congruent to products and services are largely inelastic to the innovative differentiations introduced by the competitors for a sustainable period for the homogeneous consumer segments. Such segments provide companies the opportunity to develop uniform marketing strategies in distribution, retailing and sales, pricing, promotions, and advertising to serve the market area. Consumers of certain age, interest, propensity of buying, and cognitive attributes form homogeneous markets. Market segmentation process in a company is woven indirectly around the consumer and his values, which helps companies to increase their market share and profitability in the selected market segment (Golub et al., 2000).

Market segmentation, targeting, and positioning are the key functions for a company to implement marketing-mix strategies in a marketplace. Market segmentation is specific to the consumption pattern and the consumer behavior within the region. There are different types of consumer segments including homogeneous, heterogeneous, and consumers with varied socio-economic profiles. Most consumer-centric companies develop market segments by evaluating the socio-economic profile, spending propensity, and consumption pattern of consumers, and their desire for vogue brands. The segments developed with the above criteria are classified as premium, mass (upper and lower), and bottom-of-the-pyramid consumer segments. In addition, companies considering the intensity of market competition, and the market players also segment markets (Cui, 2009). The classification of market segments based on the socio-economic profiles of consumers is presented in Table 1.1.

Age, gender, income, ethnicity, marital status, education, occupation, household size, length of residence, and type of residence, etc., constitute

Table 1.1 Socio-economic segmentation of consumers in Mexico

Socio-economic level	*Attributes of consumers*
A/B	Household income per month over US $7000 on an average. Members of family possess checking bank accounts and more than two credit cards. Live in homes or apartments with more than three or four bedrooms and two or three bathrooms
C+	Household income ranges between $3000 and $7000 per month. One or two credit cards will be available in the family. Live in homes or apartments with two or three bedrooms and one or two bathrooms. Family members own one or two cars, two telephone lines and two television sets. About 20 per cent of households in this category own a computer
C	Household income ranges between $1000 and $3000 per month. Some families have a credit card. Live in homes or apartments with two bedrooms and one bathroom. Own one basic automobile, one telephone line, one television set and one audio system
D+	Household income ranges between $600 and $1000 per month. Family members do not possess credit cards. Live in homes or apartments with one or two bedrooms and one bathroom. Do not own any automobile but have one telephone line and one radio
D	Household income ranges between $200 and $600 per month. No credit cards. Live in homes or apartments with one bedroom and one bathroom. Use public transport and communication means. Own one television set and one radio
E	Household income stays under $200 per month. Families live in small homes, a third of which have a bathroom, but most do not have a connection to a municipal sewage system. Household in the class do not possess a telephone but most have only one television set and one radio

Source Adapted from (a) Grupo Elektra (2000) *Annual Report*; (b) Chu, M., & Garcia-Cuellar, R. (2007). *Farmacias Similares: Private and Public Health Care for the Base of Pyramid in Mexico*. Boston, MA: Harvard Business School Case

the demographic variables used for segmenting the market. The territorial determinants comprise city, state, zip code, census tract, county, region, metropolitan or rural location, population density, climate, etc. The psychographic variables include attitudes, lifestyle, hobbies, risk aversion, personality traits, leadership traits, magazines read, and television programs watched. The behavioral variables include brand loyalty, usage level, benefits sought, distribution channels used, and reaction to marketing factors, etc. All these variables influence the market segmentation process of multinational companies. On commercial websites and search engines like Google, Bing, etc., every click on the links of digital communities, leads companies to gain unprecedented insights into individual consumers. The companies then target them with tailored advertisements, hands-on experience tools, and social metrics to develop brand association. However, the scope of liberal communication on digital space might be invasive to people, and it can prompt a strong backlash. Therefore, Marketers today need to understand where to draw the line in the hybrid-marketing environment (John et al., 2018).

Segmentation based on buying behavior reveals a tremendous differential among consumers toward propensity to spend on preferred product attributes such as convenience, status, and quality. Customer-centric segments can be identified by analyzing price sensitivity, product attributes, customer perceptions, and tradeoffs of competitors with customers. Building right market segments assures creating the right customer value in the marketplace (Cross & Dixit, 2005).

Micro- and Macro-Environments

Population, spending capacity of consumers, consumption pattern, and the market competition also contributes to the macroeconomic environment. Therefore, competitive advantages need to be designed in view of corporate goals, the macro-environment comprising politico-economic conditions, and the market competition. The micro-business environment consists of consumers, market segments, employees, organizational design, supply chain and operations management, market competition, investment, and stakeholders. These factors contribute to the internal marketing decision of the company.

The micro-and macro-environment factors affecting the marketing strategies and operations within the socio-economic market segments are illustrated in Table 1.2. These factors have been explained in the context of three retailing companies in Mexico-Elektra, Liverpool, and Palacio de Hierro in the services industry segment.

In Mexico, online and hybrid companies operate simultaneously in the marketplace. The hybrid companies operate on both digital platforms and brick-and-mortar infrastructures, which often create an invisible threat to the competing companies operating in the marketplace. Such markets are identified as ***hybrid market segments***. Hybrid market segments deliver convenience to consumers and build on price-value convergence business model. In this business model, any demographic, geographic,

Table 1.2 Micro- and macro-environment factors in selected companies in Mexico

Environmental indicators		*Elektra*	*Liverpool*	*Palacio de Hierro*
Macro	Demographic	Socio-economic segment—D+, D, and E	Socio-economic segment—C+ and C	Socio-economic segment—A/B
	Customer Spending	Credit linked (daily, weekly, monthly EMIs)	Cash and credit (monthly)	Cash and credit (monthly)
	Consumption Pattern	Subsistence	Economic and moderately high	Luxury or conspicuous
	Market competition	Lower niche, bottom-of-the-pyramid	Mass market competition	Mass and premium segment competition
Micro	Consumer Preferences	Low-cost technology and perceived use value	Contemporary trends, technology, and overseas brands	Vogue, signature brands, high value technology, status
	Price	Low price	Moderate price	Moderate to High Price
	Promotions	Credit- linked promotions, high frequency	Periodical promotions-discounts and credit promotions	Selective promotions
	Customer services	Credit-verification, and post-sales services	Post-sales, delivery, and customer relations	Delivery, customer relations
	Loyalty programs	Selective	Loyalty cards, memberships	Loyalty cards, memberships
	Augmented services	Negotiable	Guarantee, insurance	Guarantee, insurance
	Virtual sales	None	Yes	Yes

Source Author Research

psychographic, or behavioral variable can be used to classify people into segments. The target segments are chosen by the companies in reference to age, gender, economic profile, social relations, and peer influence. A differentiated and focused target segment serves for specific brands in a region, and over time. The market segmentation is also done in reference to the consumer preferences for product attributes, which are significantly linked to their lifestyle. The lifestyle theory suggests that the consumers' perceived hedonic attributes and social identity factors determine the shopping behavior of urban consumers (Zhu et al., 2009).

Industrial consumers transact products and services in the business-to-business market segment. The business-to-business clients buy products and services that are needed to perform business in their company. Public consumers have needs that are less defined. Larger companies have marketing departments that identify market segments and customer needs. In smaller companies, marketing is performed by engineering, sales, and management. Industrial markets include industrial markets consisting of intermediaries where all buyers are identified except the end buyers. Industrial clients buy raw material for production process and infrastructure development. The buying process is performed through negotiation between manufacturers, wholesalers, and the client following a direct transaction or via intermediaries. Many consumer product companies develop business-to-business marketing strategies for industrial clients. Furniture manufacturers often do this, opening up their tables, chairs, and couches to businesses that may want them for their corporate offices. This typically happens when the manufacturer's business grows to a large enough scale to accommodate larger orders. Service providers expand to industrial clients to take advantage of more lucrative contracts to deal with the services that contribute to an increase in the performance of clients. Most suppliers focus on customized procurement preferences of industrial clients and are governed by the client-specific Terms of Reference (TOR). Rather than trying to sell standardized products or services to the biggest possible set of buyers, B2B companies develop ways to help specific customers achieve better outcomes (Ettenson et al., 2018).

Three prominent products in the business-to-business segment are food and beverages, office supplies, and data and communication services. Food and energy production are competing within proximity to compete in the business-to-business market segment. Corn and sugar are becoming increasingly important for procurement in both sectors. These products are sold to industrial client on reverse auction business model. This model is based on the Monopsony principles where many suppliers target to one buyer. The buyers are segmented by the industrial needs, procurement policies, and locations while most supplier companies target them based on the buying potential, purchasing power, and propensity of buying. Agricultural technologies augment productivity even in difficult conditions, which drive price and supply benefits. The food-and-agribusiness value chain comprises a wide range of companies, from suppliers of agricultural machinery, seeds, chemicals, animal-health tests and vaccines, and packaged foods to data providers for precision agriculture (Goedde et al., 2015).

Office Supplies are technology-driven today. Some technologies created as many problems as they solved. Manufacturing-resource-planning (MRP) systems, for example, promised a fully automated solution to difficult production-scheduling activities. The office supplies range from stationery to electronic multifunctional systems that provide photocopying, printing, scanning, binding, and advanced office presentation services. In addition, Radio-frequency identification (RFID) tags were intended to provide a real-time view of the progress of every item from production line to customer, revolutionizing supply chain management in the process. In practice, high cost and difficulties in implementation have limited the use of the technology to a few niche areas (Alicke et al., 2017).

Data management and communication has been the major requirements of clients in the business-to-business market. The demand for data management in companies (especially banking, insurance, and capital businesses) has shifted from conventional mainframe management to Big Data and Cloud management. Big data is far more powerful than the analytics and communications of the past. These services make better predictions and smarter decisions in the companies. The notable data and communication companies are Microsoft, IBM, HP, Cisco, Oracle, and AT&T. They target more effective interventions in areas that so far have been dominated by gut and intuition rather than by data and rigor. The differences between big data and analytics are a matter of volume, velocity, and variety. Nearly real-time information makes it possible for a company to be much more agile than its competitors (McAfee & Brynjolfsson, 2012).

Traditionally, the companies based on demographic attributes of a market form market segments. Segmentation analysis allows the companies to understand buyer attitudes, motivations and values, patterns of usage, competitive preferences, and degree of association with the products. Current practices of market segmentation for consumer and industrial products show that most companies are relying on demographic and anthropomorphic segmentation by focusing on the cognitive dimensions of the consumers mapping their perceptions, attitudes, and behavior toward buying (Young & Javalgi, 2007). Market segmentation, targeting, and positioning are the key functions for a company to implement marketing-mix strategies in a marketplace. Market segmentation is specific to the consumption pattern and the consumer behavior within the region. There are different types of consumer segments, which include homogeneous, heterogeneous, and consumers with varied socio-economic profiles. Conducting a methodical marketing research is necessary for the companies to level the market segmentation, targeting, and positioning strategies; and intensify competitiveness among all firms, with the results of improved market efficiency and benefits to consumers and society (Guo, 2004).

Disruptive Product Development Process

Idea generation in the process of new product development is a major exercise. This technique calls for listing of all major attributes of the existing product and the needed attributes in order to improve the same product. Brainstorming has a major role in the idea generation process. Contemporary methods for ranking the relative merits of ideas generated by brainstorming sessions rely on comparing average scores across members of the group. Ideation process for new product development can be stimulated through metaphors, pictures, and experience. It is rooted in the philosophy of rationalism and empiricism, implying 'the truth is out there' approaches (Barczak & Kahn, 2012). It is observed that defining cognitive idea generation is based on personal experiences and beliefs driven by individual and social information. However, these forms of idea generation process are individualistic and not amenable to team contexts (Bhatt, 2000). Mentors provide motivations, set goals, develop entrepreneurial mindset, and resolve budget constraints in reference to the new product development or innovation projects.

Product ideas have to be turned into concept, and product concept can be turned later in to the brand concept. The concept testing calls for testing of these competing concepts with an appropriate group of target consumers. The concepts can be presented physically or symbolically. The consumers' response may be summarized, and the strength of the concept may be judged. The need-gap and product-gap levels may be checked and modified thereafter. The concept testing and product development methodology applies to any product or service. The business analysis includes estimating the sales as it would be of one-time purchase, frequently purchasing product or at regular interval purchase product. Consumer oriented innovation is an increasingly important source of new product development and the competitive advantage in reference to the speed with which product innovations are introduced to the market. In many cases, aesthetic properties are as important as technical functions (Petiot & Grognet, 2006).

Technology growth and consumerism are synchronized in the contemporary times. New ideas are need based and technology oriented, which, upon transforming into products, attract categorical geodemographic segments. The 3-dimensional printers are one of such innovations, which is positioned in the up-stream markets to cater to the high-end customers. The attributes and applications of 3-D printing enable partial customization at relatively low costs. However, this product is currently serving efficiently in the business-to-business market segment. 3-D printers can be identified as disruptive technologies that enable consumers to opt for either online services or owning the printer for personal or business use. However, such high-end products might significantly narrow down the scope of sales, user values, and competitive leverage in the markets of developing economies. Consequently, it is difficult for the high-end disruptive products to achieve the economies of scale in low-income countries (Berman, 2012). Disruptive technologies tend to underperform on attributes if they do not fit into the broad strategies of marketing-mix elements. However, reconfiguring the customer value propositions as a way to overcome the technological inferiority or superiority of disruptive technologies appears to be a major challenge (Pinkse & Bohnsack, 2017).

Product mix constitutes a bi-dimensional metric comprising product width (portfolios) and product line within the portfolio. An effective product proliferation in a company needs to be based on several principles that include asking consumers whether a greater assortment is required, arraying products into consumer-behavior-based strata, evaluating the associated stretching and pruning strategies for the new products, and measuring the leverage of mass customization. Wherever appropriate, companies need to offer more product choice while expanding the product mix, and implement effective strategies for managing the products across the consumer segments (Berman, 2011). A store may intentionally have a shallow product depth to keep inventory costs down. In other words, the product depth indicates the volume of products displayed in the shelf of retail outlets. Product mix is a sensitive matrix in the context of marketing, inventory management, and profit contribution. Often, the product mix is not managed objectively as top managers tend to associate with it emotionally. It causes disequilibrium in the product-market dynamics creating a rift between the fast- and slow-moving products. Therefore, product mix has to be handled efficiently to lower the costs and increase the profit contribution of each product within the product mix. The length and width of the product mix need to be aligned to identify the fast- and slow-moving products of the company for optimizing the product line. The slow-moving products should be pooled, and suitable product management strategy should be developed by measuring their market share and volume of sales. Based on product-metrics analysis in reference to the market share of products, consumer behavior, market competition, and corporate appropriate strategy can be selected by the companies. The product line can be stretched downward or upward, or both ways, depending upon the range of competitors, and the simultaneously existing product lines in the market. The downward stretch results in selling the upper-end products initially at cheaper rates. Product featuring is another strategy to promote the slow-moving products in a company. Consumer-centric companies highlight the use value of successful brands in each product portfolio by communicating the user-generated contents and consumer experience. In advertising the slow-moving products, companies generally endorse the name of the company like '*From the manufactures of Nestle Quality Products*' or endorse the name of successful brand of their own product portfolio such as '*From the manufacturer of Nescafe…*'.

It is necessary to control the overlap of products in the product line. Companies introduce new products with marginal differentiation within the product portfolio that create overlap of brands. Such product overlap strategy is developed and implemented by the companies to attract more customers to the product thereby increasing the overall market. This strategy leads to the long product line within a product portfolio, causing major problem toward the low market share and the profitability of products. Consequently, the product overlap strategy poses the threat of cannibalization of brands within the product line. The company should have a close understanding of consumer needs and uses of the products for effective implementation of the strategy. Implementation of this strategy helps companies in increasing business growth, market share, and profits. With system-of-products strategy, the company achieves monopolistic control over the market, which may lead to some problems and emphasize on its product/market opportunities.

Front-end activities comprising concept development, concept-design alignment, and concept-commercialization allow customer-centric firms to validate strategies accordingly. The combination and synchronization of these elements largely influence the process and performance of new product development. Firms create new ideas through any means such as the internal ideation process, crowdsourcing, or hybrid insights comprising internal ideation, collective intelligence, and aligned technology design. Such systematic approach provides firms not only the design-thinking perspectives for products, but also enables them to develop design-to-market strategies, which give the firms directions to gain competitive leverage, enhance customer outreach, and the product dynamics in the marketplace (Floren & Frishammar, 2012).

Social motivations to consumers are revealed as social self-concept, which drive consumers in developing consumption behavior. Hence, to enhance the scope of social brand, marketing firms stimulate perceptions of consumers and help in developing attitudes across geo-demographic consumer segments. Most consumer-centric companies implement educational marketing campaigns through social media and informal networks to reinforce the ethical, environmental, and societal benefits of organic production (McEachern & McClean, 2002). Social media has transformational effects on consumers, and it often alters their conventional consumption behavior. Consequently, the technological affordances of social media and indulgence of consumers in sharing and believing user-generated contents have engendered new forms of consumption practices in the utilitarian and hedonic products and services segments. Nonetheless, the community interactions through social media empower consumers to analyze shared experiences on digital network and form consumption opinions on social marketers. Producing new cultural and sustainable products, and socializing access to sustainable luxury brands (Rajagopal, 2020; Zhang, 2017).

Behavioral touch points like self-reference, family, peers, society, ethnicity, culture, education, communication, and community values influence consumers in developing and streamlining their perceptions and attitudes toward buying and consumption. Customer-centric companies develop corporate strategies to create consumer behavior and implement repeatability formulas to expand homogeneity in the consumption pattern. Due to the accessibility of information technology, consumer behavior tends to shift geo-demographically. Most companies, therefore, prefer to develop crowd-based business involving consumers, society, and stakeholders. Alternatively, companies are also engaged in developing hybrid approaches. The conventional consumer behavior has two common characteristics that exhibit consumption discipline and socio-psychological factors affecting consumption economics (Rajagopal, 2020; Zook & Allen, 2003).

Pricing Regulation: A Case of Mexico

In the competitive marketplace, prices of products and services are decided by the companies in the context of market trend and competitive leverage to the brands. Many companies tend to develop consumer value by creating the experience of value for money to increase product demand in every transaction. Contemporarily, firms lean on developing strategic pricing in order to gain competitive advantage in the market. The strategic perspective on pricing includes price objectives, price strategy, price structure, price levels, and price promotions. Globalization has driven various routes to market. Successful pricing strategies could create shared value in reference to augmenting consumer relationships, communicating the concept of value for money, and set proactive prices to encourage consumer buying behavior (Bertini & Gourville, 2012). Pricing structure is largely affected by the profit and cost center attributes that are immensely pushed by the firms to gain advantage over the competitors tactically. One of the pertinent problems in the profit-center structure is that it makes it impossible for the firm to consider a product's revenues and costs separately. Different price structures may be constructed based on various states of price equilibrium. A firm may engage in price competition if it has some sort of advantage enabling it to move first (Bryce et al., 2011).

Pricing plays a key role in the marketing strategy. Strategic choices about market targets, products, and distribution set guidelines for both price and promotion strategies. Product quality and features, type of distribution channel, end-users served, and the functions of intermediaries together help to establish a feasible price range. When an organization forms a new distribution network, selection of the channel and intermediaries may be driven by price strategy. Pricing regulation helps in controlling the fluctuations in prices and determining the customer value.

However, In Mexico the consumer pricing regulation as a public policy is not effective. The industry regulates consumer prices and maintains the competitive edge of pricing. The credit transaction and working capital buffer, borrowed from the primary market and banks, help companies in managing the credit and transactional gaps in business operations.

The food products prices remain uncontrolled in the country. The strict price controls were a feature of past regulations, recent regulations have been aimed at opening pharmaceutical pricing to allow more flexibility. Regulation of pharmaceutical prices in Mexico dates back to 1951, when the Act on Federal Executive Attributions in Economic Matters established maximum prices for drugs and other products. In 1984 a separate regulation for pharmaceutical prices was established in the General Health Law. Article 31 of the law conferred responsibility to the Secretaria de Comercio y Fomento Industrial (SECOFI, Ministry of Commerce and Industrial Development) to fix maximum retail prices for drugs. Based on this regulation, the maximum retail sales price for a drug was at that time based on analysis of the manufacturer's cost and operating expenditures with predetermined margins for manufacturers, wholesalers, and retailers (Moïse & Docteur, 2007).

Disruptive Pricing Effects

Companies in Mexico tend to play pricing as a customer-sensitive strategy to attract customers and offer pricing discounts, consumer credit, and promotions as major strategies to stimulate demand and acquiring new customers. The Mexican consumer economy is largely supported by a credit-driven consumption culture. Most companies attract sales through the credit incentives, loyalty programs, and direct discounts. Such marketplace strategy requires enough price attractions, sales promotions, and simple credit transactions. In addition, pricing strategy must play a pivotal role in curbing the switching behavior of shoppers in alternative channels or price sensitive markets (Roth, 2008). Many researchers argue that the increasing globalization is reducing heterogeneity in buying behaviors of young consumers as the consumer credit facilities are leading to augment the purchasing power. The increasing credit-led retailing has expanded the opportunity among consumers to access trendy products and stay tuned to fashion in the society. In addition, services like higher credit limits and domicile services are helping retail shops to acquire and retain customers with their brand tags (Srivastava, 2008).

Pricing regulation is effective in Mexico for sectoral products and services, which include pharmaceutical products and public utility services such as energy and water consumption. The authority responsible for applying and enforcing the regulatory framework in relation to pharmaceutical and medical devices is the Federal Commission for Protection against Sanitary Risks (COFEPRIS), which is a decentralized agency of the Ministry of Health. Price control in the private sector is based on a scheme of self-regulated maximum retail price (MRP) only covering patented products, overseen by the Ministry of Economy. Nonetheless, the participation of pharmaceutical companies in the price regulation process is voluntary. Under the price control norms, the MRP of predetermined products must not exceed an international reference price, which is estimated as the average price in six major markets in the North America and Latin America, plus a market factor. These reference markets change according to the consumer price indices, inflation, and demand and supply equilibrium. The MRP policy is not strictly reinforced in the country and there are no established sanctions for violations of the MRP.

The credit facilities and promotions attract customers of bottom-of-the-pyramid (socio-economic segment of D, D+, and E). According to evolutionary psychology (Griskevicius & Kenrick, 2013), conspicuous consumption may represent a means of competition in mate attraction. Consumers with low income tend to buy conspicuous goods on credit, as it signals high status to compensate for their feelings of economic powerlessness and the relatively inferior social value and lifestyle. The credit-led buying behavior among consumers in Mexico also promotes conspicuous buying behavior besides the other social and cognitive variables. Social comparisons drive conspicuous consumption effectively for those consumers who do not have a clear and well-articulated self-concept. Companies borrow finance from banks and primary markets manage the working capital emerging out of the credit gap. To achieve their extended goals, the companies use extended brands of high value products with affordable prices and credit-linked promotions for the mass market consumers (Immorlica et al., 2017).

Disruption and Strategic Thinking

Multinational companies are practicing reverse innovation as one of the best practices suggested by General Electric Company, in which products are designed first for consumers in low-income countries, and then adapted into disruptive offerings for developed economies. Companies adapting to the reverse innovation practices tend to market products at low price as it requires low technical requirements. Such reverse innovation products are created for low-income markets, but could have global appeal (Winter & Govindarajan, 2015). Disruptive innovation is linked to reverse innovation that drives the firms back to the consumers' buying behavior in reference to 4As paradigm comprising awareness, acceptability, adaptability, and affordability. Reverse innovation refers to developing ideas in emerging markets and persuading them in the existing markets, which drives tough challenges. Such innovation requires a company to overcome the institutionalized thinking that guides its actions and acquires ideas through the social media. Firms following reverse innovation develop a radically simpler and cheaper way of creating products in emerging markets and then position them in the desired consumer segments (Govindarajan, 2012; Rajagopal, 2014).

Implementation of effective marketing strategy is a 'building-block' exercise, which requires perfect coordination among various elements of marketing-mix and associated attributes like emotions, validity of decisions, and consumer value. Such architecture of marketing strategies helps companies in developing a brilliant breakthrough of their products and services in the competitive marketplace. There are several ways to develop and implement a successful marketing strategy experimented by the companies in the past century. Marketing strategies are developed by the companies to fit into organizational design of the companies. Design of a marketing organization is founded on the structural variables, organizational resources including human capital and finance, capabilities and competencies, and the workplace culture. The performance of marketing strategies varies for the companies with different organizational designs representing prospectors, analyzers, low-cost defenders, and competitive differentiation oriented company policies (Rajagopal, 2021).

As the competition of disruptive products increases, most companies tend to spend more in advertisement, promotions, and deliveries of products. However, the companies face the dilemma to trade-off between full-cost and marginal-cost (Christensen et al., 2008). As the competition is increasing, companies are shifting from category-focused marketing to an ecosystem-focused strategic mindset, which accounts for the network-based marketing engaging consumers in co-designing market performance and values. Such shifts in corporate philosophies have altered consumer preference, strategy choices, and customer networks from conventional platforms. The impact of the shift in strategic mindset toward ecosystems on competitive structure analysis has induced companies to follow strategies of successful brands, competitive strategy analysis, promotion planning, new product development, customer valuation, strategic alliances, and market segmentation (Dass & Kumar, 2014).

Strategic planning is a long-term approach in managing various perspectives of organizational growth and administering managerial activities to reach prolonged goals. In strategic planning process firms document managerial approaches and establish a direction to reach out the long-term goals by assessing various linear and discrete activities. The strategic plan helps firms to build and refine organizational mission, vision, objectives, and values to achieve them collectively. The strategy determinants aim to evaluate how the company visualizes the activity integration within the broad organizational framework that embeds mission, vision, and objectives. In the strategic planning firms aim to create value through the following elements (Gomes-Teixeira & Junior, 2019):

- Approach—develops long-term mission, vision, and objectives of the firm in various business portfolios categorically,
- Objective—identifies the purpose of the growth and activity integration,
- Support—assesses senior managerial relationship to integration,
- Importance—evaluates the commitment and maturity that the company has to integration, and
- Decision-making—evaluates the degree of influence across the areas of work within the organization.

The organizational parameter focuses on evaluating how the values, beliefs, behaviors, and mission of the company are converged with organizational design, function and culture. A strategic planning system is a structured process, which helps firms in organizing and coordinating the activities of managers who plan. A strategic planning system develops an integrated, coordinated, and consistent growth through a long-term plan of action, and facilitates adaptation of the change management within the company. Among many factors, communication of corporate performance goals, the goal-setting process, organizational design, managerial roles, the corporate planner's tasks, and the linkage of planning and budgeting affect the strategic planning in an organization to carry out its administrative activities (Lorange & Vancil, 1976).

Over the years, strategic planning has evolved to build organizational culture, group dynamics, and leadership. Strategic planning originated in the management literature. It can be defined as breaking down a goal to achieve it into steps over predetermined time, formalizing those steps so that they can be implemented almost automatically, and articulating the anticipated consequences or results of each step (Mintzberg, 1994). By identifying basic trends and uncertainties, a manager constructs a series of scenarios that helps in overcoming the usual errors in decision-making. A strategic planning system is a structured process that organizes and coordinates the activities of managers who plan. A strategic planning system develops an integrated, coordinated, and consistent long-term plan of action, and facilitates adaptation of the corporation to environmental change. Successful strategic planning requires analyzing managerial goals, diffusing strategic knowledge, and developing operational resources. It is argued that though operational effectiveness is necessary to superior performance, is not sufficient, because its techniques are easy to imitate. In contrast, the essence of strategy is choosing a unique and valuable position in the systems of activities in an organization that can be synchronized with the goals of organizational growth (Porter, 1996).

Low-end competitors pose a major threat to the companies in an industry. A company operating in the marketing at relatively lower prices for a similar or identical product disrupts the growth of the product as it cannibalizes the market share of principal competing brands. Many such low-end companies exhibit a taxonomy of disruptors, which include bare-bone companies, raiders, improvers, or challengers. Bare-bone firms operate with emphasis of low price and limited functions focused on the customer convenience, while raiders enter the market as attackers. These firms apply quick response strategies including features of product attractiveness, low prices, rapid and convenient deliveries, and multi-layers product promotions to gain the market share by cannibalizing the market share of competitors within proximity. Companies entering the market with disruptive products as an incremental innovation are less harmful to competitors. These firms play the role of improvers in the market and deliver positive effects of disruption. Challenger companies penetrate a market with strong financial support, strategies, and crowd cognition. However, disruptive tactics may serve effectively during short term, but low-end challenges are inevitable and remain in the market (Potter, 2004).

Strategic thinking helps new entrants adjust ecosystem with the socio-economic, cultural, and market-led factors that influence one another and stimulate the management of the design cube comprising design-to-market, design-to-society, and design-to-value. Business ecosystem is fundamentally based on these triadic design pillars. Large companies tend to explore radically new technology to disrupt existing markets, while new entrants focus on pursuing value-adding improvement in the existing products and technologies on the frugal innovation platform. In this process of orchestrating business ecosystems, multinational companies and joint ventures follow an integrative and long-term perspectives in business embedding business goals and strategic interests in decision-making. Such strategic business goals help these firms develop backward and forward linkages with suppliers and buyer-groups to develop operational integration (Zahra & Nambisan, 2012).

References

Alicke, K., Benavides, L., & Sankur, A. (2017). *The game changing supply-chain technologies*. McKinsey & Co.

Baker, W. L., Marn, M. V., & Zawada, C. C. (2010). *Do you have a long-term pricing strategy*. McKinsey & Co.

Barczak, G., & Kahn, K. B. (2012). Identifying new product development best practice. *Business Horizons*, *55*(3), 293–305.

Beckman, S. L., & Barry, M. (2007). Innovation as a learning process: Embedding design thinking. *California Management Review*, *50*(1), 25–56.

Berman, B. (2011). Strategies to reduce product proliferation. *Business Horizons*, *54*(6), 551–553.

Berman, B. (2012). 3-D printing: The new industrial revolution. *Business Horizons*, *55*(2), 155–162.

Bertini, M., & Gourville, J. T. (2012). Pricing to create shared value. *Harvard Business Review*, *90*(6), 96–104.

Bhatt, G. (2000). Organizing knowledge in the knowledge development cycle. *Journal of Knowledge Management*, *4*(1), 15–26.

Bianchi, C., Mingo, S., & Fernandez, V. (2019). Strategic management in Latin America: Challenges in a changing world. *Journal of Business Research*, *105*, 306–309.

Bryce, D. J., Dyer, J. H., & Hatch, N. W. (2011). Competing against free. *Harvard Business Review*, *89*(6), 104–110.

Christensen, C. M., Cook, S., & Hall, T. (2005). Marketing malpractice: The cause and the cure. *Harvard Business Review*, *83*(12), 74–83.

Christensen, C. M., Kaufman, S. P., & Shih, W. C. (2008). Innovation killers: How financial tools destroy your capacity to do new things. *Harvard Business Review*, *86*(1), 98–105.

Christensen, C. M., Raynor, M. E., & McDonald, R. (2015). What is disruptive innovation? *Harvard Business Review*, *93*(12), 44–53.

Cross, R. G., & Dixit, A. (2005). Customer-centric pricing: The surprising secret for profitability. *Business Horizons*, *48*(6), 483–491.

Chu, M., & Larangeira, C. (2019). *GENTERA: Facing the digital age*. Harvard Business School Press.

Cui, G. (2009). Segmenting China's consumer market. *Journal of International Consumer Marketing*, *11*(1), 55–76.

Dass, M., & Kumar, S. (2014). Bringing product and consumer ecosystems to the strategic forefront. *Business Horizons*, *57*(2), 225–234.

Downes, L., & Nunes, P. F. (2013). Big-bang disruption. *Harvard Business Review*, *91*(3), 44–56.

ECLAC. (2020). *Digital transformation in Latin American and Caribbean logistics. Economic Commission for Latin America and Caribbean*. Facilitation of Transport and Trade in Latin America and the Caribbean, Bulletin 381, No. 5, 1–17.

Ettenson, R., Grove, H., Knowles, J., & Sellers, K. (2018). Selling solutions isn't enough. *MIT Sloan Management Review*, *60*(1), 55–59.

Floren, H., & Frishammar, J. (2012). From Preliminary ideas to corroborated product definitions: Managing the front end of new product development. *California Management Review*, *54*(4), 20–43.

Fracaro, G., Vakkilainen, E., Hamaguchi, M., & Souza, S. (2012). Energy efficiency in the Brazilian pulp and paper industry. *Energies*, *5*(9), 3550–3572.

Gilbert, N. (2007). *Agent-based models: Quantitative applications in the social sciences*. Sage Publications.

Goedde, L., Horii, M., & Sanghvi, S. (2015). *Pursuing the global opportunity in food and agribusiness*. McKinsey & Co.

Golub, H., Henry, J., Forbis, J. L., Mehta, N. T., Lanning, M. J., Michaels, E. G., & Ohmae, K. (2000). Delivering value to customers. *McKinsey Quarterly*, June.

Gomes-Teixeira, G. F., & Junior, O. C. (2019). How to make strategic planning for corporate sustainability? *Journal of Cleaner Production, 230,* 1421–1431.

Govindarajan, V. (2012). A reverse innovation play book. *Harvard Business Review. 90*(4), 120–124.

Griskevicius, V., & Kenrick, D. T. (2013). Fundamental motives: How evolutionary needs influence consumer behavior. *Journal of Consumer Psychology, 23*(3), 372–386.

Guo, C. (2004). Marketing research: Cui Bono? *Business Horizons, 47*(5), 33–38.
Iansiti, M. (2020). From disruption to collision: The new competitive dynamics. *MIT Sloan Management Review, 61*(3), 34–39.
Immorlica, N., Kranton, R., Manea, M., & Stoddard, G. (2017). Social status in networks. *American Economic Journal: Microeconomics, 9*(1), 1–30.
John, L. K., Kim, T., & Barasz, K. (2018). *Ads that don't overstep.* Harvard Business School Publication.
Kaplan, R. S., & Norton, D. P. (1992). Balanced scorecard: Measures that drive performance. *Harvard Business Review, 70*(1), 172–180.
Katz, R., & Callorda, F. (2018). Accelerating the development of Latin American digital ecosystem and implications for broadband policy. *Telecommunications Policy, 42*(9), 661–681.
Lorange, P., & Vancil, R. F. (1976). How to design a strategic planning system. *Harvard Business Review, 54*(5), 75–81.
McAfee, A., & Brynjolfsson, E. (2012). Big Data: The management revolution. *Harvard Business Review, 90*(10), 60–68.
McEachern, M. G., & McClean, P. (2002). Organic Purchasing Motivations and Attitudes: Are they Ethical? *International Journal of Consumer Studies, 26*(2), 85–92.
Mintzberg, H. (1994). The fall and rise of strategic planning. *Harvard Business Review, 72*(1), 107–114.
Moïse, P., & Docteur, E. (2007). *Pharmaceutical pricing and reimbursement policies in Mexico* (Health Working Papers #25). Paris: Organization for Economic Co-operation and Development.
Pérez-Chacón, R., Asencio-Cortés, G., Martínez-Álvarez, F., & Troncoso, A. (2020). Big data time series forecasting based on pattern sequence similarity and its application to the electricity demand. *Information Sciences, 540*(1), 160–174.
Petiot, J. F., & Grognet, S. (2006). Product design: A vectors field-based approach for preference modeling. *Journal of Engineering Design, 17*(3), 217–233.
Pinkse, J., & Bohnsack, R. (2017). Value propositions for disruptive technologies: reconfiguration tactics in the case of electric vehicles. *California Management Review, 59*(4), 79–96.
Porter, M. E. (1996). What is strategy. *Harvard Business Review, 74*(6), 61–78.
Potter, D. (2004). Confronting low-end competition. *MIT Sloan Management Review, 41*(3), 41–49.
Radnejad, A. B., & Vredenburg, H. (2019). Disruptive technological process innovation in a process-oriented industry: A case study. *Journal of Engineering and Technology Management, 53*(1), 63–79.
Rajagopal. (2012). *Darwinian fitness in the global marketplace.* Palgrave Macmillan.

Rajagopal. (2014). *Architecting enterprise: Managing innovation, technology, and global competitiveness*. Palgrave Macmillan.
Rajagopal. (2020). *Sustainable businesses in developing economies—Socio-economic and governance perspectives*. Palgrave Macmillan.
Roth, A. E. (2008). What have we learned from market design? *The Economic Journal, 118*(527), 285–310.
Srivastava, R. K. (2008). Changing retail scene in India. *International Journal of Retail & Distribution Management, 36*(9), 714–721.
Strikwerda, J., & Stoelhorst, J. W. (2009). The emergence and evolution of the multidimensional organizations. *California Management Review, 51*(4), 11–31.
Vendrell-Herrero, F., Gomes, E., Mellahi, K., & Child, J. (2017). Building international business bridges in geographically isolated areas: The role of foreign market focus and outward looking competences in Latin American SMEs. *Journal of World Business, 52*(4), 489–502.
Watanabe, C., Naveed, N., & Neittaanmäki, P. (2018). Digital solutions transform the forest-based bioeconomy into a digital platform industry—A suggestion for a disruptive business model in the digital economy. *Technology in Society, 54,* 168–188.
Winter, A., & Govindarajan, V. (2015). Engineering reverse innovations. *Harvard Business Review, 93*(7), 80–89.
Yang, Z., Jiang, Y., & Xie, E. (2019). Buyer-supplier relational strength and buying firm's marketing capability: An outside-in perspective. *Industrial Marketing Management, 82*(1), 27–37.
Yankelovich, D. (1964). New criteria for market segmentation. *Harvard Business Review, 42*(2), 83–90.
Young, R. B., & Javalgi, R. G. (2007). International marketing research: A global project management perspective. *Business Horizons, 50*(2), 113–122.
Zahra, S. A., & Nambisan, S. (2012). Entrepreneurship and strategic thinking in business ecosystems. *Business Horizons, 55*(3), 219–229.
Zhang, L. (2017). Fashioning the feminine self in "prosumer capitalism": Women's work and the transnational reselling of Western luxury online. *Journal of Consumer Culture, 17*(2), 184–204.
Zhu, H., Wang, Q., Yan, L., & Wu, G. (2009). Are consumers what they consume? - Linking lifestyle segmentation to product attributes: An exploratory study of the Chinese mobile phone market. *Journal of Marketing Management, 25*(3–4), 295–314.
Zook, C., & Allen, J. (2003). Growth outside the core. *Harvard Business Review, 81*(12), 66–73.

CHAPTER 2

Disrupting Video Games: A Conceptual Framework for Managerial Skills Building

Pável Reyes-Mercado

Introduction

New technologies have changed the way actors interact in markets. Particularly, disruptive innovations are new products that change the fundamental ways of competing and attending customers. These disruptive innovations have a twofold effect on markets. On one hand, disruptive innovations create new markets. These innovations accomplish this goal by including less-than-optimal attributes that relate to lower prices. Due to this reason, fringe markets are the first to adopt this type of product since they look for basic functionality at a low price. The new product may be oversighted by big incumbent companies that typically overshoot their products by increasingly adding attributes that lack delivering marginal value to consumers. On the contrary, disruptive innovations as low-price,

P. Reyes-Mercado (✉)
School of Economics and Business, Marketing Department, Universidad Anáhuac México, Mexico City, Mexico
e-mail: pavel.reyes@anahuac.mx

Rajagopal and R. Behl (eds.), *Managing Disruptions in Business*, Palgrave Studies in Democracy, Innovation, and Entrepreneurship for Growth, https://doi.org/10.1007/978-3-030-79709-6_2

low-performance products can jump from the market fringe to the mainstream market and displace incumbent companies (Christensen et al., 2018). Additionally, disruptive innovations create new value networks by altering competition dynamics in this way that new players—even from outside traditional industries—and offer completely new products. New entrant to industries changes interaction not only by offering a new product, but also by developing networks with suppliers and customers in new organizational arrangements (Christensen et al., 2018). Examples of products considered as disruptive include personal computers, which were initially disregarded by manufacturers of mainframes as a threat to their product. Eventually, personal computers became the standard of computers. In this line, video games may represent a disruption to markets, not only due to their high economic value, but also due to the different audiences being attracted to the product. Video games were originally designed for kids, but more mature audiences have also been engaged to spend time playing different genres of video games. In this line, the product may become a disruptive innovation for activities outside the gaming industry.

Technology has gained a prominent place in the current global business environment. Learning is not aside. Half of worldwide population has access to Internet. Although Internet penetration rates show heterogeneity among countries, developing information and communication technologies (ICT) have taken the ubiquitous form of networked mobile devices as tablets and mobile phones, as well as laptops and video game consoles. Young people depend profoundly on technology to accomplish both utilitarian goals (e.g., search for car maintenance or learn how to fix water pipes) and hedonic activities (e.g., watch a movie or play a video game). Workplaces now include two generations: digital natives—the younger generation who "flow" and "immerse" in technology on an all-day-connected basis—engage in activities as social networking, texting, and video gaming, dimensions that shape digital competencies and skills (Prensky, 2001). Alongside this generation, digital immigrants—for whom technological development may represent a disruption—also use technology at varying degrees of skillfulness. These two groups may engage in workplace activities as problem-solving, team building, data analysis, and, hence the degree to which generations acquire and develop skills while playing video games, may be transferred to the workplace.

Existing research shows that managers acquire and develop skills through formal training, courses, coaching, and mentoring. The results of these sometimes mandatory interventions are related to job performance and career progression. Little is known about more leisure-like activities as video gaming and its impact on managers' skills formation. Existing research focuses on classroom settings for young generations (Adachi & Willoughby, 2013; Blumberg & Fisch, 2013) and hence this paper borrows from such literature. Specifically, researchers have studied how skills as spatial performance (Okagaki & Frensch, 1994), speed of processing (Dye et al., 2009), and learning, and attentional control (Green & Bavelier, 2012).

By discussing flow theory, theory of reasoned action, and personality traits theory, and using the manager as study unit, this paper aims to analyze relationships between video games usage and the resulting outcomes at the workplace. Flow theory maintains that people may engage in a state of focused attention while performing a task. Using such theoretical approaches, this paper aims to frame research proposals worth investigating:

- What is the antecedent relationship between video games usage and managers' flow?
- What are the effects of flow while video gaming on acquisition and development of managerial performance?
- What is the degree to which skills acquired and developed through flow are transferred toward workplace settings?

This paper is structured as follows: section two offers a discussion of relevant learning theories suitable to analyze how managers may acquire skills and proposes a conceptual framework along with research proposals. Section three discusses some possible paths for further testing the conceptual model. Section four closes the paper with concluding comments.

Literature Review

This section analyzes three theories deemed as suitable to research aspects of learning, personality, self-efficacy to leverage managerial skills at the workplace. Theory of flow helps explain how managers can achieve flow moments, which are important to further elaborate on learning outcomes. Personality traits may explain regarding individuals more prone to achieve flow instants and thus more prone to develop managerial performance.

Finally, theory of reasoned action helps include variables that may close a volitional gap for managers not so prone to get involved into flow.

Theories to Analyze Skills Leverage

Flow Theory

Flow theory maintains that individuals may engage in a particular mental state while performing an activity or task. Such mental state represents a moment of complete involvement, energized focus, and is related to joy and other positive emotions (Csikszentmihalyi & Nakamura, 1979). During flow, persons channel and align these emotions with the task. As emotions flow, a number of outcomes appear as meaningful learning, self-awareness, creativity, among others. Individuals perceive the task as self-rewarding, an aspect in which performing the task seems more important than achieving a particular goal. Individuals experience flow when personal skills and task challenge balance. When personal skills are low but task challenge is high, anxiety is present. In contrast, when personal skills are high but task challenge is low, relaxation appears. According to flow theory, a low-skill, low-task challenge scenario leads to apathy, whereas a high-skill, high-task challenge presents flow appears (Csikszentmihalyi, 1997). As video games are hedonic voluntary activities in which individuals engage in a number of single and collective activities, it is reasonable to expect that they get fully immersed in the game while keeping aside other peripheral activities. Video games usually present different scenarios with increasing levels of difficulty. Individuals start playing the easier difficulty levels to get familiar with the video game logic and structure and also engage with other players with similar levels of experience. This helps them to self-adjust their own level of expertise with that of the game and hence avoid strong frustration feeling derived from playing at a difficult level. The previous suggests that experience of relaxation or anxiety in managers playing video games may be indicative of an adjustment in the video game difficulty for flow to succeed. If relaxation appears, there is opportunity to build upon previous skills, and adjust video game toward a more difficult setting so a more robust set of personal skills can be achieved. On the opposite, if anxiety appears, an adjustment toward a less difficult video game needs to be set to reach a balance on the actual skills-challenge gap.

Important assumptions are made for the flow moment to occur (Csikszentmihalyi, 2014): (1) individuals should set a clear of progress and goals upon the task, (2) immediate feedback on accomplishing goals should appear, and (3) there should be a fit between challenges posed by the task and individual skills. After the individual has entered the flow moment, there are specific subjective features that appear: focused concentration on the task, a merge of action and awareness, loss of self-awareness as main actor, a heightened sense of control, a feeling that time passes at faster pace, loss of ego, and feeling the experience as self-rewarding (Nakamura & Csikszentmihalyi, 2009). Merging action and awareness refers to the fact that full attention is devoted to the task, whereas the self and other surrounding objects are left out of awareness. This is possible by focusing attention on a limited number of external stimuli. A sense of control is also developed during flow moments, in that individuals perceive themselves as lack of anxiety during performing the task; it refers more a perceived sense of control rather than actual control of the situation. When individuals are fully involved in a task, awareness on time passing is surpassed as the task poses a challenge to be solved, and hence it is perceived as passing more quickly. Loss of ego refers to the considering ego as an interactive dimension between the external demands and the internal needs, which stops mediating when the individual is fully engaged in a task (Csikszentmihalyi, 2014).

In all, the flow experience may be associated with autotelic experience, in which the road to be followed in rewarding for its own sake, alongside with a strong intrinsic motivation. Video games appear to follow above assumptions: A clear goal for chapters and missions and it is explicitly stated at the beginning. Players know what can be considered as success or failure while they are progressing in the video game. Moreover, feedback on progress in most video games is immediate. The player is made aware of missing items and accomplished partial goals. Finally, as previously discussed, players can set the difficulty level according to their expertise. In learning contexts, flow has been found to increase team game performance in students while being in flow states while playing a 1 day educational video game; distracting activities as technology problem-solving and navigating the virtual city diminished learning levels. Moreover, the less the students were distracted, the more engaged in competition they seemed to be (Admiraal et al., 2011). From the previous discussion, it is reasonable to expect that video game players who perceive a fit between video game challenge and personal skills, immediate feedback on progress, and goal clarity may engage in cognitive processes associated with flow, as concentration, quicker passing of time, and autotelic experience. From the previous discussion, two research proposals can be framed:

RP1: Higher levels of task-challenge fit, feedback, and goal clarity lead video game players to present perceptual changes in concentration, passing of time, and autotelic experience.

RP2: Video game players who present high perceptual changes in concentration, passing of time and autotelic experience may lead to high changes in learning self-perceptions by trial and error and risk-taking attitudes.

Theory of Planned Behavior

Regarding cognitive frameworks, Theory of Reasoned Action (Ajzen, 1985) lacks complete explanations of intentions and actual behaviors, that is, individuals showing high intentions to perform a specific behavior are not effectively explained only by beliefs, attitudes, and intentions. Such gap appears to be the result of a twofold mechanism: on one hand, the individuals' incomplete volitional control lead to open the gap between intentions to perform and actual performance, on the other hand, the gap also appears because non-motivational factors—time, money, and skills—become critical limitations in performing the desired behavior. Deriving from the self-efficacy theory, Bandura (1977) argues that perceived behavioral control was a construct useful to explain the extent to which a particular behavior is perceived as easy or difficult to perform according to the person's subjective self-perception. According to this view, the more ability the individual perceives to possess to perform behavior, the more likely he will succeed in performing such behavior. In specific, the link between video gaming and self-efficacy to accomplish certain results have been researched, ranging from health-related behaviors (Baranowski et al., 2008) to knowledge (Meluso et al., 2012) and learning (Huffman et al., 2013). For example, video game players with lower levels of self-efficacy as the individual perception on personal skills to play video games and the challenge posed by a high perceived difficulty of such video game may lead to a misfit between the task challenge aspects of flow. This can be detrimental for personal outcomes as learning and attitude change. In contrast, a person with high perceived high self-efficacy may be associated with higher levels of learning and attitude change. The underlying mechanism is that they have more volitional control on their own task performance in spite of actual use of video games. From the previous discussion, a research proposal can be framed as:

RP3: Video game players with high levels of self-efficacy led to higher levels of personal outcomes as learning by trial and error and risk-taking attitudes.

Personality Traits Theory

Personality traits refer to individual features that shape enduring and consistent ways of reacting toward external stimuli and are expressed as a response to situational and contextual situations. For example, job needs, social demands, behavioral norms (Tett & Burnett, 2003). The five-factor model of personality (McCrae & Costa, 1987) provides a popular description of personality using openness, conscientiousness, extraversion, agreeableness, and neuroticism. Openness refers to imaginative, original, and daring interests. Conscientiousness relates to individuals who are hardworking, ambitious, energetic, and persevering. Individuals who score high in extraversion relate to being sociable, fun-loving, affectionate, friendly, and talkative. Agreeableness refers to ruthless, callous, antagonistic, and critical people. Neuroticism describes a worrying, insecure, self-conscious, and temperamental person. Existing literature linking personality traits and flow (Ullén et al., 2012) has found a negative relationship between flow-proneness and neuroticism, whereas the relationship between flow-proneness and conscientiousness was found positive. Other personality traits lack further relationships. Conscientiousness is associated with variables as problem coping, satisfaction with life and happiness. Hence conscientiousness people, motivational and emotional mechanisms that make them more likely to engage in flow state. The neuroticism dimension is related to negative emotions that may hinder individuals from entering flow, and their associated enjoyment, control, and focus. The same study found that flow-proneness is more associated to personality traits rather than intelligence (Ullén et al., 2012).

Another set of relevant, unexplored personality traits that may explain individual differences of the relationship between focus and performance outcomes may include innovativeness, perceived ease to use the video game, and need for cognition. Innovativeness refers to the individual preferences for engaging in novel experiences to reach the goal of stimulating the mind; individuals like spending time on thinking and solving problems they face (Venkatraman & Price, 1990). Above all, the focus is on engaging in stimulant activities that demand cognitive attention and seem to be related to flow features, and consequently individuals with high cognitive innovativeness are more likely to engage in flow moments. Perceived ease of use is a concept borrowed from technology adoption modeling. Perceived ease of use of information technologies is the extent to which technology users think using a particular information system would be free of effort (Davis, 1989; Davis et al., 1989). Perceived ease of use has been associated to higher levels of in-classroom learning (Bourgonjon et al., 2010) and gamification tasks (Koivisto & Hamari, 2014). It is reasonable to expect that the easier the video game is to use, the more likely users would engage more deeply in flow while playing video games. Need for cognition is the tendency that leads people to engage and enjoy in thinking (Cacioppo & Petty, 1982). As such, individuals high in need for cognitions are more influenced by the quality of advertisements in publicity. As video games provide new experiences, individuals may try different settings that provide high immersion levels, which are indicative of flow (Przybylski et al., 2012). It is reasonable to expect that managers who score high in need for cognition are more involved in learning new aspects of the virtual reality provided by video games. From the previous discussion, the following research proposals can be framed:

RP4: Managers with high levels of openness, conscientiousness, and extraversion are more likely to engage in flow activities whereas managers with high levels of agreeableness and neuroticism are less likely to engage in flow activities.

RP5: Managers with high levels of innovativeness, perceived ease of use, and need for cognition are more likely to engage in flow activities.

Maladaptive Behaviors

The discussion so far has dealt with what can be considered as adaptive behaviors—desirable, positive learning, and attitudinal changes. However, existing literature also shows that video game players may engage in maladaptive behaviors—antisocial, aggressive, and negative behaviors to be considered the antithesis of managerial performance. For example, in youth settings, video games may be correlated with anti-social behaviors as aggressiveness. Studies suggest that gaming cognitive and behavioral aspects play a role in developing these types of behaviors. Perfectionism, cognitive and behavioral salience, along with regret are correlated with problematic gamers (Forrest et al., 2016). Moreover, similar studies report that addition to video games associates with decreased academic performance, self-esteem, and self-confidence, mainly in males (Toker & Baturay, 2016). This suggests that there is a gaming time before which individuals can derive value from playing but, from this gaming time on, there is a decreased performance. Therefore, a research proposal linking time playing video games with maladaptive behaviors can be framed as:

RP6: Time spent by video game players present a U-inverted shape in which adaptive behaviors present (learning, team building, and problem-solving) before the upper limit of time and maladaptive behaviors present after passing such upper time limit (aggressiveness, isolation, goal confusion, and personal loss of control).

A final word on the development is to say that reaching flow moments may be moderated by a number of individual characteristics, as gender, age, and experience playing video games. Most video game players refer to young men who develop more experience than women of any age; hence it is reasonable to expect that the relationships from task challenge fit, feedback, and goal clarity toward flow may be stronger for experienced young men games. Hence, a last research proposal can be framed as:

RP7: Experienced young men present a stronger relation of flow antecedents (fit with task challenge, feedback, and goal clarity) than women of any age and experience.

Conceptual Framework

As discussed previously, a fit between task challenge and individual skills, immediate feedback, and goal clarity are antecedents of flow (research proposal 1, RP1). As second antecedents, player traits as big five (RP4) and other traits as personal innovativeness, need for cognition, and perceived ease of use of the video games represent another antecedent of flow (RP5). Flow can be represented by variables as concentration, self-efficacy, sense of time, and autotelic experience. Outcomes of flow include a three-fold instance. First, personal outcomes of keeping flow while video gaming may include learning by trial and error and risk-taking attitudes (RP2). Second, personal skills acquired and developed may be leveraged to workplace settings in the form of team-building, problem-solving, innovative thinking, and design thinking (RP8) with aid of self-efficacy (RP3). Third, spending too much time playing video games may lead to maladaptive behaviors such as isolation, goal confusion, and loss of control (RP6). Finally, drawing for information systems theory, the relationships between antecedents and flow can be moderated by player's age, gender, and experience on a particular video game (RP7) (Fig. 2.1).

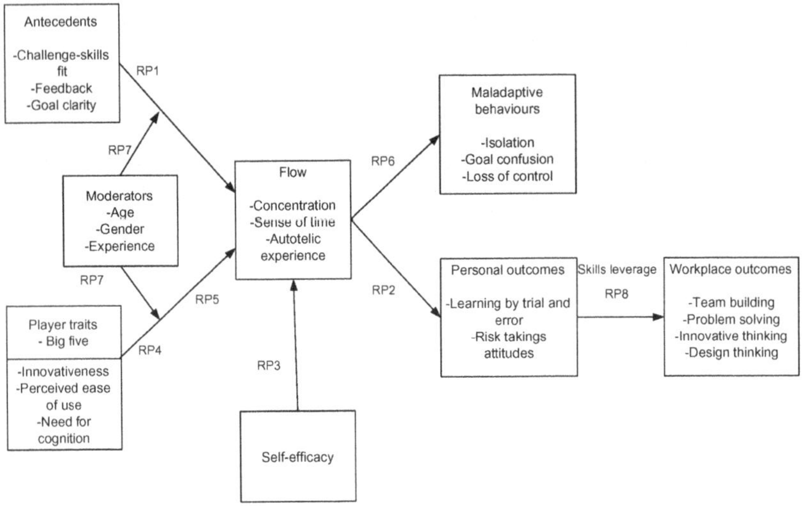

Fig. 2.1 Conceptual framework to study antecedents and consequences of video game flow (*Source* Author)

General Discussion

Prospects for Empirical Testing

There is a wide variety of multiplayer video games available in the market. One example is "Black Desert Online" in which players perform in a conflict between two countries. Through developing collaborative actions, players require to develop the skills of shooters and use limited healing capacities and potions to conquer the opponent country. While playing, there are physical obstacles and events like typhoons, which add challenges to the gaming experience. Another example is "World of the Living Dead", a game based on the actual Open Street Map platform, in which players are tasked with protecting groups of survivors after a zombie apocalypse. Players' roles include commanding troops, deploying surveillance operatives, defend survivors from zombie attacks, and radioing orders to other players. From these two examples, it seems apparent that these two video games follow the assumptions for flow to occur. So a framework can be proposed to depict the flow moments in which players engage while playing video gaming and how skills may be leveraged to the workplace.

A further empirical test may shed light of the actual antecedent influencing the formation of manager's skills. There are at least three different approaches to frame study designs on the proposed research questions. By sampling a suitable number of managers engaged in video gaming, the relationships between variables can be assessed using analytical techniques as partial least squares (PLS). This will shed light on the net effects of one variable over another. By collecting data on managers working in manufacturing, service, and professional services, interesting multi-group comparisons can be achieved. Another interesting comparison among groups would include digital natives and digital immigrants—two different generations with differing attitudes toward technology and usage levels. Items for each discussed variable may be considered as either continuous or discrete. Linear regression would be useful to test individual effects for each variable, over personal learning, attitudes, and perceived risks, as well as maladaptive outcomes. Similarly, player traits may be associated with flow, focus, and immersion. In the same line, structural equation modeling would be helpful to analyze simultaneous relationships of variables in more comprehensible models. Particularly, analytical tools as Partial Least Squares (PLS) may shed light on such relationships without restraining the data to follow stringent requirements from covariance-based models.

Alternatively, qualitative comparative analysis (QCA)—an analytical technique that departs the mainstream tools—may show all possible combinations between antecedent variables that lead to acquisition and formation of skills. Importantly, QCA does not rely on net effect and size effect as standard regression techniques and PLS does. Instead, QCA focuses on finding combinations among flow antecedents and player's traits that lead to flow. Similarly, this technique would allow analyzing which combinations of the dimensions of flow (concentration, self-efficacy, sense of time, and autotelic experience) lead to personal outcomes, workplace outcomes, and maladaptive behaviors. Noteworthy QCA would enable the researcher to analyze those antecedents leading to skill formation, but also would show those combinations which do not lead to skill formation. Another analytical approach includes performing a qualitative comparative analysis (QCA). QCA explores combinations of causal contribution of different conditions—similar to independent variables in linear regression—to a specified outcome of interest. It begins by conveying diverse configurations of conditions, i.e., the logical combinations associated with each case in which the outcome—similar to dependent variable in linear regression—can be studied. Afterward, QCA captures the simplest set of Boolean conditions that can account for all studied outcomes or their absence. For instance, the Boolean condition A and B or the combination of conditions C and D that leads to outcome X can be expressed as: $A * B + C * D = X$. In a sense, QCA answers the question what are the combinations (or groups of cases) in A, B, C, and D that produce X?

Finally, experimental designs may be framed to isolate the most relevant antecedents that lead to learning and skill development (Baranowski et al., 2008). Despite internal validity as criteria to choose experiments, video games are very diverse. Features of video games as scenarios, paths, and player teams may differ in difficulty, time, and complexity for each player. The task of designing a suitable manipulation to explore the impact of one antecedent variable on the outcome becomes challenging.

Implications for Researchers

This framework has implications for researchers. Testing the proposed framework empirically would craft an initial theory on how to deploy critical skills to the workplace through using a hedonic, non-work-related tool. This is a critical aspect for business to survive and grow. Importantly, implications for emerging economies may be even stronger since such economies are younger than more developed countries. A first implication is the link between personality-focus-learning. The number of theories addressing learning issues is vast. This paper has addressed focus theory, flow theory, immersive theory, and social cognitive theory. Future studies may shed light on learning managerial skill through video gaming, using other theories as constructivism and multiple intelligences. Second, our propositions focus on the moderating effect of age, gender, and experience, but we excluded mediating processes. Other studies may engage in analyzing other moderators as tenure, type of industry and firm, and managerial or technical roles. Third, scope for this study has included a number of outcomes, namely learning, risk attitudes, and maladaptive behaviors. A logical next step in advancing research on the topic is to include other dimensions of learning as collaborative learning, co-creating, team-building, and collaborative problem-solving.

Implications for Practitioners

This framework has also implications for managers. First, by analyzing the combinations of antecedents that lead to flow and individual skills, managers may engage in developing organizational initiatives and policies that promote using specific video games as learning tools in the workplace. Our framework assumes that video games features should be considered alongside manager traits to explore segments of managers who may benefit from new organizational policies. Second, patterns of technology usage have implications for workplaces around the world given the availability of video game consoles, Internet access, and online multiplayer games. Some tech firms and universities have engaged in such initiatives with an intuition on the benefits, but more research is needed to understand the evidence-based managerial interventions. Third, our research proposals assume that managers more prone to play video games may engage more frequently in flow, focus, and immersive behaviors. While this may suggest higher performance, we are also aware that mature managers may not be inclined to playing video games; hence they would lose such performance effect. Hybrid policies would be needed at workplaces, since firms include generations, digital natives, and immigrants. Finally, maladaptive behaviors may appear because of playing video games. Firms need to detect early signals from these behaviors and address them accordingly.

Conclusion

Video games have evolved toward pervasive, hedonic, entertaining systems. This paper has proposed a number of research questions to analyze managerial behavior in the context of alternative training tools. Our proposal links manager traits, video game features with focus, flow, and immersion, as core constructs. The outcome is learning and developing skills by trial and error, self-control, enhanced cognitive capabilities, alongside possible maladaptive behaviors as loss of control, aggressiveness, and isolation. We hope that these research questions may help advance understanding transferal of managerial skills from video games to the workplace. We also hope other researchers engage in this exciting topic.

References

Adachi, P. J., & Willoughby, T. (2013). More than just fun and games: The longitudinal relationships between strategic video games, self-reported problem solving skills, and academic grades. *Journal of Youth and Adolescence, 42*(7), 1041–1052.

Admiraal, W., Huizenga, J., Akkerman, S., & Ten Dam, G. (2011). The concept of flow in collaborative game-based learning. *Computers in Human Behavior, 27*(3), 1185–1194.

Ajzen, I. (1985). From intentions to actions: A theory of planned behavior. In J. Kuhl & J. Beckmann (Eds.), *Action control* (pp. 11–39). Springer.

Bandura, A. (1977). Self-efficacy: toward a unifying theory of behavioral change. *Psychological Review, 84*(2), 191–215.

Baranowski, T., Buday, R., Thompson, D. I., & Baranowski, J. (2008). Playing for real: Video games and stories for health-related behavior change. *American Journal of Preventive Medicine, 34*(1), 74–82.

Blumberg, F. C., & Fisch, S. M. (2013). Introduction: Digital games as a context for cognitive development, learning, and developmental research. *New Directions for Child and Adolescent Development, 139*, 1–9.

Bourgonjon, J., Valcke, M., Soetaert, R., & Schellens, T. (2010). Students' perceptions about the use of video games in the classroom. *Computers & Education, 54*(4), 1145–1156.

Cacioppo, J. T., & Petty, R. E. (1982). The need for cognition. *Journal of Personality and Social Psychology, 42*(1), 116–131.

Christensen, C. M., McDonald, R., Altman, E. J., & Palmer, J. E. (2018). Disruptive innovation: An intellectual history and directions for future research. *Journal of Management Studies, 55*(7), 1043–1078.

Csikszentmihalyi, M. (1997). *Finding flow*. Basic.

Csikszentmihalyi, M. (2014). *Flow and the foundations of positive psychology: The collected works of Mihaly Csikszentmihalyi*. Springer.

Csikszentmihalyi, M., & Nakamura, J. (1979). The concept of flow. In B. Sutton-Smith (Ed.), *Play and learning* (pp. 257–274). Gardner.

Davis, F. D. (1989). Perceived usefulness, perceived ease of use, and user acceptance of information technology. *MIS Quarterly, 13*(3), 319–340.

Davis, F. D., Bagozzi, R. P., & Warshaw, P. R. (1989). User acceptance of computer technology: A comparison of two theoretical models. *Management Science, 35*(8), 982–1003.

Dye, M. W., Green, C. S., & Bavelier, D. (2009). Increasing speed of processing with action video games. *Current Directions in Psychological Science, 18*(6), 321–326.

Forrest, C. J., King, D. L., and Delfabbro, P. H. (2016). The measurement of maladaptive cognitions underlying problematic video-game playing among adults, *Computers in Human Behavior*, *55*(Part A), 399–405.

Green, C. S., & Bavelier, D. (2012). Learning, attentional control, and action video games. *Current Biology, 22*(6), 197–206.

Huffman, A. H., Whetten, J., & Huffman, W. H. (2013). Using technology in higher education: The influence of gender roles on technology self-efficacy. *Computers in Human Behavior, 29*(4), 1779–1786.

Koivisto, J., & Hamari, J. (2014). Demographic differences in perceived benefits from gamification. *Computers in Human Behavior, 35*(6), 179–188.

McCrae, R. R., & Costa, P. T. (1987). Validation of the five-factor model of personality across instruments and observers. *Journal of Personality and Social Psychology, 52*(1), 81.

Meluso, A., Zheng, M., Spires, H. A., & Lester, J. (2012). Enhancing 5th graders' science content knowledge and self-efficacy through game-based learning. *Computers & Education, 59*(2), 497–504.

Nakamura, J., & Csikszentmihalyi, M. (2009). Flow theory and research. In C. R. Snyder & S. J. Lopez (Eds.), *Oxford handbook of positive psychology* (pp. 195–206). Oxford University Press.

Okagaki, L., & Frensch, P. A. (1994). Effects of video game playing on measures of spatial performance: Gender effects in late adolescence. *Journal of Applied Developmental Psychology, 15*(1), 33–58.

Prensky, M. (2001). Digital natives, digital immigrants. *On the Horizon, 9*(5), 1–6.

Przybylski, A. K., Weinstein, N., Murayama, K., Lynch, M. F., & Ryan, R. M. (2012). The ideal self at play the appeal of video games that let you be all you can be. *Psychological Science, 23*(1), 69–76.

Tett, R. P., & Burnett, D. D. (2003). A personality trait–based interactionist model of job performance. *Journal of Applied Psychology, 88*(6), 500–517.

Toker, S., & Baturay, M. H. (2016). Antecedents and consequences of game addiction. *Computers in Human Behavior*, *55*(Part B), 668–679.

Ullén, F., de Manzano, Ö., Almeida, R., Magnusson, P. K. E., Pedersen, N. L., Nakamura, J., Csíkszentmihályi, M., & Madison, G. (2012). Proneness for psychological flow in everyday life: Associations with personality and intelligence. *Personality and Individual Differences, 52*(2), 167–172.

Venkatraman, M. P., & Price, L. L. (1990). Differentiating between cognitive and sensory innovativeness: Concepts, measurement, and implications. *Journal of Business Research, 20*(4), 293–315.

PART II

Social Media Drivers

CHAPTER 3

Social Media Usage Behavior in Job Search: Implications for Corporate Image and Employer Branding

N. V. Subbarao, Bindu Chhabra, and Manit Mishra

Introduction

Companies tend to suitably address their organizational recruitment policies and methods in order to recruit top talent. It is a vivid pointer goading business leaders to pay more attention to Employer Branding in order to survive better. Further with social media now playing a critical role in recruiting, Employer Branding has become even more critical.

N. V. Subbarao (✉) · B. Chhabra · M. Mishra
International Management Institute, Bhubaneswar, India
e-mail: 18fpm-bhu005@imibh.edu.in

B. Chhabra
e-mail: bindu@imibh.edu.in

M. Mishra
e-mail: manit.mishra@imibh.edu.in

Rajagopal and R. Behl (eds.), *Managing Disruptions in Business*, Palgrave Studies in Democracy, Innovation, and Entrepreneurship for Growth, https://doi.org/10.1007/978-3-030-79709-6_3

According to Randstad Employer Brand Research (2019) Global Report: (i) 78% of candidates consider the overall job seeking experience an indicator of how a company values its employees (ii) 55% of job seekers abandon their application processes after reading negative reviews (iii) 99% of employers believe managing the employer brand is important when attracting top talent and (iv) 91% of companies believe employer brand and reputation could impact revenue, among other points. Thus it can be seen that Employer Branding is a strategic business need for organizations to emerge as 'preferred employer' (Barrow, 1990).

Brand and human capital have long been acknowledged as important assets of a firm (Aaker, 1996; Backhaus & Tikoo, 2004) for gaining competitive advantage in the marketplace (Sutherland et al., 2002). While the role of branding has received significant attention, there is very little research on the role that branding plays in retaining and attracting employees that constitute the firm's human capital. Studies on human capital strategy have shown that the performance of firms depends on finding, hiring and retaining talented workers (Coff & Kryscynski, 2011). The firms find talent by relying on, search behaviors of their designated workers and or recruiters, referrals from existing employees, and or post job advertisements to search and choose from among the applicants (Fernandez et al., 2000; Jovanovic, 1979; Mortensen & Vishwanath, 1994; Petersen et al., 2000). Other studies examined the impact of employer branding on recruitment outcomes using customer brand equity models (Keller, 1993). They suggest creating favorable employee perceptions and to build strong employer brand equity (EBE) for gaining talent advantage (Collins & Stevens, 2002). However, the rapid adoption of social media and the advent of social media recruitment from around 2010 appears to have added more complexity to employer branding and human capital (Cappelli, 2019). Complexity that seems to be arising from influence effects of perceived trendiness and perceived imagery, triggering rapid and large-scale information exchanges between employer and job aspirants (Taylor et al., 2007). Consequently, Employer Branding (EB) has emerged as a distinct topic of strategic importance for both organizations and academia to pursue and understand more. Specifically, the aspects that signal unique and compelling value propositions to attract and/or retain talent. Accordingly, building Employer Brand Equity (EBE) using social media has emerged as a strategic priority. Published literature however on employer branding in contexts of social media and job search is scarce.

This quantitative study attempts to bridge the gap by ascertaining job search behaviors using Technology Acceptance Model (TAM) as a theoretical framework. Three antecedent constructs; *Information Provisioning (IP), Perceived Image (IM) and Perceived Trendiness (TR),* exemplifying social media usage behaviors in job search were thus studied. The constructs identified from literature, in effect are the predictors of the endogenous variables; *Perceived Usefulness (PU)* and *Perceived Ease of Use (PE),* which are the predictors for *Intent to Use (IU). Intent to Use in turn leads to Actual Use (AU) of social media in job search* (Davis & Venkatesh, 1996; Venkatesh & Davis, 2000). Ergo, a theoretical model of *Social Media Usage Behavior in Job Search* is proposed and studied using Structural Equation Modelling (SEM), post specifying the Measurement Model using Confirmatory Factor Analysis (CFA). The study has its primary objective to 'understand the influence of the three antecedent constructs on job seeking behavior and thereby the implications on Employer Branding thereof. In sum, behavioral patterns are identified from the test model and inferred for implications on Employer Branding and Corporate Image. The paper is structured as follows: as conceptualisation via the theoretical framework and hypotheses development for quantitative assessment, research methodology, analysis of results, discussions of managerial and other implications, and concludes with comments on the limitations of the study.

Theoretical Framework and Hypotheses Development

The topic of employer branding has been an evolving one and is a topic of much interest in strategy, marketing and HR. Aaker (1996) stated Employer Branding to have its origins in the proven methods of branding of goods and services, from the traditional era of brand marketing.

Employer Branding and the Job Market Mechanism

Ambler and Barrow (1996). defined Employer Branding in the context of people management as the "*the package of functional, economic and psychological benefits provided by employment and identified with the employing company*". In this it has largely been identified as the projection of the image of an organization as a great place to work for both external (potential) and internal (existing) employees. Later Branham

(2000) suggested employer branding as a means of building reputation as a credible employer and great place to work implying that an organization with a strong employer brand would attract more qualified candidates and become a preferred employer. Employer brand is thus to be understood as the set of distinctive images of a prospective employer, which are manifested in the minds of potential employees (Petkovic, 2004). It is the sum total and more, of the values, systems, policies and behaviors of the firm toward the objectives of attracting and retaining current and future employees' (Dell, et al., 2001). With the advent and widespread use of social media in recruitment, the role of Employer Branding appears to have become even more important. However, there appears to be not enough understanding of job search behaviors with social media and their implication on employer branding. Past studies indicate *information provisioning (IP), perceived image (IM) and perceived trendiness (TR),* as three exogenous constructs of social media usage that exemplify job search behaviors (Esch & Black, 2019; Raunier & Yang, 2014; RoyChowdhury & Srimannarayana, 2013). Thus, a fundamental understanding of the job search behaviors using a conceptual framework to measure these constructs could help understand and create more effective employer branding. Hence, we quantitatively studied the 3 antecedent constructs; *IP, IM and TR* using the Technology Acceptance Model (TAM) as a theoretical framework. Ergo, understanding job seeking behaviors could convey the relevant information needed for identifying the credible brand signals for Employer Branding.

Social Media Usage Behavior in Job Search—Conceptual Framework

TAM derived from the Theory of Reasoned Action (TRA), has its roots in sociological and psychological research (Fig. 3.1). It is a widely accepted

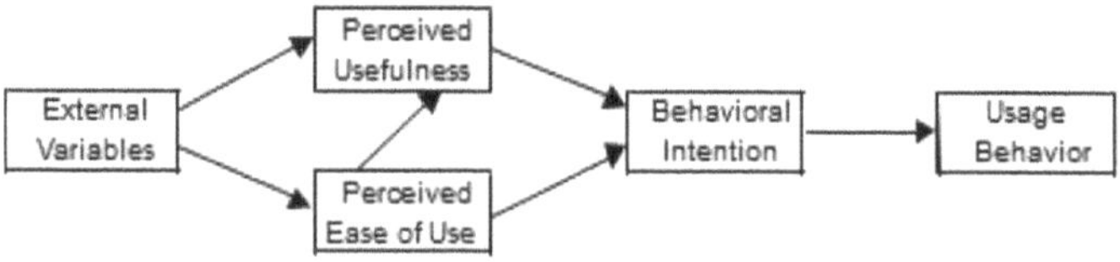

Fig. 3.1 Technology acceptance model (TAM)

theory of usage, behavior and acceptance, and aims to explain behavioral intentions to use an information system with two primary factors: *Perceived usefulness and Perceived ease of use* as its antecedents (Davis & Venkatesh, 1996; Venkatesh & Davis, 2000). TAM has been shown to have proven applicability across both digital and non-digital contexts (Bond et al., 2012), and so is a good place to start.

Proposed Model—Social Media Usage Behavior in Job Search Model

The above TAM mode (Fig. 3.1) was thus adopted with the antecedent constructs IP, IM and TR from literature review as external variables to propose a Theoretical Model of *Social Media Usage Behavior in Job Search* (Fig. 3.2). Hypotheses along the path lines were thus suitably constructed and statistically tested to check causality.

Relevant Constructs and Hypotheses Proposed

The seven constructs from the above proposed model are discussed next to arrive at the definitions of the respective constructs and the proposed hypotheses for testing and confirmation.

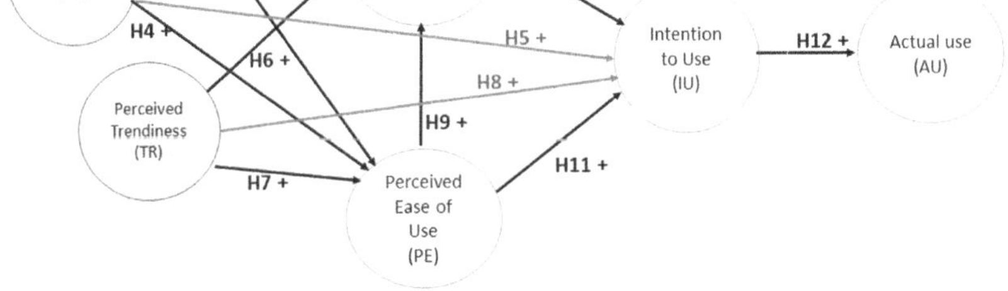

Fig. 3.2 Theoretical model and hypotheses (*Source* Authors' research)

Information Provisioning (IP)

We define IP in terms of the amount of information that is provided by the job seeker (or recruiting organization) on the social media site, that contribute to their job search experience.

Cober et al. (2003) suggested information provisioning to be an important factor in employment-related contexts as is part of the applicant's expectations. For online recruitments, applicants typically have more access to information on organizations from multiple sources like discussion boards and forums (RoyChowdhury & Srimannarayana, 2013). Thus it's beneficial for job search mechanisms to be perceived as useful and even easy to use. This gives rise to the following propositions;

H1: *Better Information Provisioning (IP) leads to increased Perceived Usefulness (PU) of a job post or company (i.e., IP on social media sites for job search is positively related to PU)*

H2: *Better Information Provisioning (IP) leads to increased Perceived Ease of Use (PE) of a job post or company (i.e., IP on social media sites for job search is positively related to PE)*

Image Perception (IM)

We define IM as the degree to which the use of social media in job search is perceived to enhance the appeal of the job seeker and motivate him or her to respond for furthering their employment status. Moore and Benbasat (1991) studied use of an innovation and its perceptions to enhance individual's status in social systems. Sinar et al. (2003), described this construct as a useful reflection of a candidate's image of companies that use the internet for applicant selection purposes. Venkatesh and Davis (2000) provide evidence for a positive effect of subjective norm on image and found a positive relation between image and perceived usefulness. Studies by Sylva and Mol (2009) and RoyChowdhury and Srimannarayana (2013), posit that applicants image perception affects process satisfaction of the online application systems in e-recruitment and so influences their perceived ease of use and usefulness. This thus gives rise to the following propositions:

H3: *Better Perceived Image (IM) leads to increased Perceived Usefulness (PU) of a job post and or company (i.e., IM on social media sites for job search is positively related to PU)*

H4: *Better Perceived Image (IM) leads to increased Ease of Use (PE) of a job post or company (i.e., IM on social media sites for job search is positively related to PE)*

Employer Branding studies also indicate that firms perceived to be more innovative and trendy garner higher mind share and attract more candidates than others (Backhaus & Tikoo, 2004; Dell et al., 2001). Hence we propose:

H5: *Greater Image (IM) of a company or a job post leads to increased Intention to Use (PU) of job post and or social media site for job search (i.e. IM on social media sites for job search is positively related to IU, as a direct relationship)*

Perceived Trendiness (TR)

We define TR as the extent to which the job seeker using social media on a site might be perceived as not just novel (i.e., new and different), but also trendy in pursuing his job hunting efforts.

Esch and Black (2019) suggest that the new digital or any AI-enabled job application process could likely be perceived as trendy by both job seekers and organizations. Earlier, Esch and Mente (2018) stated that participating with a trendy technology bestows all the cool, novel, and leading-edge characteristics, and promotes higher engagement levels. Dixit and Prakash (2018) stated that a trendy technology inherently implies new, and so bestows trendiness, often to garner higher usage. This gives rise to the following propositions:

H6: *Greater Trendiness (TR) leads to increased Perceived Usefulness (PU) of a job post and or company (i.e., TR on social media sites for job search is positively related to PU)*

H7: *Greater Trendiness (TR) leads to increased Perceived Ease of Use (PE) of a job post and or company (i.e., TR on social media sites for job search is positively related to PE)*

Further the literature on Perceived Trendiness (TR) suggests that the new, trendy and/ or innovative technologies are perceived to have leading-edge characteristics which promote high engagement by the direct intention to use (Esch & Mente, 2018). Hence we also propose;

H8: *Greater Trendiness (TR) leads to increased Intention to Use (IU) of a job post or social media site for job search (i.e., TR on social media sites for job search is positively related to IU, as a direct relationship)*

Perceived Usefulness (PU)

We define PU as the extent to which the social media user believes that using a particular social media technology in job search is perceived as being useful and thus help him in the process. Gutman (1982) shows PU to represent advantageous results derived from attributes of the technology being used. Dhar and Wertenbroch (2000) state that the utilitarian value drawn from the usage of technology is cognitively driven, instrumental, goal oriented and accomplishes a functional or practical task of the users. The extent to which this utilitarian value of social media uses, and application is perceived beneficial, determines the PU.

Perceived Ease of Use (PE)

We define PE as the degree to which the social media site is considered free of effort and as such is easy to use for job search purposes. The social media site should be intuitive and efficient in getting tasks done to the principle of least effort (Zipf, 1949). Zeithaml et al. (2002) showed that PE signifies the degree to which an innovation is perceived easy to understand or operate. Past studies by Rauniar et al. (2009), Molla and Licker (2001), Yoo and Donthu (2001) and Zeithaml (2000) indicate that an easy to use website enhances the users experience. This gives rise to the following propositions:

H9: *Greater Perceived Ease of use (PE) leads to increased Perceived Usefulness (PU) of job post or social media site for job search (i.e.PE for job search is positively related to PU)*

Intention to Use (IU) and Actual Use (AU)

We define IU as the continued intention to perform job search using one or more of the social media sites by the job seeker. We define AU as the actual use or deployment of social media in job search by the job seeker. The TAM model is based on the relationship of PU, PE, IU and AU. Davis (1989) states Intention reflects a decision that the person has made about whether to perform a behaviour or not. Davis (1989) and Venktatesh and Davis (2000), state that beliefs or attitudes about PU and PE determine IU of that technology, which in turn leads to actual usage (AU). This gives rise to the following propositions:

- *H10*: *Greater Perceived Usefulness (PU) leads to increased Intention to Use (IU) of a job post or social media site for job search (i.e., PU of social media for job search is positively related to IU)*
- *H11*: *Greater Perceived Ease of Use (PE) leads to increased Intention to Use (IU) of a job post or social media site for job search (i.e., PE of social media for job search is positively related to IU)*
- *H12*: *Greater Intention to Use (IU) leads to greater Actual Use (AU) of a job post or social media site for job search (i.e., IU of social media for job search is positively related to AU)*

Research Methodology

Sample

A representative sample of job seekers was chosen for the study. Both first time job seekers (from any academic discipline), and experienced candidates (from any industry sector with a minimum of 1 year work experience) were chosen. The data from the cross section of the population was collected via a structured questionnaire fielded online and shared on social media platforms. In all 578 responses were obtained over a period of 4 months and 552 responses were accurately completed (response rate 95%). The sample consists of 35% first time job seekers and 65% having work experience (with 56% employed and 9% unemployed and looking for job). 60% of the respondents age was in the '20–25' and '25–30 years' range, while 25% indicate 'more than 40 years'. The maximum number of respondents (36%) fell in the age range of 20–25 years. The gender ratio was 61% male and 39% female. 86% of the respondents indicated they had used social media at least once for job search and or for career-related purposes.

Measures

The study uses covariance-based structural equation modeling (CB-SEM) to assess the measurement model followed by evaluation of structural relationships. Covariance-based SEM was chosen for analysis because the three antecedent constructs and four endogenous constructs were measured using previously developed scales, thus requiring construct validation. Further, as the study emphasizes upon theory testing, CB-SEM could help better explain the model and the multiple relationships that could exist with their respective causalities (Hair et al., 2014). Analysis of Moment Structures (AMOS) Version 21 was used for testing the causal relationships and examining the hypothesized research model. A two-stage model building approach was used. First, the measurement model was tested to assess validity and reliability of the constructs. Second, the structural model was examined using path estimates. The estimation of the measurement model and structural model was conducted using Maximum Likelihood Estimation (MLE). Also a bootstrapping procedure with 1000 bootstrap samples at 95% bias-corrected confidence intervals was employed.

Research Instruments

The research instruments used in the study are borrowed from extant research. The social media behavior constructs of job seeking: *Information Provisioning (IP)*, *Perceived Image (IM)* and *Perceived Trendiness (TR)* were measured using scales adopted from Sylva and Mol (2009), Raunier and Yang (2014), and Esch and Black (2019), respectively. Similarly, the technology acceptance related constructs of Perceived Usefulness (PU), Perceived Ease of Use (PE), Intention to Use (IU) and Actual Use (AU) were operationalized using the scales developed by Davis (1996).

Accordingly, the final questionnaire with 31 items was designed. To prevent common method bias, negatively worded items were included. Following the data collection, box plot analysis was conducted to examine outliers and based on it, 35 cases were eliminated. Next reliability testing of constructs and their respective items was done to check acceptance via Cronbach alpha (α) values.

Control Variables

Control variables included gender, age, industry type, employment status, years of work experience, whether used social media for job or career related and number of social media accounts. The survey instrument used is attached as Appendix A.

Results and Discussion

Measurement Model Development (Assessing Reliability and Validity)

The purpose of the measurement model is to determine the reliability and validity of a set of items in each latent construct. Confirmatory Factor Analysis (CFA) was conducted to offer evidence of unidimensionality of the items of each measurement. The assessment is typically to ensure the measurement model does not contain correlated errors or loadings from other latent variables (Heene et al., 2011). The construct validity was examined by investigating convergent (Table 3.1) and discriminant validity (Table 3.2).

Convergent validity was measured utilizing Composite Reliability (CR) and Average Variance Extracted (AVE) (Fornell & Larcker, 1981). A commonly used value for Composite reliability should be at least 0.7 whereas the Average Variance Extracted (AVE) should be 0.5 or higher to be considered acceptable (Hair et al., 2006). As can be seen in Table 3.1. The loading value of each factor is greater than or equal to 0.5 and also reach the significance level of $p < 0.001$. The factors IM and AU, both show AVE values less than 0.5, but CR values are higher than 0.60. In the case of AVE being less than 0.50 and CR is higher than 0.60 (factors IM and AU in Table 3.1), the convergent validity of the construct is still adequate (Fornell & Larcker, 1981). Hence we conclude all model constructs show good convergent validity as the convergent validity criterion is met.

Discriminant validity measures the difference between a construct and its indicators from another construct and its indicators (Bagozzi, 1992). It is also used to measure the extent to which a construct is different from other constructs (Hair et al., 2006). Fornell and Larcker (1981) state that the correlations among items in any two constructs should be less than the square root of the AVE shared by items within a construct. For acceptable discriminant validity, each indicator highly measures its intended constructs (Garson, 2009). Additionally, the AVE

Table 3.1 Convergent validity assessment (AVE & CR)

Factor	*Item*	*Factor loading*	*AVE*	*CR*	*Cronbach alpha (α)*
Perceived usefulness (PU)	PU1	0.764	***0.564***	***0.866***	0.869
	PU2	0.739			
	PU3	0.756			
	PU4	0.795			
	PU5	0.696			
Perceived ease of use (PU)	PE1	0.766	***0.597***	***0.816***	0.824
	PE2	0.802			
	PE4	0.749			
Information provisioning (IP)	IP1	0.766	***0.579***	***0.804***	0.804
	IP2	0.818			
	IP3	0.693			
Perceived image (IM)	IM1	0.755	**0.448**	***0.801***	0.756
	IM2	0.603			
	IM3	0.680			
	IM4	0.646			
	IM5	0.652			
Perceived trendiness (TR)	TR1	0.798	***0.536***	***0.775***	0.766
	TR2	0.737			
	TR4	0.655			
Intent to use (IU)	IU1	0.771	***0.665***	***0.888***	0.887
	IU2	0.834			
	IU3	0.850			
	IU4	0.804			
Actual usage (AU)	AU1	0.785	***0.453***	***0.803***	0.715
	AU2	0.546			
	AU3	0.652			
	AU4	0.715			
	AU5	0.642			

Note CR = composite reliability; AVE = average variance extracted

shared between a construct and its measures should be higher than the AVE shared by the constructs in the model, and the correlation between the constructs should be lower than 0.85 (Gefen & Straub, 2005).

Thus, from Tables 3.2 and 3.3, we observe that the criteria for conver-

Table 3.2 Discriminant validity assessment

	Correlation between the variables in the model:		
	IP	*IM*	*TR*
Information provisioning (IP)	1.00		
Perceived image (IM)	0.696	1.00	
Perceived trendiness (TR)	0.540	0.582	1.00
	Fornell & Larker Criterion Check (AVE based):		
Information provisioning (IP)	**0.761**		
Perceived image (IM)	0.696	**0.669**	
Perceived trendiness (TR)	0.540	0.582	**0.732**

Note Numbers on diagonal are the Square root AVEs and off-diagonal numbers are the inter-constructs correlations

Table 3.3 Results of the theoretical model goodness-of-fit

Model fit index	*Criteria*		*Values*	*References*
	Good fit	Level of acceptance		
Root mean square error of approximation (RMSEA)	<0.08		***0.065***[a]	Hair et al. (1995)
Standardized RMR (SRMR)	<0.08		***0.0598***[a]	Hair et al. (1998)
Comparative fit index(CFI)	≥0.9	0.88–0.90 adequate	**0.904**[a]	Hair et al. (1998)
CMIN (χ^2)/DF	<3.0	3.00–5.00 adequate	***3.201***[b]	Hair et al. (1998)

[a]Good fit
[b]Close to good fit(RMSEA: 0.080–0.083, SRMR: 0.080–0.083, CFI: 0.90), and
[c]Implies adequate fit(CMIN: 3.0–3.1)

gent validity is fully met for all the constructs. We therefore concluded that the model's constructs were reliable and valid. Apropos the next step is to construct the structural model and examine its results (Fig. 3.3).

Structural Model Evaluation

In order to assess the structural relationships, the study evaluated following goodness of fit indices; CMIN/DF, Root mean square

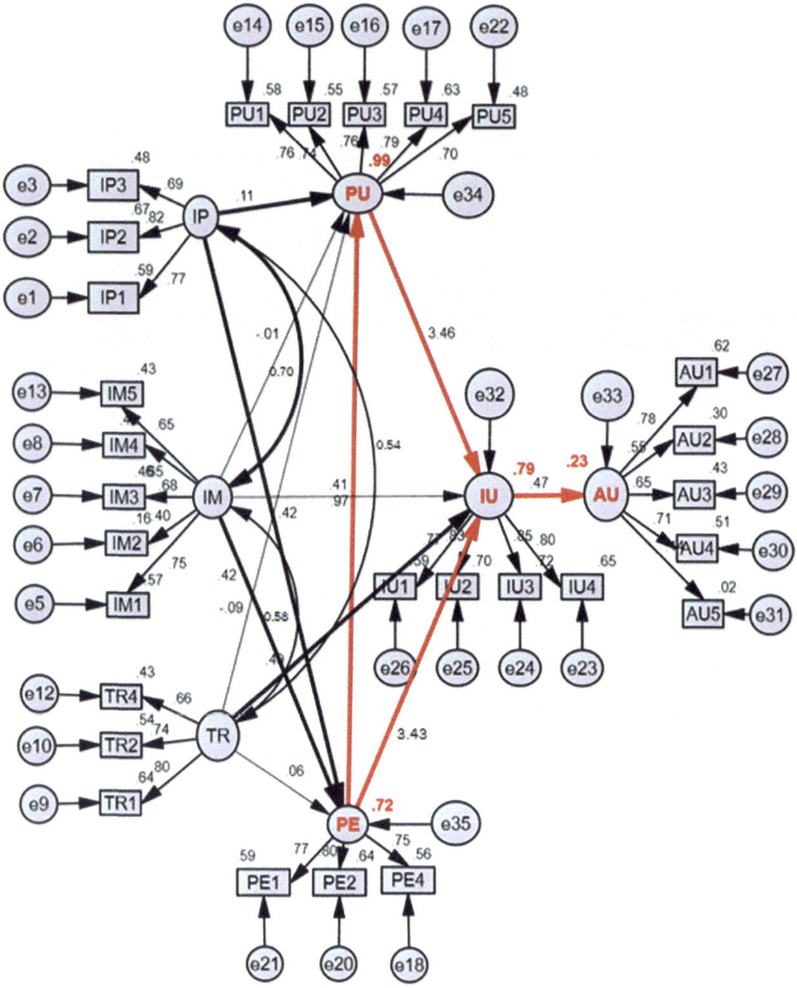

Fig. 3.3 Structural model and path coefficients (with standardized estimates) (Authors' data analysis [SEM] results)

error approximation (RMSEA), Standardized root mean square residual (SRMR) and Comparative fit index (CFI). For a good model fit the CFI should be greater than or equal to 0.90 and *CMIN/DF* should be less than 3 (Hair et al., 1995). Moreover, RMSEA and RSMR should be less than 0.08 (Hair et al., 1998). Common criteria for (AMOS) along with the outcomes are shown in Table 3.3.

Overall we observe that the normed chi-square for the hypothesized model is 3.201, CFI is 0.904, RMSEA is 0.065 (and $L_0 = 0.061$), SRMR is 0.0598 and the p-value is < 0.001. The structural model was also therefore judged to have acceptable goodness of fit (Hair et al., 2010) at minimum. Further, the test offers the path coefficients and the squared multiple correlation (R^2), which indicate the variance of the dependent constructs which can be shown by independent constructs.

Results of Hypotheses Testing

The regression weights of the models are shown in Table 3.4 and in effect show the results of the structural model. The test produces the standardized path coefficients between model constructs, and also their statistical significance. Further, the test offers the squared multiple correlation (R^2), which indicate the variance of the dependent constructs which can be

Table 3.4 Regression estimates

Path Relationship	*Regression estimates*			
	Unstandardized	p(*<0.001)*	*Beta (standardized)*	p(*<0.001)*
IP → PU	**0.114**	***	**0.111**	
PE → PU	**1.051**	***	**0.971**	
PE → PU	−0.01	0.913	−0.009	
TR → PU	−0.081	0.151	−0.086	
IP → PE	**0.397**	***	**0.417**	
IM → PE	**0.410**	***	**0.418**	
TR → PE	0.053	0.423	0.061	
IM → IU	0.470	0.175	**0.412**	
TR → IU	**0.483**	***	**0.486**	
PU → IU	**3.629**	***	**3.462**	
PE → IU	**3.901**	***	**3.434**	
IU → AU	**0.597**	***	**0.475**	

Source Authors' data analysis results *** Implies p value <0.001 (statistically significant)

shown by independent constructs. The hypothesized relationships can thus be examined:

Thus, from the above regression estimates we infer the following:

Perceived Usefulness (PU) of social media usage in job search was predicted by Information provisioning (IP) ($\beta = 0.111$, $p < 0.001$) and Perceived Ease of Use (PE) ($\beta = 0.971$, $p < 0.001$). These variables together explained 99% of the Perceived Usefulness ($R^2 = 0.991$). We also observe Perceived Image (IM) and Perceived Trendiness (TR) have no statistically significant relationship with PU and so are not predictors of same. Therefore:

- Hypothesis H1: *IP of social media sites for job search is positively related to PU, is supported.*
- Hypothesis H9: *PE of social media sites for job search is positively related to PU, is supported.*
- Hypothesis H3: *IM of social media sites for job search is positively related to PU, is not supported.*
- Hypothesis H6: *TR of social media sites for job search is positively related to PU, is not supported.*

Perceived Ease of Use (PE) of social media usage in job search was predicted by Information Provisioning (IP) ($\beta = 0.417$, $p < 0.001$) and Perceived Image (IM) ($\beta = 0.418$, $p < 0.001$). These variables together explained 72% of the Perceived Ease of Use ($R^2 = 0.719$). We also observe Perceived Trendiness (TR) has no statistically significant relationship with PE and so does not predict the same. Therefore:

- Hypothesis H2: *IP on social media sites for job search is positively related to PE, is supported.*
- Hypothesis H4: *IM of social media sites for job search is positively related to PE, is supported.*
- Hypothesis H7: *TR of social media sites for job search is positively related to PE, is not supported.*

Intention to use (IU) of social media usage in job search was predicted by Perceived Usefulness (PU) ($\beta = 3.462$, $p < 0.001$), Perceived Ease of Use (PE) ($\beta = 3.434$, $p < 0.001$) and Perceived Trendiness (TR) ($\beta = 0.486$, $p < 0.001$). These variables together explained 79% of the

Perceived Usefulness ($R^2 = 0.788$). We also observe Perceived Image (IM) to have no statistically significant relationship with IU and so is not a predictor for same. Therefore:

- Hypothesis H5: *IM of social media for job search is positively related to IU, is not supported.*
- Hypothesis H8: *TR of social media for job search is positively related to IU, is supported.*
- Hypothesis H10: *PU of social media for job search is positively related to IU, is supported.*
- Hypothesis H11: *PE of social media for job search is positively related to IU, is supported.*

Actual Use (AU) of social media usage in job search was predicted by Intention to Use (IU) ($\beta = 0.475$, $p < 0.001$). Intention to Use explains 23% of the Perceived Usefulness ($R^2 = 0.226$). Therefore:

- Hypothesis H12: *IU of social media for job search is positively related to AU, is supported.*

(Note: It is observed that the R^2 of AU (0.226) is relatively lower vs. that of PU (0.991), PE (0.719) and AU (0.788). This may possibly be due to the loading of AU 5 items (whose R^2 is 0.02 vs. the other four for items AU1 (0.616), AU2 (0.298), AU3 (0.426) and AU4 (0.411).

The results thus indicate the following causal paths to exist; (i) IP contributes to both PU and PE (ii) IM contributes to PE (and not PU), nor has any direct relationship with IU (iii) TR has no causal paths to PE or PU but has a direct path to IU (underscoring the intent of job seekers, even without information of the job role or company). The causal relationship with the variable has been measured through the structural model and path coefficients as exhibited in Fig. 3.4.

Summarizing the above results, we observe eight of the twelve proposed alternate hypotheses have strong statistical support, and as the coefficients are all positive, the influence would also be positive.

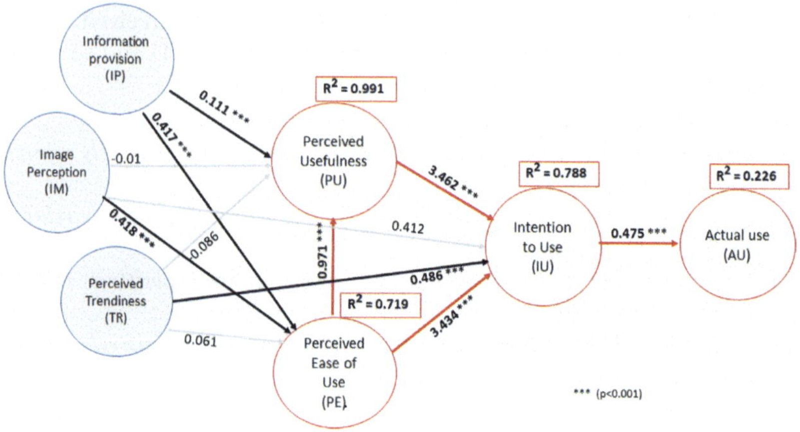

Fig. 3.4 Structural model and path coefficients: Causal relationships (*Source* Authors' data analysis results)

Discussion

This study found that social media usage behavior of job seeker tends toward positive perceptions from Information provisioning (IP), Perceived Image (IM) and Perceived Trendiness (TR). Moreover, the study finds a reasonable (and near good) fit for the hypothesized model. The three antecedent constructs are shown to have causal relationships that contribute significantly to both *Perceived Usefulness* and *Perceived Ease of Use* that cause the *Intention to use*. Thus establishing the framework for the *Actual use*. The antecedent constructs including IP, IM and TR, measured on dimensions of their observable items (Table 3.5), indi-

Table 3.5 Employer branding dimensions of social media

Information provisioning (IP)	*Perceived imagery (IM)*	*Perceived trendiness (TR*
• Explains job roles adequately • Contributes to job application process • Offers a holistic view of firm • Get reliable and credible information	• Futuristic and innovative • Prestige connotations • Peer recognition • Top jobs	• Cool • Exciting • Fun • Trendy

Theoretical Implications

This empirical study contributes to the extant literature by investigating social media usage behaviors in job search and studies their implications to Employer Branding using TAM as a theoretical framework. The research explores the antecedents of social media behaviors in job search and found that the outcomes bear significant implications to employer branding. The empirical findings from the study suggest that the hypothesized model provides a suitable basis from which to conceptualize social media usage behaviors in job search and its implications to Employer Branding. However, the model could require modifications specific to the industry/ employer context. Further, the model does not directly address the role of employer branding in the creation of employer brand equity. Future studies in Employer Branding can be conducted to understand more the behaviors of both potential employees and employers, and their effect on corporate image and firm productivity. This could also provide insights into identifying the brand signals from different segments in the job market to enable focused Employer Branding efforts.

Managerial Implications

We infer from our study that job seekers want to associate more with companies that are perceived to be trendy, provide relevant information, have a positive image and provide top jobs. The overt implications of these studied behaviors suggest employers would need to integrate these very elements into their employability propositions, to attract and retain talent. Projecting the same in job market could keep them effective and adopt a strategic path to employer branding for attracting talent. This study provides a model-based framework to suitably address Employer Branding efforts. However, this model may require modifications to the employer context, depending on the characteristics and competitiveness of the industry sector that they operate in. Thus the employer branding approach for consumer goods industry could be very different from that of services, technology, manufacturing or other industry sectors. Employers could thus use this framework to gain knowledge of the perceptions of the job seekers to suitably develop their employer branding strategies and methods. Such an approach could help the firm to accrue a strategic advantage in the job market and help it to become an employer of choice.

Limitations and Scope for Future Research

One of the limitations that appears with this study is to be its cross sectional attributes and the causal relationships cannot be generalized for the 'job market', which has diverse sets of employers and job seekers. Accordingly sector specific studies using this framework approach can be conducted to avail sector rich implications. Also, there could be other antecedent constructs from other social theories, beyond the three chosen in our model (such as trustworthiness, privacy violation, etc.). Such behavioral constructs could also influence job search behaviors directly or indirectly with associated implications to Employer Branding.

Further, though the sample size of this study is large, we cannot fully rule out the biases of respondents, procedural or desirability related. Future studies could thus also employ qualitative techniques to identify emergent themes in this area. Lastly this study is an inference of employer branding from social media usage in job search behaviors. Future empirical studies could directly ascertain employer responses to employer branding on variables that could comprehensively explain their employer branding approach and methods. Future studies could also shed more light on employer branding based on size of organization (as large, medium or small) for the constraints and challenges faced by these organizations could differ significantly, for reasons of culture norms, ethnicity, work motivations, competitiveness, etc.

Appendix A

Study measures for the measurement and structural model.

Information Provisioning (IP):	I think the information posted on jobs on social media sites.

IP1 Explains the job roles adequately.

IP2 Contributes to my job application experience.

IP3 Offers me a holistic view of the company.

IP4 Is not realistic nor believable (*negative worded item*).

[All items measured using 5 point Likert scale: 1 (strongly disagree) to 5 (strongly agree)].

Perceived Image (IM): I feel using social media for job search:

IM1 Makes the companies to look more innovative and futuristic (by the use of multi-media etc.)

IM2 Is not a very innovative approach (*negative worded item*).

IM3 Offers more prestige to companies that use social media.

IM4 More candidates tend to join prestigious companies.

IM5 Helps me to find a top job (which my friends are also telling me.

[All items measured using 5 point Likert scale: 1 (strongly disagree) to 5 (strongly agree)].

Perceived Trendiness (TR): I think applying for jobs using social media:

TR1 Is cool.

TR2 Is exciting.

TR3 Is not as fun.

TR4 Is trendy.

[All items measured using 5 point Likert scale: 1 (strongly disagree) to 5 (strongly agree)].

Perceived Usefulness (PU): I feel job search using social media:

PU1 Is faster.

PU2 Is better, as can get more information.

PU3 Connects me with a wide range of companies.

PU4 Connects me with right companies (that matter to me).

PU5 Helps me to fit better into a company, if selected.

[All items measured using 5 point Likert scale: 1 (strongly disagree) to 5 (strongly agree)].

Perceived Ease of Use (PE): I think job search using social media:

PE1 Is easier.

PE2 Makes it easy to interact with companies.

PE3 Does not allow me to find a job quickly (*negative worded item*).

PE4 Enables me to apply to right companies.

[All items measured using 5 point Likert scale: 1 (strongly disagree) to 5 (strongly agree)].

Intention to Use (IU): I intend to use social media:

IU1 For searching and for applying for jobs.

IU2 By taking the support of various social media apps and tools.

IU3 As it allows me to communicate better.

IU4 As it allows me to brand myself better.

[All items measured using 5 point Likert scale: 1 (strongly disagree) to 5 (strongly agree)].

Actual Use (AU):

AU1How often per week do you visit social media sites for job related reasons?

[Item measured using 5 point Likert scale: 1 (Not at all visit: nil), 2 (Rarely visit: 1–2 times) 3 (Occasionally visit: 3–4 times) 4 (Often visit: 4–5 times) and 5 (Frequently visit: 6 or more times)].

AU2How often per week do you post on your personal social media accounts.

[Item measured using 5 point Likert scale: 1 (Not at all post: nil), 2 (Rarely post: 1–2 times) 3 (Occasionally post: 3–4 times) 4 (Often post: 4–5 times) and 5 (Frequently post: 6 or more times)].

AU3How many job postings have you seen in the last 1 month on social media sites.

[Item measured using 5 point Likert scale: 1 (Not seen any: nil), 2 (Not seen many :1–2 jobs), 3 (Seen few: 3–5 jobs), 4 (Seen many: 6–9) and 5 (Seen very many:10 or more jobs)].

AU4How many job postings have you applied for in the last 1 month using social media sites.

[Item measured using 5 point Likert scale: 1 (Not applied to any: nil), 2 (Applied to some: 1–2 jobs), 3 (Applied to few: 3–5 jobs), 4 (Applied to many: 6–9) and 5 (Applied to very many:10 or more jobs)].

AU5How much time do you spend on social media every day?

[Item measured using 5 point Likert scale: 1 (Not much: 0–2 h), 2 (Spend somewhat time: 2–4 h) 3 Spend reasonable time: 4–6 h) 4 (Spend much time: 6–8 h) and 5 (Spend very much more time: more than 8 h)].

References

Aaker, D. A. (1996). Measuring brand equity across products and markets. *California management review*, *38*(3), 102–120.

Ambler, T., & Barrow, S. J. (1996). The employee brand. *The Journal of Brand Management.*, *4*(3), 185–206.

Backhaus, K., & Tikoo, S. (2004). Conceptualizing and researching employer branding. *Career Development International*, *9*(4/5), 501–517.

Bagozzi, R. P. (1992). The self-regulation of attitudes, intentions, and behavior. *Social Psychology Quarterly*, *55*, 178–204.

Barrow, S. (1990). Turning recruitment advertising into a competitive weapon. Paper delivered at the *CIPD Annual Conference*, Harrogate, UK.

Berthon, P., Ewing, M., & Hah, L. L. (2005). Captivating company: Dimensions of attractiveness in employer branding. *International Journal of Advertising, 24*(2), 151–172.

Branham, L. (2000). *Keeping the people who keep you in business: 24 ways to hang on to your most valuable talent*. AMACOM/American Management Association.

Bond, R. M., Fariss, C. J., Jones, J. J., Kramer, A. D., Marlow, C., Settle, J. E., & Fowler, J. H. (2012). A 61-million-person experiment in social influence and political mobilization. *Nature, 489*(7415), 295–298.

Cappelli, P. (2019). Your approach to hiring is all wrong. *Harvard Business Review, 97*(3), 48–58.

Cober, R. T., Brown, D. J., Levy, P. E., Cober, A. B., & Keeping, L. M. (2003). Organizational web sites: Web site content and style as determinants of organizational attraction. *International Journal of Selection and Assessment, 11*(2–3), 158–169.

Coff, R., & Kryscynski, D. (2011). Invited editorial: Drilling for microfoundations of human capital-based competitive advantages. *Journal of Management, 37*(5), 1429–1443.

Collins, C. J., & Stevens, C. K. (2002). The relationship between early recruitment-related activities and the application decisions of new labor-market entrants: A brand equity approach to recruitment. *Journal of Applied Psychology, 87*(6), 1121.

Davis, F. D. (1989). Perceived usefulness, perceived ease of use, and user acceptance of information technology. *MIS quarterly, 13*(3), 319–340.

Davis, F. D., & Venkatesh, V. (1996). A critical assessment of potential measurement biases in the technology acceptance model: Three experiments. *International Journal of Human-Computer Studies, 45*(1), 19–45.

Dell, D., Ainspan, N., Bodenberg, T., Troy, K., & Hickey, J. (2001). Engaging employees through your brand (*Research Report* 1288-01-RR). The Conference Board.

Dhar, R., & Wertenbroch, K. (2000). Consumer choice between hedonic and utilitarian goods. *Journal of Marketing Research, 37*(1), 60–71.

Dixit, R. V., & Prakash, G. (2018). Intentions to use social networking sites (SNS) using technology acceptance model (TAM) an empirical study. *Paradigm, 22*(1), 65–79.

Fernandez, R. M., Castilla, E. J., & Moore, P. (2000). Social capital at work: Networks and employment at a phone center. *American Journal of Sociology, 105*(5), 1288–1356.

Fornell, C., & Larcker, D. F. (1981). Evaluating structural equation models with unobservable variables and measurement error. *Journal of Marketing Research, 18*(1), 39–50.

Garson, G. (2009). Validity. [Online]. Available: http://faculty.chass.ncsu.edu/garson/PA765/validity.htm.

Gefen, D., & Straub, D. (2005). A practical guide to factorial validity using PLS-graph: Tutorial and annotated example. *Communications of the Association for Information Systems, 16*(1), 5.

Gutman, J. (1982). A means-end chain model based on consumer categorization processes. *Journal of Marketing, 46*(2), 60–72.

Hair, J. F., Anderson, R. E., Tatham, R. L., & Black, W. C. (1995). *Multivariate date analysis with readings* (4th ed.). Prentice Hall.

Hair, J. F., Black, W. C., Babin, B. J., Anderson, R. E., & Tatham, R. L. (1998). *Multivariate data analysis* (Vol. 5, No. 3, pp. 207–219). Prentice hall.

Hair, J. F., Black, W. C., Babin, B. J., Anderson, R. E., & Tatham, R. L. (2006). *Multivariate data analysis* (6th ed.).Pearson Prentice Hall.

Hair, J. F., Black, W. C., Babin, B. J., & Anderson, R. E. (2010). *Multivariate data analysis* (7th ed.). Prentice Hall.

Hair, J. F., Hult, G. T. M., Ringle, C. M., & Sarstedt, M. (2014). *A primer on partial least squares structural equation modeling (PLS-SEM)*. Sage.

Heene, M., Hilbert, S., Draxler, C., Ziegler, M., & Bühner, M. (2011). Masking misfit in confirmatory factor analysis by increasing unique variances: A cautionary note on the usefulness of cutoff values of fit indices. *Psychological Methods, 16*(3), 319.

Jain, S. P., & Posavac, S. S. (2001). Prepurchase attribute verifiability, source credibility, and persuasion. *Journal of Consumer Psychology, 11*(3), 169–180.

Jovanovic, B. (1979). Firm-specific capital and turnover. *Journal of Political Economy, 87*(6), 1246–1260.

Keller, K. L. (1993). Conceptualizing, measuring, and managing customer-based brand equity. *Journal of Marketing, 57*(1), 1–22.

Kotler, P. (1997). *Marketing management: Analysis, planning, implementation and control*. Prentice Hall.

Molla, A., & Licker, P. S. (2001). E-commerce systems success: An attempt to extend and re-specify the Delone and MacLean model of IS success. *Journal of Electronic Commerce Research, 2*(4), 131–141.

Moore, G. C., & Benbasat, I. (1991). Development of an instrument to measure the perceptions of adopting an information technology innovation. *Information Systems Research, 2*(3), 192–222.

Mortensen, D. T., & Vishwanath, T. (1994). Personal contacts and earnings: It is who you know! *Labour Economics, 1*(2), 187–201.

Petersen, T., Saporta, I., & Seidel, M. D. L. (2000). Offering a job: Meritocracy and social networks. *American Journal of Sociology, 106*(3), 763–816.

Petkovic, M. (2004). Geschickte markenpolitik. *Personal, 56*(4), 6–9.

Randstad Report. Randstad Employer Brand Research. (2019). *Download Randstad Employer Branding Global Report (Randstad.com website)*, 16.2, Employer Brand Research (2019), Global Report (2019).

Rauniar, R., Rawski, G., Crumbly, J., & Simms, J. (2009). C2C online auction website performance: Buyer's perspective. *Journal of Electronic Commerce Research, 10*(2), 56–75.

Raunier, R., & Yang, J. (2014). Technology acceptance model (TAM) and social media usage: An empirical study on Facebook. *Journal of Enterprise Information Management, 27*(1), 6–30.

RoyChowdhury, T., & Srimannarayana, M. (2013). Applicants' perceptions on online recruitment procedures. *Management and Labour Studies, 38*(3), 185–199.

Sinar, E. F., Reynolds, D. H., & Paquet, S. L. (2003). Nothing but 'Net'? Corporate image and web-based testing. *International Journal of Selection and Assessment, 11*(2–3), 150–157.

Sutherland, M. M., Torricelli, D. G., & Karg, R. F. (2002). Employer-of-choice branding for knowledge workers. *South African Journal of Business Management, 33*(4), 13–20.

Sylva, H., & Mol, S. T. (2009). E-recruitment: A study into applicant perceptions of an online application system. *International Journal of Selection and Assessment, 17*(3), 311–323.

van Esch, P., & Black, J. S. (2019). Factors that influence new generation candidates to engage with and complete digital AI-Enabled Recruiting. *Business Horizons, 62*(6), 729–739.

van Esch, P., & Mente, M. (2018). Marketing video-enabled social media as part of your e-recruitment strategy: Stop trying to be trendy. *Journal of Retailing and Consumer Services, 44*, 266–273.

Taylor, S., Hunter, G., & Lindberg, D. (2007). Understanding (customer-based) brand equity in financial services. *Journal of Services Marketing, 21*(4), 241–252.

Venkatesh, V., & Davis, F. D. (2000). A theoretical extension of the technology acceptance model: Four longitudinal field studies. *Management Science, 46*(2), 186–204.

Yoo, B., & Donthu, N. (2001). Developing a scale to measure the perceived quality of an Internet shopping site (SITEQUAL). *Quarterly Journal of Electronic Commerce, 2*(1), 31–45.

Zeithaml, V. A. (2000). Service quality, profitability, and the economic worth of customers: What we know and what we need to learn. *Journal of the Academy of Marketing Science, 28*(1), 67–85.

Zeithaml, V. A., Parasuraman, A., & Malhotra, A. (2002). Service quality delivery through web sites: A critical review of extant knowledge. *Journal of the Academy of Marketing Science, 30*(4), 362–376.

Zipf, G. (1949). *Human Behavior and the Principle of Least Effort: An Introduction to Human Ecology*. Addison-Wesley.

CHAPTER 4

Social Media—The Emotional and Mental Roller-Coaster of Gen Z: An Empirical Study

Lakshmi Kannan and T. Praveen Kumar

Introduction

Generation Z today is said to adapt to everything and anything rapidly and not only this they learn about new products and various other developments on social media quicker than anyone else does. They are also 59% more likely than older generations to connect socially with friends and families and build the network. Being socially connected to others can ease stress, anxiety, and depression, boost self-worth, provide comfort and joy, and prevent loneliness. On the other side, lacking strong social connections can pose a serious risk to the mental and emotional health and feel completely left out and aloof, which is where the harm begins.

L. Kannan · T. P. Kumar (✉)
Faculty, Ramaiah Institute of Management, Bangalore, India
e-mail: praveen@msrim.org

L. Kannan
e-mail: lakshmikannan@msrim.org

Rajagopal and R. Behl (eds.), *Managing Disruptions in Business*, Palgrave Studies in Democracy, Innovation, and Entrepreneurship for Growth, https://doi.org/10.1007/978-3-030-79709-6_4

Everyone is different and there is no specific amount of time spent on social media and no one can control the time one spends over social sites or the frequency one checks for updates, or the number of posts one makes and likes but these don't indicate by any means that the user is being unhealthy, but if this excess use causes one to neglect face-to-face relationships and the society, causes distractions at work school, or is developing feelings of envy, hatred, or one is posting pictures to show others or make others jealous, its time one thinks and relooks into their social behavior and social media habits. For this current generation using social media has become a substitute for a lot of offline social interactions. Even if one is out with friends, one still feels the need to constantly check social media. Post regular content about oneself, get comments, or likes on the posts, or respond quickly and enthusiastically to friends' posts. These days' people check social media last thing at night, first thing in the morning, or even when they wake up in the night?, and the light from phones and other devices can disrupt one's sleep and cause sleepless nights and does affect mental health. All of our understanding is that Millennials were excited about social media, but Gen Z brings this to an entirely different level.

The generation replacing the Millennials is Generation Z or Gen Z for brief. The mid-to-late-1990s are widely used by demographers and researchers as beginning birth years, though at the end of the years a consensus has not been reached. Generation Z has used technological generation from a younger age for its inspiration and is comfortable with the Internet. Gen Z has started to collect awareness and insights on buying power and social media, and they are generating attention that has been put on Millennials for a long period. This makes Gen Z and their use of social media very accurate. In parenting and adulthood, millennials develop equally, so Gen Z can emerge. They will be the number one age to be raised within the mobile and social media globe without a doubt. Generation Z is passionate about social media users and has emerged as an efficient force for social change. Technological developments (i.e., smartphones and social media) have changed how Gen Z was relative to previous generations in communicating, socializes, and gets statistics. Because dwelling through these events and seeing their impact affects how they could perceive and take the attitude of others, precise reports and characteristics encouraged generation Z's empathy. In addition to testing its effect on them as an individual, business enterprise, and society, the paper seeks to highlight how the current generation Z uses social media. The paper describes the emotional equilibrium of the distinction of generation Z in their attitudes, norms, and choices that may change continuously over time. It explains their use of social media and their intra-generational differentiation that stems from environmental and private influences. The paper reveals how the use of social media impacts on their emotional attitudes in the Gen Z. It aims to pick out some questions about Gen Z's and their social media usability, as well as sketches rational insights into emotional behavior that causes the younger generation's different choices, choices, and emotional choices. The Research questions stood in the present study is: What is the role of social media in the emotional and mental health of Gen Z during pre- and current pandemic situation? More specifically we ask two research questions as stated below:

- RQ_1: Would Gen Z usage pattern (fixed and varied period) and addiction toward social media affect their emotional and mental health?
- RQ_2: How the mental and emotional health of Gen Z varies between pre- and current pandemic situations.

To answer these questions, we conducted a literature review, from which hypotheses were formulated. Social media addiction, mental well-being, and emotional behavior questionnaires were then taken, based on contributions from the literature, to test these hypotheses. The questionnaire was given to Gen Z in Bangalore city. Descriptive analysis, paired sample *t*-test and ANOVA (randomized block experiment), and partial least-square were used to obtain the results. This research paper is categorized as follows: first, grounded on the research question the review of literature is discussed second, the study objectives identified, next the model and hypothesis are developed. Then, the study methodology is described. Finally, analysis is carried out and results are obtained and discussed.

Theoretical Background

Gratification Theory

Katz et al. (1973) pointed out that the gratification theory (U&G) is based on the social and psychological roots of needs that create perceptions from mass media or other outlets that contribute to unequal patterns of media visibility, resulting in the need for gratification and other consequences. U&G is linked to the use of mass media by people. U&G was also concerned with how individuals fulfilled or satisfied their needs in terms of content when using the media. The U&G theory suggests that the social and psychosocial consequences of the use of the Internet depend largely on the user's motivations and objectives for using the technology (Weiser, 2001). Shao (2009) reported that individuals use user-generated media for a variety of purposes: consuming content to meet their knowledge, entertainment, and mood management needs; engaging through engagement with content and other users to improve social connections and virtual communities and creating their content for self-expression and self-actualization. Colás et al.'s (2013) study findings indicate that for young people, online social networks are a source of resources used to meet both psychological and social needs There are common reasons for people to use social networks. Omar et al. (2014) described the following motivations: finding information, seeking entertainment, social contact, personal identification, and self-disclosure. As McQuail (1987) said, "seeking information" is a basic need for people to understand the relevant events and conditions in the world. "Seek entertainment" is seen to get rid of the tension of daily life and relax as well as to fill your spare time.

Social interaction and incorporation provide an insight into the circumstances of others or social sympathy. Personal identity involves enhancing personal beliefs, discovering behavioral trends, connecting with other values (in the media), and gaining insight into one's self (Omar et al., 2014). Jourard (1964) listed self-disclosure, made the individual visible to others, and enabled others to see the person as a special or common human being. Several studies have explored the motives of the Internet and SNS (Stafford & Gillenson, 2004), socialization and entertainment (Curras-Perez et al., 2014), alienation (Petrocchi et al., 2015), social integration (Weiser, 2001), self-expression and self-actualization (Shao, 2009), work-life balance, etc. (Kim et al., 2014). Scheepers et al. (2014) applied more motivational aspects to the usage of social networks. These behaviors are the quest for knowledge, hedonistic habits, the preservation of strong connections, and the extension of weak ties. Another research conducted in Turkey by Calisir et al. (2013) found that 155 participants had a behavioral intention to use, perceived pleasure, perceived ease of use, perceived utility, and social impact, either directly or indirectly, on the use of social networks on smartphones among students.

Social Displacement Theory

The Social Displacement Theory, as originally suggested, claimed that when individuals were affected, they spend more time on the Internet and spend less time on personal relationships with near family and friends. This argument claimed that while the contact was increased Internet opportunities decreased social interaction and psychological wellness (Kraut et al., 1998; Nie, 2001). Subsequent empiric investigations have stopped these complaints (Kraut et al., 2002; Nie & Hillygus, 2002), and only a meta-analysis was found poor evidence of a cross-sectional correlation between Internet usage and well-being (Huang, 2010). As of its initial wording, the displacement hypothesis new life has been identified in the study of online discussion groups (Cummings et al., 2002). There are four forms of indirect evidence of social displacement as related to the use of social media. First, a recent meta-analysis, involving 9000 Facebook users, reported a poor positive correlation between use and loneliness but challenged the causal relationship (Song et al., 2014). This establishes a connection between the Usage of social media and depression as stated by the displacement hypothesis. Second, to the association, the face-to-face relationships and positive psychosocial results are better than the relationship between online-only relationships and psychosocial result (Ahn & Shin, 2013; Dunbar, 2014; Pollet et al., 2011; Shakya & Christakis, 2017). Short-term longitudinal methods (e.g., Hinsch & Sheldon, 2013; Sheldon et al., 2011) and experience sampling methods (ESMs) have been utilized to explore the association between social media use and well-being (Kross et al., 2013; Verduyn et al., 2015). Although Shakya and Christakis (2017) explored the positive association with the number and quality of close relationships, they did not explore whether social media use predicted change in interactions with close others.

Effect on Social Media on Well-Being

Aparicio (2020) analyzes the effects of communication with cell phones and web-based media stages that influence the psychological wellness and prosperity of teenagers as they progress from existence with guardians to life on their own. Convenience test of no under 50 and close to 100 people between the ages of 18–25 reacting to a poll using a Qualtrics online survey. Findings show that although web-based media is not the main pointer of sadness, web-based media has a factually huge relationship with expanded CES-D scores. Xu et al. (2020) research investigates the utilization of multimodal prompts present in online media presents on foresee clients' psychological well-being status. Few characterization tests expecting to separate between (1) sound clients and clients influenced by a psychological wellness ailment; and (2) solid clients and clients inclined to mental illness. The exploratory outcomes show that utilizing different modalities can improve the exhibition of this grouping task when contrasted with the utilization of each methodology in turn and can give significant signals into a client's psychological status. Zhang et al. states that such examination means to analyze research subjects, the part of web-based media, and exploration techniques in web-based media-based general well-being research distributed from 2000 to 2018. A dataset of 3419 legitimate investigations was created by looking through the top-notch of applicable catchphrases in the Web of Science and PubMed information bases. Furthermore, this investigation utilizes an unaided book mining method and subject displaying to remove research topics of the distributed studies. Social media empowers researchers to concentrate on new wonders and propose new examination inquiries in general well-being research. Zhang and Ma (2020) analyze the prompt effect of the COVID-19 pandemic on psychological wellness and personal satisfaction among nearby Chinese inhabitants matured ≥18 years in Liaoning Province territory, China. An online overview was disseminated through a web-based media stage between January and February 2020. Members finished an altered approved poll that surveyed the Impact of Event Scale (IES), pointers of negative emotional wellness effects, social and family uphold, and psychological well-being connected way of life changes. In the end, the COVID-19 pandemic was related with a gentle upsetting effect in the example, although the COVID-19 pandemic is as yet continuous. Twenge and Farley (2021) try to look at the relationship between changed kinds of screen exercises (online media, web, gaming, and TV) and mental health indicators independently for young men and girls. It drew from a broadly delegate test of 13–15-year-old teenagers in the UK (n = 11,427) getting some information about hours of the day spent on explicit screen media activities. It has been observed that time spent via web-based media and Internet use were all the more unequivocally connected with self-hurt practices, burdensome manifestations, loser fulfillment, and low confidence than hours spent on electronic gaming and TV viewing. Young women generally demonstrated a more grounded relationship between screen media time and emotional well-being pointers than young men. Nop (2020) investigates the breaks down of what the impacts are and how correspondence is affected by these youngsters. It doubts how youngsters can use web-based media and abatement harm. The study will be directed through a writing audit and analysis. Its objective is to orchestrate the current information via online media prosperity and how it identifies with youngsters, explicitly Millennials and Generation Z, to at last prescribe methodologies to streamline prosperity in the advanced age. Cooks (2020) connects essential points to analyze these pathways between online media use and discouragement and to decide if such connections equal what is perceived about the relationship between burdensome manifestations and up close and personal relational working. Keles et al. (2020) discuss audit blended proof as online media use to overcome gloom, nervousness, and mental trouble in adolescents. A search of PsycINFO, Medline, Embase, CINAHL, and SSCI information bases procured 13 qualified investigations, of which 12 were cross-sectional. All spaces are related to discouragement, uneasiness, and mental misery. Rasmussen et al. (2020) explored the relationship between social media use and mental well-being through difficulties with emotion regulation and perceived stress among a sample of US college-student emerging adults. Findings suggest that social media use may be a risk factor for mental health among adults and that social media use may be an activity to which adults resort when dealing with difficult emotions.

Yadav and Rai attempt to investigate the consciousness of how the current Generation Z is utilizing the online media just as to survey its repercussion on them as an individual's association and society as a system. This research is significant for tending to the real importance for associations looking to comprehend and attempting to exploit Gen Z' web-based media collaborations. Çiçek et al. (2018) distinguish the impact of web-based media advertising on brand faithfulness of the shoppers, given that the idea is getting expanding consideration from promoting the scholarly community and professionals. The extent of the investigation comprise of clients who follow at any rate one brand on the online media in Turkey and the information were gathered through the organization of an organized survey with an example of 338 individuals and tried using stepwise different relapse analysis. The consequences of the examination indicated that brand dependability of the clients is emphatically influenced when the brand (1) offers invaluable missions, (2) offers pertinent substance, (3) offers famous substance, and (4) shows up on different stages and offers applications via web-based media.

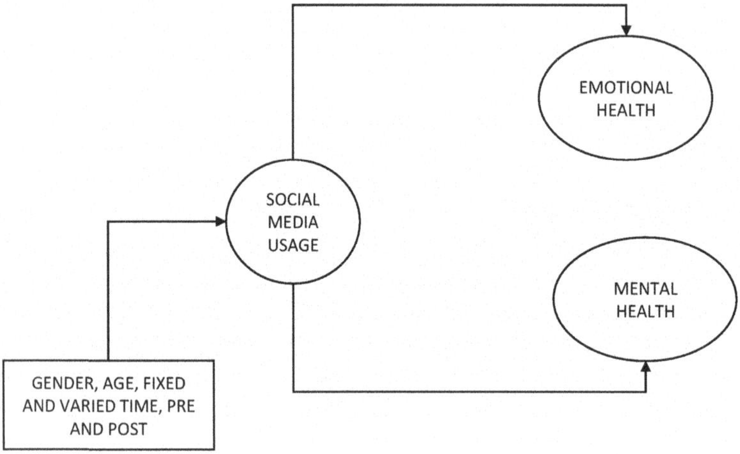

Fig. 4.1 Conceptual model (*Source* Authors)

Objectives of the Study

To observe the part played by social media in Gen Z emotional and mental well-being the empirical analysis is needed to:

1. measure the mental and emotional health of Gen Z in fixed and varied time usage of mobile phones.
2. measure the mental and emotional health of Gen Z in pre- and current pandemic situations.
3. investigate the impact of social media usage pattern on mental and emotional health among a section of Gen Z (Fig. 4.1).

Hypothesis Development

Homogeneity Test—Hypothesis

H1a: *There is no homogeneity across the different levels of time (Fixed and Varied) concerning the Pre- and Post-Pandemic on mental health and emotional health.*

H2a: *There is no homogeneity across the Pre- and Post-Pandemic situations and mobile phone usage on mental health and emotional health of Gen Z.*

SEM—Measurement Hypothesis

H0: Impact of social media usage pattern on emotional and mental health.

Methodology

Participants

The research design is the technique of finding answers to the research questions. This study encompasses investigating the impact of social media on the mental and emotional health of Gen Z in pre- and current pandemic situations. As it efforts to measure the phenomena as they exist. The researcher conducted a randomized controlled trial (RCT) in investigating the impact of social media on mental and emotional health among a section of Gen Z pre- and current pandemic situations. This study is carried out in Bangalore city, where a higher number of Gen Z studying in Higher educational institutions. Four educational institutions in Bangalore were chosen based upon the number of Gen Z categories studying in this institution. After obtaining consent from the educational intuition and voluntariness of participants, In February 2020 the Gen Z were included in the experiment. The inclusion criteria are participant must be frequent users of social media use, and at least have three or more different social media account. The reasons for selecting the criteria of social media usage in part because previous research has shown that there is a relationship between the use of social media and mental health (Fuller et al., 2017).

Procedure

Totally 420 Gen Z showed interested in participating in the experiment and received an information sheet explaining the study and an informed consent form. And this was signed by 350 people. So a total of 350 Gen Z participants were randomly assigned to the following two groups with two-time period: measuring mental health and emotional health condition on March 2020 with fixed time on social media usage ($n = 175$) and varied/increase time on social media usage ($n = 175$) (pre-first period—pre-pandemic with intervention) and August 2020 (Post—second period—current pandemic—with intervention) fixed time on social media usage ($n = 175$) and varied/increase time on social media usage ($n = 175$). Block randomization was carried out for the two groups with stratification on gender, location, education level, and age using computer-generated random sequences of numbers.

Measures

All respondents finished measures on two occasions: at baseline (Pre-first period—March 2020 with pre-pandemic with intervention) and completed line (Post-second period—current pandemic—with intervention). Structured questionnaires were used to measure mental health, emotional health, and social media addiction, and questionnaires were administered online to collect data from the respondents. The outcome measures mental health measured through well-being (WHO-5 Well-Being Index), depression (Depression module of Health Questionnaire [PHQ-9]; Kroenke et al., 2001), anxiety (Generalized Anxiety Disorder 7 scale [GAD-7]; Löwe et al., 2008), stress (perceived stress scale [PSS-10]; Cohen & Williamson, 1991), and sleep quality (SQI). Another measure of emotional health measured through Emotional Behavioral Scales—Generalized Anxiety disorder (GAD), Separation anxiety disorder (SAD), Major Depressive disorder (MDD), social anxiety disorder (social phobia) (SP), Attention-deficit hyperactivity disorder (ADHD), oppositional-defiant disorder (ODD), and Conduct disorder (CD) (Laura Duncan et al., 2018). The social media addiction through Bergen Social Media Addiction Scale (BSMAS; Andreassen et al., 2012).

Results and Discussions

Demographic Analysis

The respondents were taken for the study concerning the gender with the same proportion in both pre- and post-pandemic situations concerning the fixed time and varied time. The total number of 350 samples was blocked based on the above proportion (50%) (Table 4.1).

> *Objective 1: To measure the mental and emotional health of Gen Z in fixed and varied time usage of mobile phones.*

To test if these different levels of time (fixed and varied/ pre- and post-pandemic) concerning mobile phone usage had an impact on mental

Table 4.1 Demographic profile

			Pre-pandemic		*Post-pandemic*	
S. No	*Demographic Variable*		*Fixed time*	*Varied time*	*Fixed time*	*Varied time*
1	Gender	Male	87	87	87	87
2		Female	88	88	88	88
	Total		175	175	175	175

Source Primary Data

health (well-being, depression, anxiety, stress, and sleep quality) and emotional health (Separation anxiety disorder, Major Depressive disorder, Social phobia—social anxiety disorder, Attention-deficit hyperactivity disorder, Conduct disorder, and Generalized Anxiety disorder) of Gen Z, one-way analysis of variance was carried out. Since testing each measure of emotional and mental health of Gen Z will provide concrete results regarding the impact of different levels of time (fixed and varied/pre- and post-pandemic), the consolidated hypothesis formulated for the same is given below (Table 4.2):

> H1a: There is no homogeneity across the different levels of time (Fixed and Varied) concerning the Pre- and Post-Pandemic on mental health and emotional health

Testing of homogeneity across different levels of time concerning pre-pandemic.

The level of the study belongs to a fixed and varied level of time concerning mobile phone usage The hypothesis formulated is given below:

> H1a: There is no homogeneity across the different levels of time (Fixed and Varied) concerning the Pre-Pandemic on mental and emotional health.

The ANOVA results of mental health and emotional health measures across two levels of mobile phone usage time (fixed and varied) concerning pre-pandemic are presented in Table 4.2. The test results for all the measures in mental and emotional health were found to be insignificant as p values are higher than 0.05. Therefore, failed to reject the null

Table 4.2 Analysis of variance (ANOVA)—fixed time a varied time (pre- and post-pandemic)

Study variables	*Measurement*	*Levels*	*N*	*Mean*	*ANOVA*	
					F-value	*P-value*
Mental health	Well-being	Fixed Time—Pre	175	17.25	2.003	**0.158**
		Varied Time—Pre	175	17.82		
		Fixed Time—Post	175	15.22	3.025	**0.083**
		Varied Time—Post	175	14.61		
	Depression	Fixed Time—Pre	175	13.75	0.984	**0.322**
		Varied Time—Pre	175	14.37		
		Fixed Time—Post	175	13.59	0.026	**0.873**
		Varied Time—Post	175	13.53		
	Anxiety	Fixed Time—Pre	175	11.07	1.411	**0.236**
		Varied Time—Pre	175	11.68		
		Fixed Time—Post	175	10.51	1.021	**0.313**
		Varied Time—Post	175	10.19		
	Stress	Fixed Time—Pre	175	26.70	0.422	**0.516**
		Varied Time—Pre	175	26.03		
		Fixed Time—Post	175	20.11	0.064	**0.801**
		Varied Time—Post	175	20.24		
	Sleep quality	Fixed Time—Pre	175	9.91	1.595	**0.207**

(continued)

Table 4.2 (continued)

Study variables	*Measurement*	*Levels*	*N*	*Mean*	*ANOVA*	
					F-value	*P-value*
		Varied Time—Pre	175	10.71		
		Fixed Time—Post	175	10.55	0.087	**0.768**
		Varied Time—Post	175	10.64		
Emotional health	Separation anxiety disorder	Fixed Time—Pre	175	19.23	0.566	**0.452**
		Varied Time—Pre	175	19.85		
		Fixed Time—Post	175	14.07	1.653	**0.199**
		Varied Time—Post	175	13.55		
	Major Depressive disorder	Fixed Time—Pre	175	25.25	1.853	**0.173**
		Varied Time—Pre	175	26.67		
		Fixed Time—Post	175	17.33	0.429	**0.513**
		Varied Time—Post	175	17.67		
	Social phobia -social anxiety disorder	Fixed Time—Pre	175	13.14	1.826	**0.178**
		Varied Time—Pre	175	14.13		
		Fixed Time—Post	175	9.99	0.269	**0.604**
		Varied Time—Post	175	9.82		
	Attention-deficit hyperactivity disorder	Fixed Time—Pre	175	21.84	0.789	**0.375**
		Varied Time—Pre	175	22.70		
		Fixed Time—Post	175	16.20	0.183	**0.669**
		Varied Time—Post	175	16.37		
	Conduct disorder	Fixed Time—Pre	175	27.77	0.364	**0.547**

(continued)

Table 4.2 (continued)

Study variables	*Measurement*	*Levels*	*N*	*Mean*	*ANOVA*	
					F-value	*P-value*
		Varied Time—Pre	175	27.19		
		Fixed Time—Post	175	19.84	0.007	**0.935**
		Varied Time—Post	175	19.88		
	Generalized Anxiety disorder	Fixed Time—Pre	175	16.18	1.282	**0.258**
		Varied Time—Pre	175	17.07		
		Fixed Time—Post	175	11.98	0.408	**0.151**
		Varied Time—Post	175	12.22		
	Oppositional-defiant disorder	Fixed Time—Pre	175	14.56	0.648	**0.421**
		Varied Time—Pre	175	15.19		
		Fixed Time—Post	175	12.42	2.071	**0.524**
		Varied Time—Post	175	11.87		

hypothesis and rejected the alternate hypothesis. It means there is homogeneity across the different levels of time (fixed and varied) concerning the pre-pandemic on mental and emotional health.

Testing of homogeneity across different levels of time concerning post-pandemic effects:

The level of the study belongs to a fixed and varied level of time concerning mobile phone usage. The hypothesis formulated is given below:

> H1b: There is no homogeneity across the different levels of time (Fixed and Varied) concerning the Post-Pandemic on mental and emotional health.

The ANOVA results of mental health and emotional health measures across two levels of mobile phone usage time (fixed and varied) concerning post-pandemic are presented in Table 4.2. The test results for all the measures in mental and emotional health were found to be insignificant as *p* values are higher than 0.05. Therefore, failed to reject the null hypothesis and rejected the alternate hypothesis. It means there is homogeneity across the different levels of time (fixed and varied) concerning the post-pandemic on mental and emotional health. So, in general, there is a significant impact on mobile phone usage time on the mental and emotional health of Gen Z (Table 4.3).

Table 4.3 Analysis of variance (ANOVA)—pre- and post-pandemic

Study variables	*Measurement*	*Levels*	*N*	*Mean*	*ANOVA*	
					F-value	*P-value*
Mental health	Well-being	Pre-pandemic	175	17.53	97.289	**0.000**
		Post-Pandemic	175	14.91		
	Depression	Pre-pandemic	175	14.06	1.970	**0.161**
		Post-Pandemic	175	13.56		
	Anxiety	Pre-pandemic	175	11.38	11.555	**0.000**
		Post-Pandemic	175	10.35		
	Stress	Pre-pandemic	175	26.37	117.68	**0.000**
		Post-Pandemic	175	20.18		
	Sleep quality	Pre-pandemic	175	10.31	0.630	**0.428**
		Post-Pandemic	175	10.59		
Emotional health	Separation anxiety disorder	Pre-pandemic	175	19.54	157.10	0.000
		Post-Pandemic	175	13.81		
	Major depressive disorder	Pre-pandemic	175	25.96	201.88	0.000
		Post-Pandemic	175	17.83		
	Social phobia -social anxiety disorder	Pre-pandemic	175	13.63	87.66	0.000
		Post-Pandemic	175	9.91		
	Attention-deficit hyperactivity disorder	Pre-pandemic	175	22.27	129.840	0.000
		Post-Pandemic	175	16.29		
	Conduct disorder	Pre-pandemic	175	27.48	204.58	0.000
		Post-Pandemic	175	19.86		
	Generalized anxiety disorder	Pre-pandemic	175	16.63	108.66	0.000
		Post-Pandemic	175	12.10		
	Oppositional-defiant disorder	Pre-pandemic	175	14.87	39.357	0.000
		Post-Pandemic	175	12.15		

Objective 2: To measure the mental and emotional health of Gen Z in pre- and current pandemic situations.

The consolidated hypothesis formulated for the above objectives is given below:

> H2a: There is no homogeneity across the Pre- and Post-Pandemic situations and mobile phone usage on mental health and emotional health of Gen Z.

The ANOVA results of mental health and emotional health measures pre- and post-pandemic are presented in Table 4.3. The test results for all the measures in mental and emotional health were found to be significant as p values are lesser than 0.05. Except depression ($p = 0.161$) and sleep quality ($p = 0.428$). Therefore, reject the null hypothesis and accept the alternate hypothesis H2a for mental health (Well-Being, Anxiety, Stress) and emotional health (Separation anxiety disorder, Major Depressive disorder, Social phobia—social anxiety disorder, Attention-deficit hyperactivity disorder, Conduct disorder, Generalized Anxiety disorder). It means there is no homogeneity across the pre- and post-pandemic on mental health (Well-Being, Anxiety, Stress) and emotional health (Separation anxiety disorder, Major Depressive disorder, Social phobia—social anxiety disorder, Attention-deficit hyperactivity disorder, Conduct disorder, Generalized Anxiety disorder) and there is homogeneity across pre- and post-pandemic on sleep quality and depression. It means there is no significant mean difference in depression and sleep quality of Gen Z in pre- and post-pandemic situations.

Objective 3: To investigate the impact of social media usage pattern on mental and emotional health among a section of Gen Z.

Structural equation modeling (SEM), also known as path analysis, is now a regularly used method for representing dependency relations in multivariate data in the behavioral and social sciences. SEM refers to a diverse set of mathematical models, computer algorithms, and statistical methods that fit networks of constructs to data. SEM includes confirmatory factor analysis, path analysis, and partial least squares path analysis. We have done the SEM and taken the measurement model. SEM was tested using AMOS software. The measurement model defines relationships between the observed and unobserved variables. It provides the link between scores on a measuring instrument (i.e., the observed indicator variables) and the underlying constructs they are designed

Table 4.4 SEM—Hypothesis verification

Hypothesis	*Hypothesis*	*Standardized estimate*	*S.E*	*C.R*	*P*
H1	SMAA → WELL-BEING	0.016	0.136	0.413	0.679
H2	SMAA → DEPRESSION	0.597	0.336	4.312	***
H3	SMAA → ANXIETY	0.630	0.385	4.330	***
H4	SMAA → STRESS	0.707	0.608	4.363	***
H5	SMAA → SLEEP QUALITY	0.555	0.397	4.286	***
H8	SMAA → GAD	0.755	0.817	4.379	***
H7	SMAA → SAD	0.772	0.774	4.384	***
H8	SMAA → MDD	0.791	0.791	4.389	***
H9	SMAA → SOCIAL PHOBIA	0.770	0.901	4.383	***
H10	SMAA → ATTENTION DISORDER	0.791	0.784	4.389	***
H11	SMAA → OPPOSITIONALDEFIANT-DISORDER	0.738	0.764	4.374	***
H12	SMAA → CONDUCT DISORDER	0.537	0.558	4.343	***

to measure. The hypothesized framework was constructed with mental health, emotional health, social media addiction, pre- and post-pandemic, fixed and varied period level, and demographic variables. The hypothesis is formulated and tested, and verification values are given below (Table 4.4):

SEM—Measurement Model

The Hypotheses from H2 and H12 are accepted since all their Critical ratios (CR) are greater than 1.96 and *p*-values are lesser than 0.05. So therefore the factor covariance of those hypotheses is accepted. The hypothesis H1 is rejected because the Critical ratios (C.R) are 0.413 not greater than 1.96 and the *p*-value 0.679 is not less than 0.05. The above results were supported by Twenge and Farley's (2021) study results, which has shown that social media addiction impacting mental and emotional health. All variables were included with significant covariance's for error terms from the results of confirmatory factor analysis, and the model was tested for goodness of fit, and the results are as follows. CMIN/df = 3.567, CFI = 0.988, GFI = 0.967, NFI = 0.908, CLOSE = 0.549, RMSEA = 0.061. The values well abide by the prescribed limits thus ensuring that the SEM has a good fit acquired from this study are within the recommended values of Hair et al. (2009).

Discussions

Social media is considered a very important tool in dissemination of information among young adults and teens today. Due to its brevity, cost, and instant mass communication, it has been gaining momentum in the recent past. The information diffused through this can be a positive or a negative influence in the minds of the recipients. The positive impression can be used as a powerful instrument in marketing goods and services addressing the specific segments or even niche market (Urban Gen Z in this study). The study of the negative impression can help alleviate the stress and other related disorders among the said population. This study views social media and its influence from both the seller and buyer perspectives. It also gives scope to understand the psychosomatic disorders caused by extensive use of internet-based communication tools. Further analysis from more angles using different variables would take the research into the next level.

Implication and Future Directions

The impact on the mental and emotional health of Gen Z could be reduced if that generation is educated about the hazardous outcome of mobile phone usage. The adaptability of Gen Z to technology can be used positively to disseminate the negative effect of over usage of mobile phones. This could be done with self-regulated usage (in terms of time) by the users to mitigate the health outcome. The pandemic brought the world to a grinding halt. Even during such an extreme situation, Gen Z did not reduce the usage of social media which deteriorated the quality of sleep and enhanced depression. More facts and figures on the health issues could be highlighted to the current generation on social medial usage. This would help in consciously reducing the time and channelize the energy and efforts into something more constructive. Future research could focus on identifying which social media handle has a maximum impact on Gen Z and how could that be used positively in building the generation. It could also emphasize the role played by educational institutions to redefine responsibility in using social media.

Conclusion and Limitations

To conclude, it is evident that Gen Z popularly known as the Internet generation has both gained and lost due to the use of social media. The gains, however, can be harnessed positively as a powerful marketing and communication tool. The concern here is the dark side of social media usage which has resulted in emotional and mental disorders. If these disorders are not mended at an early stage or prevented in its nascent stage, they can lead to threatening situations in the future. This will affect all the stakeholders of Gen Z, namely parents, teachers, society, educational institutions, and their peers. A deeper study could reveal finer reasons for this impact and help arrive at suggestions that would help resolve the volatility in the behavior of Gen Z.

Limitations

The scope of the study is limited only to four educational institutions in Bangalore city, which is very narrow and limits the universality of the entire population. The sample population has been considered only from the urban stratum which negates the usage and impact of social media among the rural Gen Z population. Only few variables have been considered that gives a skewed perspective of the study. Consideration of other variables could give a holistic and deeper outlook of the study. This opens up opportunities for future studies that would augment the cause and effect of social media on Gen Z.

References

Ahn, D., & Shin, D.-H. (2013). Is the social use of media for seeking connectedness or for avoiding social isolation? Mechanisms underlying media use and subjective well-being. *Computers in Human Behavior, 29*, 2453–2462. https://doi.org/10.1016/j.chb.2012.12.022

Andreassen, C. S., Torsheim, T., Brunborg, G. S., & Pallesen, S. (2012). Development of a Facebook addiction scale. *Psychological Reports, 110*(2), 501–517.

Aparicio, J. (2020). *The effect of social media uses via a mobile device on the mental health of young adults*. Doctoral dissertation, California State University.

Calisir, F., Atahan, L., & Saracoglu, M. (2013, October). Factors affecting social network sites usage on smartphones of students in Turkey. In *Proceedings of the World Congress on Engineering and Computer Science* (Vol. 2, No. 1, pp. 23–25).

Çiçek, M., Eren-Erdoğmuş, İ., & Daştan, İ. (2018). How to increase the awareness of in-app mobile banner ads: exploring the roles of banner location, application type and orientation. *International Journal of Mobile Communications, 16*(2), 153–166.

Cohen, S., & Williamson, G. M. (1991). Stress and infectious disease in humans. *Psychological Bulletin, 109*(1), 5.

Colás, P., González, T., & de Pablos, J. (2013). Young people and social networks: Motivations and preferred uses. *Comunicar, XX*(40), 15–23.

Cooks, J. A. (2020). Understanding social media and the complex interplay between use and depressive symptoms. Doctoral dissertation, Kent State University.

Cummings, J. N., Butler, B., & Kraut, R. (2002). The quality of online social relationships. *Communications of the ACM, 45*(7), 103–108.

Curras-Perez, R., Ruiz-Mafe, C., & Sanz-Blas, S. (2014). Determinants of user behaviour and recommendation in social networks: An integrative approach from the uses and gratifications perspective. *Industrial Management & Data Systems.*

Duncan, L., Georgiades, K., Wang, L., Van Lieshout, R. J., MacMillan, H. L., Ferro, M. A., ... & Boyle, M. H. (2018). Psychometric evaluation of the mini international neuropsychiatric interview for children and adolescents (MINI-KID). *Psychological Assessment, 30*(7), 916.

Dunbar, R. I. (2014). The social brain: Psychological underpinnings and implications for the structure of organizations. *Current Directions in Psychological Science, 23*(2), 109–114.

Fuller, C., Lehman, E., Hicks, S., & Novick, M. B. (2017). Bedtime use of technology and associated sleep problems in children. *Global Pediatric Health, 4*, 1–8.

Hair, B., Black, W. C., Babin, B. J., & Anderson, R. E. (2009). *Multivariate data analysis.* Prentice Hall.

Hinsch, C., & Sheldon, K. M. (2013). The impact of frequent social Internet consumption: Increased procrastination and lower life satisfaction. *Journal of Consumer Behaviour, 12*(6), 496–505.

Huang, C. (2010). Internet use and psychological well-being: A meta-analysis. *Cyberpsychology, Behavior, and Social Networking, 13*, 241–249. https://doi.org/10.1089/cyber.2009.0217

Jourard, S. M. (1964). *The transparent self: Self-disclosure and well-being* (Vol. 17). Van Nostrand.

Katz, E., Gurevich, M., & Haas, H. (1973). On the use of the mass media for important things. *American Socialogical Review, 38*, 164–181.

Keles, B., McCrae, N., & Grealish, A. (2020). A systematic review: The influence of social media on depression, anxiety, and psychological distress in adolescents. *International Journal of Adolescence and Youth, 25*(1), 79–93.

Kim, D., Chun, H., Kwak, Y., & Nam, Y. (2014). The employment of dialogic principles in website, Facebook, and Twitter platforms of environmental nonprofit organizations. *Social Science Computer Review, 32*(5), 590–605.

Kraut, R., Kiesler, S., Boneva, B., Cummings, J., Helgeson, V., & Crawford, A. (2002). Internet paradox revisited. *Journal of Social Issues, 58*, 49–74. https://doi.org/10.1111/1540-4560/00248

Kraut, R., Patterson, M., Lundmark, V., Kiesler, S., Mukopadhyay, T., & Scherlis, W. (1998). Internet paradox: A social technology that reduces social involvement and psychological wellbeing? *American Psychologist, 53*, 1017–1031. https://doi.org/10.1037/0003-066x.53.9.1017

Kroenke, K., Spitzer, R. L., & Williams, J. B. (2001). The PHQ-9: Validity of a brief depression severity measure. *Journal of General and Internal Medicine, 16*(9), 606–613.

Kross, E., Verduyn, P., Demiralp, E., Park, J., Lee, D. S., Lin, N., & Ybarra, O. (2013). Facebook use predicts declines in subjective well-being in young adults. *Plos One, 8*(8), e69841. https://doi.org/10.1371/journal.pone.0069841

Löwe, B., Decker, O., Müller, S., Brähler, E., Schellberg, D., Herzog, W., & Herzberg, P. Y. (2008). Validation and standardization of the Generalized Anxiety Disorder Screener (GAD-7) in the general population. *Medical care, 46*, 266–274.

McQuail, D. (1987). *Mass communication theory: An introduction*. Sage Publications, Inc.

Nie, N. H. (2001). Sociability, interpersonal relations, and the internet: Reconciling conflicting findings. *American Behavior Scientist, 45*, 420–435. https://doi.org/10.1177/00027640121957277

Nie, N. H., & Hillygus, D. S. (2002). The impact of Internet use on sociability: Time-diary findings. *IT & Society, 1*(1), 1–20.

Nop, A. (2020). Young people, social media, and impacts on well-being. *School of Professional Studies*, 44. https://commons.clarku.edu/sps_masters_papers/44

Omar, A. S., Rashid, W. E. W., & Majid, A. A. (2014). Motivations using social networking sites on quality work life. *Procedia-Social and Behavioral Sciences, 130*, 524–531.

Parks, M. R. (2011). Boundary conditions for the application of three theories of computer-mediated communication to MySpace. *Journal of Communication, 61*(4), 557–574.

Petrocchi, N., Asnaani, A., Martinez, A. P., Nadkarni, A., & Hofmann, S. G. (2015). Differences between people who use only Facebook and those who use Facebook plus Twitter. *International Journal of Human–Computer Interaction, 31*(2), 157–165.

Pollet, T. V., Roberts, S. G. B., & Dunbar, R. I. M. (2011). Use of social network sites and instant messaging does not lead to increased offline social network size, or to emotionally closer relationships with offline network members. *Cyberpsychology, Behavior, and Social Networking, 14*, 253–258. https://doi.org/10.1089/cyber.2010.0161

Rasmussen, E. E., Punyanunt-Carter, N., LaFreniere, J. R., Norman, M. S., & Kimball, T. G. (2020). The serially mediated relationship between emerging adults' social media use and mental well-being. *Computers in Human Behavior, 102*, 206–213.

Roberti, J. W., Harrington, L. N., & Storch, E. A. (2006). Further psychometric support for the 10-item version of the perceived stress scale. *Journal of College Counseling, 9*(2), 135–147.

Scheepers, C. E., Wendel-Vos, G. C. W., Den Broeder, J. M., Van Kempen, E. E. M. M., Van Wesemael, P. J. V., & Schuit, A. J. (2014). Shifting from car to active transport: A systematic review of the effectiveness of interventions. *Transportation Research Part A: Policy and Practice, 70*, 264–280.

Shakya, H. B., & Christakis, N. A. (2017). Association of Facebook uses with compromised wellbeing: A longitudinal study. *American Journal of Epidemiology, 185*(3), 203–211. https://doi.org/10.1093/aje/kww189

Shao, G. (2009). Understanding the appeal of user-generated media: A uses and gratification perspective. *Internet Research, 19*(1), 7–25.

Sheldon, K. M., Abad, N., & Hinsch, C. (2011). *A two-process view of Facebook use and relatedness need-satisfaction: Disconnection drives use, and connection rewards it.*

Song, H., Zmyslinski-Seelig, A., Kim, J., Drent, A., Victor, A., Omori, K., & Allen, M. (2014). Does Facebook makes you lonely? A meta-analysis. *Computers in Human Behavior, 36*, 446–452. https://doi.org/10.1016/j.chb.2014.04.011

Stafford, T. F., & Gillenson, M. L. (2004). Motivations for mobile devices: Uses and gratifications for m-commerce. *SIGHCI 2004 Proceedings, 7*.

Twenge, J. M., & Farley, E. (2021). Not all screen time is created equal: Associations with mental health vary by activity and gender. *Social Psychiatry and Psychiatric Epidemiology, 56*(2), 207–217.

Verduyn, P., Lee, D. S., Park, J., Shablack, H., Orvell, A., Bayer, J., & Kross, E. (2015). Passive Facebook usage undermines affective well-being: Experimental and longitudinal evidence. *Journal of Experimental Psychology: General, 144*(2), 480.

Weiser, E. B. (2001), The functions of internet use and their social and psychological consequences. *Cyberpsychology and Behavior, 4*(6), 723–743.

Xu, Z., Pérez-Rosas, V., & Mihalcea, R. (2020). Inferring Social Media Users' Mental Health Status from Multimodal Information. *Proceedings of the 12th Language Resources and Evaluation Conference* (pp. 6292–6299). Marseille.

Zhang, Y., & Ma, Z. F. (2020). Impact of the COVID-19 pandemic on mental health and quality of life among residents in Liaoning Province, China: A cross-sectional study. *International Journal of Environmental Research and Public Health, 17*(7), 2381.

CHAPTER 5

Social Media Competence: An Assessment of Male and Female Users in India

Sourabh Sharma and Megha Sharma

Introduction

Social Media is a platform used for sharing ideas, information, and content. Social media generates wide range of content on the Internet as different social media platforms allow anyone and everyone with an Internet connection to generate their own content and share them effortlessly on their network. Several studies have revealed the different benefits and usages of social media platforms. Social media is widely used to share information. It has benefits for consumers as well as for producers. Consumers may directly interact with the brand and influence others by sharing their feedbacks. The produces may know the response instantly

S. Sharma (✉)
International Management Institute, Bhubaneswar, India
e-mail: sourabh@imibh.edu.in

M. Sharma
Department of Management Studies, NIIS Institute of Business Administration, Bhubaneswar, India

Rajagopal and R. Behl (eds.), *Managing Disruptions in Business*, Palgrave Studies in Democracy, Innovation, and Entrepreneurship for Growth, https://doi.org/10.1007/978-3-030-79709-6_5

and may create a better customer engagement for the brand. Traditional marketing cannot generate such kind of engagement (Trusov et al., 2009). A framework was proposed by Grewal and Levy's (2014) 4E model, which describes the actual usage of social media in real time. As per the proposed framework, there are four purposes of social media to:

- motivate users with relevant content,
- inform them about the brand and product/services,
- facilitate users to interact with the brand, product/services online; and
- keep them engaged online.

IAMAI (Internet and Mobile Association of India) 2019 data reveals that, in India, out of 560 million Internet users, half of them are very diligently using different social media platforms. Facebook and YouTube are the two most used social media platforms in India. WhatsApp is also gradually becoming popular among the active social media users. Popularity of Facebook is increasing day by day and it is expected that the users in India for Facebook will be close to 319 million by the end of 2021. Globally, women dominate the activities on major social media platforms but in India the trend is reversed. In India, male users have dominance over female users on Facebook and is very much gender skewed.

Although the trend in India is skewed more toward male users, it will be interesting to find out the different social media dimensions which are impacting the usage pattern of male and female users in the developing country like India. The present research is proposed to compare the same and finds the insight for future references.

Literature Review

Social media has improved the role of users from passive users to active users. Users are actively participating on social media platforms to share their views and thoughts. The active users are not only participating but are also involved in content creation (e.g., photos, videos, and stories) and sharing the same to their network. Around 30% of the users are involved in self-created content sharing on their news feeds (Lenhart et al., 2010). The users on social media are not constrainted to only interpersonal communication but they also use the platforms to interact with the business organizations and brands to share their experiences (Prahalad & Ramaswamy, 2004). Presently, the management is using social media platforms and integrating the same with their existing customer relationship management (CRM) systems to improve customer satisfaction (Trainor et al., 2014). For managing customer relations, this integration of social media with CRM has given a new approach, which is network-focused (Trainor et al., 2014).

As defined earlier, Facebook is the most used social media platform in India. Sacide Güzin Mazman and Yasemin Koçak Uslue (2010) designed a model to describe the educational use of Facebook for its users. In this model, a direct relationship was established between users' purposes in using Facebook and the educational usage of Facebook whereas an indirect relationship was established between users' Facebook adoption processes and their educational use of Facebook.

Twitter is another social media platform in India, which is used and followed by many of the users. Java et al. (2007) define the type of users available for Twitter. For this study, user's Twitter data was analyzed to derive the classification of user's intents like "daily chatter," "conversations," "sharing information/URLs," and "reporting news," Teevan, Ramage and Morris (2011) examined why people search Twitter and found that users were looking for current events and "social information" related to other Twitter users. Approaching the issue from the other side, Hurlock and Wilson (2011) studied which tweets users found most helpful in a search. The authors found that the most useful tweets contained facts/common knowledge; direct recommendations/insights; humor; shared perspective; temporally relevant information; or trustworthy links. Building on the research, Elsweiler and Harvey (2014) discovered that Twitter search is about "both achieving and maintaining the state of being informed."

Social media, such as Facebook, Twitter, LinkedIn, YouTube, WhatsApp, Instagram, etc., facilitate users/brands to create their own profile/page, add friends and followers to connect, and exchange content (user-generated content) with them. Pew Research Center's Internet & American Life Project (PRCI & ALP) in a research concluded that in USA, young adults are more connected to social media sites. Internet users under the age group of 18–29 are mostly using the social networking site of any kind. Women are dominating and are more likely than men to be on these sites. People living in urban settings are the main users of social networking sites as compare to rural Internet users. Women are more active on social media sites like Pinterest, Instagram in Africa, America, and Latino.

Gianfranco, Walsh et al., (2016) have conceptualized five dimensions of social media competence: technical competency, visibility awareness competency, knowledge competency, impact assessment competency, and social media communication competency. By using these dimensions, a scale was created to analyze the social media competency. They described that "for convergent, discriminant and nomological validities, exploratory factor analyses, confirmatory factor analyses, and structural equation modeling were implemented." The same scale (Annexure 1) has been explored and used to compare these five factors between male and female in Indian context.

Social media is playing a very important role in the change of Indian lifestyles. Social Media Sites (SMS) have become an essential part of life of every Indian who now have access to Internet and want to be socially connected through these mediums (Jehangir, 2018). These virtual social media platforms are very popular among the teenagers and young adults but at the same time, these social media platforms are gradually showing their presence in the life of the entire population (Oberst et al., 2017).

Research Gap

From an extensive literature review, it was found that ample research studies are available on social media and its influence on individual within the organization and society at large. The usage of social media, in general, was studied in some of the research studies. It has been observed that there is a research gap to identify the social media competence dimensions and may further be used to evaluate the competence level (gender wise) of social media users in the developing country like India. This study is an honest attempt to map the social media competence of male and female users on various identified dimensions of social media usage. It will be a comparative research to identify the level of competence and analyze the social media usage behavior of Indian users (male and female). This study is going to address this gap by implementing the social media competence scale for the Indian users in the Indian context.

Objective of the Study

Following objectives have been derived from the identified research gap:

- To explore the social media competence dimensions (scale).
- To check the validity and reliability of the social media competency evaluation scale.
- To compare the social media competence dimensions for male and female users.

Data and Methodology

Scale developed by Gianfranco Walsh et al. (2016) of 21 items is used to measure the social media competence. There are five dimensions in this scale: "Technical Competence, Visibility awareness competence, Knowledge competence, Impact assessment competence, and Social media communication competence." A brief description about the dimensions[1]:

1. **Technical Competence (TC):** Technical competence is all about using the technical aspects of social media in an efficient manner.
2. **Visibility Awareness Competence (VAC):** This competence is to acknowledge once presence on social media platforms which is perceptible to all at large.
3. **Knowledge Competence (KC):** It is the competence of involving oneself in the ongoing conversations on social media only when one has the knowledge on the subject matter.
4. **Impact Assessment Competence (IAC):** it's a realization of the impact of social media contents shared on social media platforms.
5. **Social Media Communication Competence (SMCC):** The way of expressing the views and thoughts in the most appropriate and non-argumentative manner on social media platforms.

The research methodology used for this study is descriptive.

[1] Items of these dimensions are shown in Annexure 1.

Sampling Technique

As discussed above, the scale comprises 21 items related to social media usage under five competence aspects that were circulated in the form of a questionnaire to the Internet users who are active on social media platforms in India. In response, the data was collected from 445 respondents, segregated among 244 males and 201 females. Many of the respondents were between 22 and 40 years of age group.

Data Analysis and Finding

To check the construct validity, correlation and exploratory factor analysis are used, whereas for reliability check, Cronbach's alpha test of reliability is used. The correlation analysis was used to check the validity of social media competence scale in the Indian context. To identify the convergent and discriminant validity, a correlation tool was applied.

Exploratory factor analysis was also performed on 21 items scale of social media competence to confirm the validity of the construct. The factor analysis results are depicted in Tables 5.2 and 5.3. The KMO value is more than the requisite (0.5) and the significance level for the Bartlett's test is below 0.05 as exhibited in Table 5.1. Therefore, it is pertinent to apply factor analysis. The standard extraction method wherein principal component with Varimax rotation was applied to get the factors. Factors are constructed based on the Eigenvalues greater than 1.0 (Field, 2009).

Table 5.2 shows the factor loading of all five dimensions. These dimensions together represent 57.29% of the variance. The first dimension "Technical Competence (TC)" comprised five items and explained 17.884 percent of the total variance. This factor has Eigenvalue of 3.756 and the items TC1, TC2, TC3, TC4, and TC5 are paired up together. Four items with 12.762% of the total variance and 2.680 Eigenvalue were clubbed in the second dimension "Visibility Awareness Competence

Table 5.1 KMO and Bartlett's test

Kaiser-Meyer-Olkin measure of sampling adequacy		0.693
Bartlett's test of sphericity	Approx. Chi-Square	3006.654
	Df	210
	Sig	0.000

Source Authors computation

Table 5.2 Factor analysis for social media competence scale

Factor 1		*Factor 2*		*Factor 3*		*Factor 4*		*Factor 5*	
TC		*VAC*		*KC*		*IAC*		*SMCC*	
Items	*Loading*	*Items*	*Loading*	*Items*	*Loading*	*Items*	*Loading*	*Items*	*Loading*
TC2	0.781	VAC3	0.821	KC3	0.831	IAC3	0.781	SMCC4	0.612
TC3	0.776	VAC1	0.779	KC2	0.826	IAC4	0.775	SMCC2	0.575
TC4	0.709	VAC2	0.731	KC1	0.821	IAC2	0.761	SMCC1	0.563
TC5	0.691	VAC4	0.622	KC4	0.668	IAC1	0.493	SMCC3	0.475
TC1	0.681								
EigenValue 3.756		EigenValue 2.680		EigenValue 2.254		EigenValue 1.965		EigenValue 1.377	
Percentage of variance 17.884		Percentage of variance 12.762		Percentage of variance 10.733		Percentage of variance 9.357		Percentage of variance 6.558	
Total variance: 57.294									

Source Authors computation

(VAC)." The items VAC1, VAC2, VAC3, and VAC4 are combined in this dimension.

The third dimension "Knowledge Competence (KC)" comprises of four items, i.e., KC1, KC2, KC3, and KC4 and explained 10.733% of the total variance with an Eigenvalue of 2.254. The fourth dimension "Impact Assessment Competence (IAC)" also has four items IAC1, IAC2, IAC3, and IAC4 and explained 9.357% of the total variance with an Eigenvalue of 1.965. Fifth dimension "Social Media Communication Competence (SMCC)" comprised four items and explained 6.558 percent of the total variance. It has an Eigenvalue of 1.377. The items SMCC1, SMCC2, SMCC3, and SMCC4 loaded on this dimension.

According to Kaura et al. (2013), high loading on the same factor and no substantial cross-loading confirms convergent and discriminant validity, respectively. Further, the Cronbach's alpha test is used to check the reliability of the scale. The values in Cronbach's alpha coming at higher side depict the internal consistency of all items in each factor (Wang & Ahmed, 2009, p. 23). Table 5.3 shows the results of the reliability analysis.

Table 5.3 represents the Cronbach's alpha value of all five dimensions. The Cronbach's alpha value of first dimension, *i.e.*, "Technical Competence" is 0.786. The value shows a high reliability. The next

Table 5.3 Result of reliability analysis on social media competence scale

Item-total statistics

	Scale mean if item deleted	Scale variance if item deleted	Corrected item-total correlation	Cronbach's alpha if item deleted
Technical Competence				
TC1	14.64	10.786	0.502	0.765
TC2	14.79	9.693	0.623	0.727
TC3	14.77	9.184	0.628	0.723
TC4	14.71	9.792	0.541	0.752
TC5	15.13	8.864	0.545	0.758
Cronbach's alpha = 0.786				
Visibility Awareness Competence				
VAC1	13.29	4.192	0.616	0.693
VAC2	13.13	4.998	0.593	0.705
VAC3	13.24	4.288	0.623	0.687
VAC4	12.95	5.765	0.484	0.76
Cronbach's alpha = 0.770				
Knowledge Competence				
KC1	12.16	7.921	0.688	0.745
KC2	12.07	7.887	0.662	0.757
KC3	12.13	7.547	0.711	0.733
KC4	11.89	9.588	0.495	0.829
Cronbach's alpha = 0.817				
Impact Assessment Competence				
IAC1	11.6	6.623	0.303	0.722
IAC2	11.76	5.103	0.503	0.608
IAC3	11.69	5.54	0.537	0.587
IAC4	11.69	5.253	0.569	0.563
Cronbach's alpha = 0.691				
Social Media Communication Competence				
SMCC1	11.88	4.192	0.229	0.386
SMCC2	11.13	4.624	0.348	0.27
SMCC3	10.85	5.301	0.294	0.342 ara>
SMCC4	12.17	4.504	0.16	0.467
Cronbach's alpha = 0.433				
SMCC2	4.49	0.606	0.472	
SMCC3	4.22	0.91	0.472	
Revised Cronbach's alpha = 0.632				

three dimensions that are "Visibility Awareness Competence," "Knowledge Competence," and "Impact Assessment Competence" have 0.770, 0.817, and 0.691 Cronbach's alpha values, respectively. Which again shows the significant reliability of all these dimensions. Although the Cronbach's alpha value for last dimension, *i.e.*, "Social Media Communication Competence" is 0.433. This value shows a very low reliability and cannot be considered. Looking at the values of "Corrected Item—Total Correlation" column, two items SMCC1 and SMCC4 having lowest values are deleted and the Cronbach's Alpha is recalculated for reliability, the reliability is increased to an acceptable level (0.632).

Cronbach's alpha values received for social media competence dimensions show reliability varying from 0.632 to 0.817.

Comparison of Social Media Competence Dimensions for Male and Female Users

This is the third and most important objective of the present study. To address this objective, the mean of two independent samples which are male and female social media users are compared using the independent *t*-test and to determine whether the sample mean has the significant difference. The sample size is divided into 244 males and 201 females. Table 5.4 shows the result of independent *t*-test:

Independent *t*-test is applied to identify the significance and association of items by comparing the means in the group of two independent samples (Sharma & Sharma, 2018). Here the independent *t*-test states that whether there is a significant difference in the mean score of social media users (male and female) for each competence dimensions. As depicted in Table 5.4, for dimension one, i.e., "Technical Competence," the resulted significance value is 0.000 ($p < 0.05$). So, the NULL hypothesis (t value 7.409, $p < 0.05$) is rejected. It means that there is a significant difference in the Technical Competence level of male and female social media users. The difference can be identified by comparing the mean values. For this dimension, the mean values are 3.926 and 3.429 for male and female social media users, respectively. By comparing the mean values, we may be concluded that male social media users are more technically sound than female users as their mean score is comparatively higher. The technical knowhow of different social media platforms is more in the male users than the female users. Technical competence is all about using the technical features such as settings and security in the most efficient

Table 5.4 Independent t-test: A comparison of independent samples of male and female social media users

Factors	*Gender (Independent sample)*	*N*	*Mean*	*SD*	*Std. Error mean*	*t-test*	*Sig. (2-tailed) P value*
1.Technical Competence (TC)	Male	244	3.926	0.7678	0.0492	7.409	0.000
	Female	201	3.429	0.6482	0.0457		
2.Visibility Awareness Competence (VAC)	Male	244	4.371	0.6715	0.0430	−0.441	0.660
	Female	201	4.401	0.7442	0.0525		
3.Knowledge Competence (KC)	Male	244	4.043	0.9028	0.0578	0.581	0.562
	Female	201	3.991	0.9606	0.0678		
4.Impact Assessment Competence (IAC)	Male	244	3.568	0.7450	0.0477	−11.845	0.000
	Female	201	4.292	0.5432	0.0383		
5.Social Media Communication Competence (SMCC)	Male	244	4.324	0.7054	0.0452	− 0.942	0.347
	Female	201	4.391	0.7893	0.0557		

Source Authors computation

manner. As per the research findings, male users are more comfortable using technical features such as profile settings and privacy settings, whereas female users find it more complicated and cumbersome.

The "Visibility Awareness Competence," second dimension, accepts the NULL hypothesis (t-test = −0.441, $p > 0.05$) and shows that there is no significant difference between the male and female social media users. Here, the mean value of male users ($M = 4.371$) is near to the mean score of female users ($M = 4.401$). The result defines that all the social media users are aware about the visibility of their social media posts and comments to others, including the large number of social media population which are not known to them (strangers).

In the third dimension, i.e., knowledge competence, NULL hypothesis is again accepted (t-test = 0.581, $p > 0.05$). So, there is no significant difference between male and female social media users. Here the mean value of male users ($M = 4.043$) is close to the mean value of female users ($M = 3.991$). As per Knowledge Competence, both the genders, comprise of male and female users, participate in the discussions on social media platforms if they have the adequate information regarding the subject of discussion. According to the result, all the social media users understand that one should really write about a certain topic, only if they have enough wisdom in the relevant field.

Impact assessment competence does not accept the NULL hypothesis (t-test = −11.845, $p < 0.05$) which means that there is a significant difference in mean responses of male and female social media users for this dimension. So, to identify the difference, mean values are compared. Here the mean value of female social media users ($M = 4.292$) is significantly greater than male users ($M = 3.568$). According to the findings, the possible implications can be predicted in advance by the female users of their social media posts and engagements (like, comment, and share). Female users in advance imagine that how other users may react to their contributions on the social media sites. Whereas the male users on social media platforms are more vocal and write in the flow of current.

Fifth and the last dimension, i.e., "Social Media Communication Competence" accepts the NULL hypotheses. So, there is no substantial difference among both the social media users for this dimension. The mean score of male users ($M = 4.324$) is near to the mean score of female users ($M = 4.391$) at 5% significant level, ($t = -0.942$, $p > 0.05$). As per the findings, all social media users give more importance to the pleasant conversational tone in their social media conversations.

Conclusion

With reference to the five critical dimensions, this research has identified the different competence levels of male and female social media users. It was found in the research that as far as the technical knowhow, settings and security features are concerned, male social media users are more friendly and find it easy whereas female users find it a bit complex. Both the users (male and female) are cognizant that the open post and engagement in social media sites are displayed to the users to whom they know as well as they do not know or met personally. Both the users know the importance of having enough knowledge about a topic before participating in the online discussions on social media platforms. Regarding awareness about the unwanted effects that one's contributions could have on social media; research indicates that female users are quite mature and can anticipate about the impact of their engagements and posts on others mindset and feelings. Both male and female users consider that style of writing the comment on social media is the most important component and generally try to keep it appropriate on all social media platforms.

Managerial Implications

Social media plays a unique role to assess the behavioral aspects of an individual within the organization. So, it is a demand of an hour to understand the various competency parameters mentioned in the study of the social media users. This study will educate all the three stakeholders which include Social Media Users, Social media Channels, and Employers to adopt the outcome and strategies the future course of actions accordingly. Broadly, following three implications may be defined of the present study:

- This research may create an awareness among the social media users and give them an understanding of their areas for improvement. All five dimensions of social media competence are independently comparing the male and female user's behavior and showing the relevant areas of strength and weaknesses of these users.

- The social media channels may also consider the outcome of this research and may create their platforms more convenient and easier to use by removing the technical complexities and guiding users to improve their social media profiles.
- Employers may also use this result to allocate the responsibilities to the employees to manage digital marketing activities more efficiently.

The use of social media by an employee produces a wide range of monetary and non-monetary benefits to the company. All the users know the importance and power (positive and negative) of social media in an organization's reputation in real terms. Companies can better focus on their employee's strengths and weaknesses through this analysis and can get the best result.

Limitation of the Research

This research has some limitations which give an opportunity for future research.

- This study included the respondents from only one nation, i.e., India.
- The sample size also does not represent the complete population of the social media users. Because of a smaller number of respondents, it is difficult to generalize the result of this study.
- There may also have some response biasness of respondents while filling the questionnaire due to the behavioral psychology.

Future studies: For future studies, user's age, income level, qualification, economic status, etc. can also be associated in this study to understand the overall impact of user's behavior on different social media platforms.

Annexure 1

Questionnaire on Social Media Competence

Name of the Participant: ______________________________.
Gender:

- Male
- Female

Age:

- Below 18
- 18 – 35
- 36 – 50
- Above 50

Highest Qualification:

- School Level
- UG
- PG
- Doctorate

Technical Competency (TC)	*1*	*2*	*3*	*4*	*5*
TC1: I find it easy to understand the technical side of my profile settings					
TC2: I find it easy to find my way around in social media					
TC3: I find it easy to change my profile settings in social media					
TC4: It is easy to block other people from accessing my profile					
TC5: I know how to conceal personal information in social media such as pictures, texts, and personal data from other users					
Visibility Awareness Competence (VAC)	**1**	**2**	**3**	**4**	**5**
VAC1: I am conscious of the fact that my public comments in social media are read by people I do not know					
VAC2: I know that a great number of people can follow my activities in social media					
VAC3: I know that my profile is visible to people I do not know					
VAC4: I know that through social media I am connected worldwide					

(continued)

(continued)

Technical Competency (TC)	*1*	*2*	*3*	*4*	*5*
Knowledge Competence (KC)	1	2	3	4	5
KC1: I only comment on subject-specific contributions of other users when I am well-versed in the subject area					
KC2: I only participate in discussions on social media when I have knowledge of the subject area					
KC3: I only make a counter argument in a discussion on social media when I know my argument is correct					
KC4: I only post comments when I am sure that they are correct					
Impact Assessment Competence (IAC)	1	2	3	4	5
IAC1: Before I write something in social media, I try to picture possible consequences					
IAC2: I think in advance of how my comments or posts might affect other users' thoughts and emotions					
IAC3: I give thought to how other people might take to my contributions and comments					
IAC4: Before I write something in social media, I consider how other people might perceive my contribution					
Social Media Communication Competence (SMCC)	1	2	3	4	5
SMCC1: I respond to impolite and insulting messages with courtesy and respect					
SMCC2: A pleasant conversational tone is important to me when communicating in social media with other users					
SMCC3: It is important to me that my contributions, comments or posts do not attack anybody personally					
SMCC4: To emphasize what I write in social media I sometimes use expletives					

1-Strongly Disagree; **2**-Disagree; **3**-Neigher Agree nor Disagree; **4**-Agree; **5**-Strongly Agree

References

Elsweiler, D., & Harvey, M. (2014). Engaging and maintaining a sense of being informed: Understanding the tasks motivating twitter search. *Journal of the Association for Information Science and Technology*. https://doi.org/10.1002/asi.23182

Field, A. (2009). *Discovering statistics using SPSS: Introducing statistical method* (3rd ed.). Sage Publications.

Grewal, D., & Levy, M. (2014). *Marketing* (4th ed.). McGraw-Hill/Irwin. https://www.pewinternet.org/2013/02/14/the-demographics-of-social-media-users-2012/.

Hurlock, J., & Wilson, M. (2011). Searching Twitter: Separating the tweet from the chaff. *International AAAI Conference on Weblogs and Social Media*. Retrieved from https://www.aaai.org/ocs/index.php/ICWSM/ICWSM11/paper/view/2819.

Java, A., Song, X. Finin, T. & Tseng, B. (2007). Why we Twitter: Understanding microblogging usage and communities. *Proceedings of the 9th WebKDD and 1st SNA-KDD 2007 Workshop on Web Mining and Social Network Analysis (WebKDD/SNA-KDD '07)*. https://doi.org/10.1145/1348549.1348556.

Jehangir, B. (2018). Exploring education-related use of social media: Business students perspectives in a changing India. *Safer Communities*, *17*(2), 119–131.

Kaura, V., Prasad, C. S. D., & Sharma, S. (2013). Customer perception of service convenience: A comparison between public and new private sector banks. *Global Business Review*, *14*(3), 529–547.

Lenhart, A., Purcell, K., Smith, A., & Zickuhr, K. (2010). *Social media and young adults*. www.pewinternet.org/2010/02/03/social-media-and-young-adults/. Accessed on May 26, 2017.

Mazman, S. G., & Uslue, Y. K. (2010). Modeling educational usage of Facebook. *Computers & Education*, *55*(2), 444–453.

Oberst, U., Stodt, B., Brand, M., & Chamarro, A. (2017). Negative consequences from heavy social networking in adolescents: The mediating role of fear of missing out. *Journal of Adolescence*, *55*, 51–60.

Prahalad, C. K., & Ramaswamy, V. (2004). Co-creation experiences: The next practice in value creation. *Journal of Interactive Marketing*, *18*(3), 5–14.

Sharma, S., & Sharma, M. (2018). Stress level of male and female bank officials in public banks: A comparative study. *International Journal of Business Competition and Growth (IJBCG)*, *6*(2), 128–138.

Teevan, J., Ramage, D., & Morris, M. R. (2011). #TwitterSearch: A comparison of microblog search and web search. *WSDM '11: Proceedings of the fourth ACM International Conference on Web Search and Data Mining* (pp. 35–44). New York: ACM.

Trainor, K. J., Andzulis, J. M., Rapp, A., & Agnihotri, R. (2014). Social media technology usage and customer relationship performance: A capabilities-based examination of social CRM. *Journal of Business Research*, *67*(6), 1201–1208.

Trusov, M., Randolph, E. B., & Koen, P. (2009). Effects of word-of-mouth versus traditional marketing: Findings from an Internet social networking site. *Journal of Marketing*, *73*(5), 90–102.

Walsh, G., Schaarschmidt, M., & von Kortzfleisch, H. (2016). Employees' company reputation-related social media competence: Scale development and validation. *Journal of Interactive Marketing, 36*, 46–59.
Wang, Y., & Ahmed, P. K. (2009). The moderating effect of the business strategic orientation on eCommerce adoption: Evidence from UK family run SMEs. *The Journal of Strategic Information Systems, 18*(1), 16–30.

CHAPTER 6

Insights: Indian Adolescents' Social Media Usage and Life Satisfaction

Snigdha Mohapatra and Manit Mishra

Introduction

Social media has users from almost every background irrespective of their age, gender, caste, color, region, and religion. The genesis of social media resulted from the desire to stay connected. Its application got further extended to staying abreast with current events and being better informed in diverse domains. Social media usage is now integrated with modern lifestyle. Its applications are diversifying at an increasing rate. The increasing reach of social media has not only facilitated efficient communication within the existing network but has also contributed towards developing new relationships. Given social media's role in connecting

S. Mohapatra
Birla Global University, Bhubaneswar, Odisha, India
e-mail: snigdha.mohapatra@bgu.ac.in

M. Mishra (✉)
International Management Institute, Bhubaneswar, Odisha, India
e-mail: manit.mishra@imibh.edu.in

Rajagopal and R. Behl (eds.), *Managing Disruptions in Business*, Palgrave Studies in Democracy, Innovation, and Entrepreneurship for Growth, https://doi.org/10.1007/978-3-030-79709-6_6

with friends, family, co-workers, and communities, a significant part of young people's lives is lived mostly on social media platforms. At the same time, extant research offers contradictory findings on whether or not social media enhances these relationships (Dzogang et al., 2017; O'Keeffe & Clarke-Pearson, 2011). Prior research has found social media behavior to have significant influence on emotional states such as happiness and loneliness (Davis, 2001; Nalwa & Anand, 2003; Pelling & White, 2009). The emotional state of happiness is interpreted as a positive evaluation of the quality of one's life events and experiences (Diener & Seligman, 2002). Happiness consists of an affective and a cognitive part (Diener, 2009; Veenhoven, 1991). Feeling socially connected is the affective content and evaluating the worth of these connections with others is the cognitive content that users' experience on social media platforms. Loneliness, on the other hand, is a negative interpretation when users fail to find a connection with others. Perlman and Peplau (1981) define loneliness as "the unpleasant experience that occurs when a person's network of social relations is deficient in some important way."

Social networking sites (SNSs) facilitate social sharing either through purely text or through a combination of text and image. Visual images have been found to be more subtle than text. Shaw and Gant (2002) argue, based on an experiment conducted with different age group subjects, that the intention to remember and use an image-based information is more than pure text based information. Ostensibly, there is a greater traction of SNSs that allow both image- and text-based information rather than only-text-based exchange (Reid & Reid, 2007). However, there is no evidence in extant research of the differential impact of these two types of SNSs on subjective benefits to the users. Therefore, the current research is carried out to fulfill the following objective. The study evaluates how social sharing on text- and image-based SNSs influence the generalized positive emotional state of happiness, generalized negative socially disconnected state of loneliness and its cascading impact on life satisfaction. The rest of the article is divided into following parts: section "Theoretical Paradigm" establishes the theoretical paradigm of the study; section "Research Model" puts forth the research model; section "Methodology" illustrates the methodology; section "Analysis and Results" presents the result and analysis; and finally, section "Discussion" offers insights through discussion, conclusion, and implications of the study.

Theoretical Paradigm

Social Media

Social media is an online application that allows users to create and share self-generated content and/or content developed by others (Kaplan & Haenlein, 2010). With the help of web- or mobile-based technology social media comprises of sharing and organizing sites like YouTube (Pickren & Rutherford, 2010); content creation and editing medium such as blogs (Kietzmann et al., 2011; Leonardi et al., 2013); and social networking sites. The current research is based on social media usage through social networking sites (SNS). These sites facilitate interpersonal communication by providing sharing access with online contacts for different forms of content such as profile, status, private information, etc (Mitchell & Guskin, 2013). Two of the prominent SNSs are Facebook and Twitter (Steinfield et al., 2013; Stutzman et al., 2012).

Uses and Gratification Theory Approach

The uses and gratification theory (UGT) approach to study social media usage is one of the more widely established methods to understand media consumption behavior (Sundar & Limperos, 2013). It is an audience-oriented approach towards understanding mass communication and emphasizes upon users' choice of technology to fulfill their personal needs (Katz et al., 1973). The UGT approach helps in understanding why users are fond of or averse towards any mass communication technology. Social media, as compared to mass media of twentieth century, has an advantage in terms of greater control and interaction among members and this characteristic is instrumental in its ever-increasing popularity (Pittman & Reich, 2016). Extant research pertaining to UGT approach of understanding social media usage indicate towards various consequences of SNS such as happiness (Krasnova et al., 2013; Lucas & Clark, 2006; Verduyn et al., 2015); satisfaction (Bargh & McKenna, 2004; Underwood & Findlay, 2004); loneliness (Bellamy et al., 2010; Cacioppo et al., 2009); and addiction (Basilisco & Cha, 2015; Skues et al., 2012; Sundar & Limperos, 2013). This study uses the UGT approach to understand the relationship between SNS usage, happiness, loneliness, and life satisfaction.

Image and Text

UGT approach is a consumer centric approach that gives emphasis on what needs are satisfied by using a particular media (Rubin et al., 2009). This helps in analyzing the medium through which users are exchanging information (Sundar & Limperos, 2013). Differential usage of social media is natural since gratification is based on belief about the information that has been exchanged. Most of the SNSs are delivering the users' content either in the form of text, or in the form of image, or both simultaneously. The attention theories, however, emphasize that only-text information has lesser impact than image-based information. An image is said to have a better representation of fact, much louder than a bunch of words. This has led the researchers to differentiate users on the basis of only-text (Twitter) in contrast to text- and image-based (Facebook, WhatsApp) SNSs.

Life Satisfaction

Life satisfaction is the general evaluation of one's surroundings which may be positive or negative (Scheufele & Shah, 2000). This is usually interpreted as subjective happiness (Diener et al., 1985). Literature highlights that life satisfaction is an outcome of social ties (Kahneman & Krueger, 2006). Life satisfaction is a feeling that results from happiness due to having friends (Leary & Kowalski, 1990); happiness of family members (Clore & Palmer, 2009); and frequent interpersonal communications (Diener et al., 1991). A sociable and extraverted personality also contributes towards greater life satisfaction (Francis, 1999). SNSs provide an opportunity to actively interact, experience connectedness, and feel happier thereby contributing towards greater life satisfaction (Valkenburg et al., 2006). The present research explores a feeling of life satisfaction derived out of SNS usage.

Research Model

SNSs allow users to create and share content related to both personal and public happenings either in the form of only-text or both image-and-text. Text- and image-based media offer a relatively more real and intimate interpersonal experience (Pittman & Reich, 2016). As image grabs more attention and generates greater trust in the content, the use of SNSs offering a combination of image and text sharing facility is likely to be higher among the users.

Extant research indicates greater happiness among users of SNSs as a result of improved communication and enhanced social support (Tosun, 2012; Verduyn et al., 2017). On the contrary, loneliness as an emotional state has been reported to exhibit a decreasing trend due to the opportunity to have social interaction through SNSs (Shaw & Gant, 2002). The preceding discourse leads us to propose following hypotheses:

H1: Social media usage through SNSs increases the happiness of the users.

H2: Social media usage through SNSs decreases the loneliness of the users.

Prior research suggests that in the context of usage of SNSs, life satisfaction as an evaluation of personal life experiences is contingent upon enhanced happiness and diminished loneliness (Ellison et al., 2011; Longstreet & Brooks, 2017; Turel & Serenko, 2012). Based on the aforementioned arguments, we hypothesized that:

H3: Enhanced happiness due to SNS usage will increase life satisfaction.

H4: Diminished loneliness due to SNS usage will increase life satisfaction.

The proposed model is shown below (Fig. 6.1).

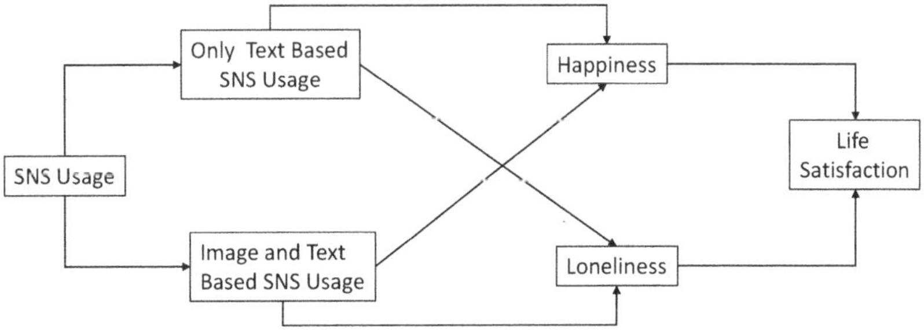

Fig. 6.1 Proposed model (*Source* Authors)

Methodology

The study investigates the linkage between different types of SNSs and the consequent constructs of happiness, loneliness, and life satisfaction. Specifically, the study assessed the usage of exclusively image-based platform (Instagram), exclusively text-based platform (Twitter), and one generalized mixed platform (Facebook). Using pre-established scales, this study captures loneliness, happiness, and life satisfaction among SNS users.

Sample

Data was collected from 255 university students from Bhubaneswar, Odisha, India, enrolled in undergraduate programs. After scrutiny, on the basis of non-response of major items, the final sample comprised 183 participants. The sample comprised 60% female and 40% male respondents. The respondents have a mean age of 20.22 years with a standard deviation of 3.32 years.

Instruments

All constructs of interest in this study were measured with previously used and validated instruments. In addition, age and gender are included as control variables in the model. Happiness was assessed using the Oxford Happiness Questionnaire (OHQ) comprising of eight questions on a six-point Likert scale (Hills & Argyle, 2002). The Cronbach's α reliability coefficient for the scale stands at 0.667. The respondent scores for happiness ranged between 17 and 46 with a mean (M) of 29.43 and standard deviation (SD) of 4.82. Hughes et al.'s (2004) shortened three-item loneliness instrument measured on a seven-point semantic differential scale was used to measure loneliness. The Cronbach's α reliability score stands at 0.801 and the respondent scores range from 3 to 21 with M = 11.46 and SD = 5.01. Life satisfaction was operationalized with the help of a life satisfaction scale comprising of 11 questions on a seven-point Likert scale (Diener et al., 1985). The Cronbach's α reliability for the scale stands at 0.753. The life satisfaction score of respondents ranges between 8 and 35, with M = 23.08 and SD = 5.59. Social media usage is measured using six items on a seven-point Likert scale borrowed from Pittman and Reich (2016). The Cronbach's α reliability score for the scale stands at 0.992. The usage scores range between 11 and 45 and have M = 37.68 and SD = 9.22.

Analysis and Results

Prior to proceeding with the assessment of relationships, the relative usage of different SNSs was evaluated. To find out the usage of different SNSs each participant was asked to respond either in "yes" or "no" regarding a particular text-based (Twitter), image-based (Instagram), and text- and image-based (Facebook) platform. In case of a "yes" response, the respondent's usage pattern was gauged using the Pittman and Reich (2016) scale. Table 6.1 presents the number of responses in case of each type of SNS. The figures in Table 6.1 suggest that use of only-text-based SNS (Twitter) is very low in comparison to use of SNS that allows image-based (Instagram) or both image- and text-based SNS (Facebook). Due to lower number of only-text-based SNS users, further analysis was carried out only on image-based and text- and image-based user responses.

The relationships were investigated using correlation analysis. Table 6.2 provides the internal consistency reliability of scales and correlation coefficients between constructs used in the study. The internal consistency reliability for each construct is above the acceptability thresholds. SNS usage was found to be significantly positively related to happiness but has a significantly negative relationship with loneliness. This finding provides support for H1 and H2. The correlation value for loneliness and happiness confirms that these two constructs are totally independent of each other. A positively significant relationship between happiness and life satisfaction leads us to surmise a positive impact of happiness on life satisfaction. Thus, there is a support for H3. On the other hand, the significantly negative correlation between loneliness and life satisfaction suggests that with increased loneliness, life satisfaction diminishes.

Table 6.1 SNS users for different platforms

Platform used	*Number of responses*
Twitter	23
Instagram	97
Facebook	122

Source Authors' research

Table 6.2 Correlation analysis

	Internal consistency reliability	*Social media usage*	*Loneliness*	*Happiness*	*Life satisfaction*
Social media usage	0.890	1			
Loneliness	0.667	−0.312**	1		
Happiness	0.801	0.440**	0.000	1	
Life satisfaction	0.753	NA	−0.205**	0.290**	1

$p < 0.01$; NA: not applicable

A statistically significant negative correlation between loneliness and life satisfaction provides evidence in support of H4.

Thus, the findings can be gainfully interpreted as follows. An enhanced usage of image-based and image- and text-based social networking sites reduces loneliness and enhances happiness among the users. Further, the heightened happiness and diminished loneliness have a positive effect on life satisfaction.

Discussion

Social media usage is found to be addictive (Fox & Moreland, 2015; Kross et al., 2013), and yet very prevalent. This study endeavored to identify the various consequences of image-based and image-and-text-based SNS usage. The study hypothesized that SNS usage increases happiness and decreases loneliness. Further, the increased happiness and decreased loneliness are expected to reflect in increased life satisfaction among adolescents. Accordingly, data were collected from adolescents using survey method with the help of established scales. With respect to image-based and image- and text-based SNS users, the study offers the following insights: (1) SNS usage is positively related to happiness but negatively related to loneliness; (2) increasing happiness contributes towards enhanced life satisfaction; and (3) decreasing loneliness boosts life satisfaction. Thus, the study found evidence in support of all the four hypotheses proposed.

The findings of this study are in alignment with the extant research. SNS usage helps the users to communicate virtually. The time spent on

SNS helps the users to stay connected with their friends and relatives (Peter & Valkenburg, 2006). Social media not only helps in interpersonal interconnectivity but is also a source of entertainment (Cheung et al., 2011). Social sharing is also known to significantly contribute towards users' well-being (Grieve et al., 2013; Shaw & Gant, 2002). The findings from present research build on these prior results to put forth more specific outcomes of SNS usage in terms of increased happiness, diminished loneliness, and enhanced life satisfaction. The feeling of connectedness due to active membership of an SNS platform facilitates happiness. On the other hand, the confidence of not being left out of the social circles decreases the sense of loneliness and thereby, enhances life satisfaction. Overall, staying connected and contributing, directly or indirectly, to the platform makes users feel happy and satisfied (McKenna et al., 2002; Oh et al., 2014).

Conclusion and Implications

Social media usage has been widely studied to identify consequences at both ends of the spectrum. Some studies have brought out the negative repercussions such as reduced attention span, increased sensitivity, mood swings, depression, social comparison, and social displacement (Donnelly & Kuss, 2016; Kabasakal, 2015; Samaha & Hawi, 2016; Van Deursen et al., 2015). On the other hand, there are studies that have argued in favor of positive outcomes of social media usage such as pleasant feeling, freedom to share, learning without barrier, and happiness (Das et al., 2018; Kim, 2014; Przybylski et al., 2013; Song et al., 2014). In this context, the present brought a fresh perspective by endeavoring to explore the mechanism for attainment of life satisfaction due to SNS usage. Though life satisfaction is a very multifaceted concept and people interpret it from myriad perspectives, this study established its connection with lowered loneliness and higher happiness in the context of SNS usage. Sharing content and receiving the content shared on social media platforms makes the users feel connected, lowers loneliness, heightens happiness, eventually leading towards greater satisfaction in life. Therefore, the objective of SNS platforms should be to facilitate greater sharing.

The study provides a platform for future research pertaining to SNS platforms. Researchers would be able to immensely contribute to the domain by exploring the consequences of SNS usage in greater detail by including not just observable but various intrinsic outcomes as well. There is also a need to delve deeper into SNS platforms and understand motives as well as consequences for the users. The reasons for greater usage of image-based SNS platforms in comparison to pure text-based platforms also need to be investigated by researchers. Going beyond survey methods, researchers also need to use unstructured data available on SNS platforms to derive insights. Even as the study contributes towards our understanding of SNS platforms, it is not free from limitations. The study has not taken into consideration pure text-based SNS platforms which are a major outlet for opinion sharing. Inclusion of antecedent constructs of SNS usage would have made the model more holistic. And finally, multivariate data analysis would have offered more insights pertaining to the relationships between the constructs. Nevertheless, the current study has provided insights related to SNS usage, loneliness, happiness, and life satisfaction. Even more importantly, insights are generated from an adolescent population. Our study sets the stage for future research involving adolescents, a vulnerable demographic group, on the mechanism for non-addictive gratification through SNS usage.

References

Bargh, J. A., & McKenna, K. Y. (2004). The Internet and social life. *Annual Review Psychology, 55*, 573–590.

Basilisco, R., & Cha, K. J. (2015). Uses and gratification motivation for using Facebook and the impact of Facebook usage on social capital and life satisfaction among Filipino users. *International Journal of Software Engineering and Its Applications, 9*(4), 181–194.

Bellamy, A. J., Williams, P. D., & Griffin, S. (2010). *Understanding peacekeeping*. Polity.

Cacioppo, J. T., Fowler, J. H., & Christakis, N. A. (2009). Alone in the crowd: The structure and spread of loneliness in a large social network. *Journal of Personality and Social Psychology, 97*(6), 977.

Cheung, C. M., Chiu, P. Y., & Lee, M. K. (2011). Online social networks: Why do students use Facebook? *Computers in Human Behavior, 27*(4), 1337–1343.

Clore, G. L., & Palmer, J. (2009). Affective guidance of intelligent agents: How emotion controls cognition. *Cognitive Systems Research, 10*(1), 21–30.

Das, S., Mishra, M., & Mohanty, P. K. (2018). The impact of customer relationship management (CRM) practices on customer retention and the mediating effect of customer satisfaction. *International Journal of Management Studies, 5*(1 (4)), 95–103.

Davis, R. A. (2001). A cognitive-behavioral model of pathological Internet use. *Computers in Human Behavior, 17*(2), 187–195.

Diener, E. (2009). Subjective well-being. In *The science of well-being* (pp. 11–58). Springer, Dordrecht.

Diener, E. D., Emmons, R. A., Larsen, R. J., & Griffin, S. (1985). The satisfaction with life scale. *Journal of Personality Assessment, 49*(1), 71–75.

Diener, E., & Seligman, M. E. (2002). Very happy people. *Psychological Science, 13*(1), 81–84.

Diener, E., Sandvik, E., & Pavot, W. (1991). Happiness is the frequency, not the intensity, of positive versus negative affect. In F. Strack, M. Argyle, & N. Schwarz (Eds.), *Subjective well-being: An interdisciplinary perspective* (pp. 119–139). Pergamon Press.

Donnelly, E., & Kuss, D. J. (2016). Depression among users of Social Networking Sites (SNSs): The role of SNS addiction and increased usage. *Journal of Addiction and Preventative Medicine, 1*, 1–6.

Dzogang, F., Goulding, J., Lightman, S., & Cristianini, N. (2017, October). Seasonal variation in collective mood via Twitter content and medical purchases. In *International Symposium on Intelligent Data Analysis* (pp. 63–74). Springer, Cham.

Ellison, N. B., Steinfield, C., & Lampe, C. (2011). Connection strategies: Social capital implications of Facebook-enabled communication practices. *New Media & Society, 13*(6), 873–892.

Fox, J., & Moreland, J. J. (2015). The dark side of social networking sites: An exploration of the relational and psychological stressors associated with Facebook use and affordances. *Computers in Human Behavior, 45*(45), 168–176.

Francis, B. (1999). Lads, lasses and (new) labour: 14–16-year-old students' responses to the laddish behaviour and boys' under achievement' debate. *British Journal of Sociology of Education, 20*(3), 355–371.

Grieve, R., Indian, M., Witteveen, K., Tolan, G. A., & Marrington, J. (2013). Face-to-face or Facebook: Can social connectedness be derived online? *Computers in Human Behavior, 29*(3), 604–609.

Hills, P., & Argyle, M. (2002). The Oxford Happiness Questionnaire: A compact scale for the measurement of psychological well-being. *Personality and Individual Differences, 33*(7), 1073–1082.

Hughes, M. E., Waite, L. J., Hawkley, L. C., & Cacioppo, J. T. (2004). A short scale for measuring loneliness in large surveys: Results from two population-based studies. *Research on Aging, 26*(6), 655–672.

Kabasakal, Z. (2015). Life satisfaction and family functions as-predictors of problematic internet use in university students. *Computers in Human Behavior, 53*, 294–304.

Kahneman, D., & Krueger, A. B. (2006). Developments in the measurement of subjective well-being. *Journal of Economic Perspectives, 20*(1), 3–24.

Kaplan, A. M., & Haenlein, M. (2010). Users of the world, unite! The challenges and opportunities of Social Media. *Business Horizons, 53*(1), 59–68.

Katz, E., Blumler, J. G., & Gurevitch, M. (1973). Uses and gratifications research. *The Public Opinion Quarterly, 37*(4), 509–523.

Kietzmann, J. H., Hermkens, K., McCarthy, I. P., & Silvestre, B. S. (2011). Social media? Get serious! Understanding the functional building blocks of social media. *Business Horizons, 54*(3), 241–251.

Kim, H. (2014). Enacted social support on social media and subjective well-being. *International Journal of Communication, 8*, 21.

Krasnova, H., Wenninger, H., Widjaja, T., & Buxmann, P. (2013, 27 February–1 March). Envy on Facebook: A hidden threat to users' life satisfaction? In *Proceedings of the 11th International Conference on Wirtschaftsinformatik (WI2013)*. Universität Leipzig, Germany.

Kross, E., Verduyn, P., Demiralp, E., Park, J., Lee, D. S., Lin, N., & Ybarra, O. (2013). Facebook use predicts declines in subjective well-being in young adults. *PloS one, 8*(8), e69841.

Leary, M. R., & Kowalski, R. M. (1990). Impression management: A literature review and two-component model. *Psychological Bulletin, 107*(1), 34.

Leonardi, P. M., Huysman, M., & Steinfield, C. (2013). Enterprise social media: Definition, history, and prospects for the study of social technologies in organizations. *Journal of Computer-Mediated Communication, 19*(1), 1–19.

Longstreet, P., & Brooks, S. (2017). Life satisfaction: A key to managing internet & social media addiction. *Technology in Society, 50*, 73–77.

Lucas, R. E., & Clark, A. E. (2006). Do people really adapt to marriage? *Journal of Happiness Studies, 7*(4), 405–426.

McKenna, K. Y. A., Green, A. S., & Gleason, M. E. J. (2002). Relationship formation on the internet: What's the big attraction? *Journal of Social Issues, 58*(1), 9–31.

Mitchell, A., & Guskin, E. (2013, November 4). Twitter news consumers: Young, mobile and educated. *Pew Research Journalism Project*.

Nalwa, K., & Anand, A. P. (2003). Internet addiction in students: A cause of concern. *Cyberpsychology & Behavior, 6*(6), 653–656.

Oh, H. J., Ozkaya, E., & LaRose, R. (2014). How does online social networking enhance life satisfaction? The relationships among online supportive interaction, affect, perceived social support, sense of community and life satisfaction. *Computers in Human Behavior, 30*, 69–78.

O'Keeffe, G. S., & Clarke-Pearson, K. (2011). The impact of social media on children, adolescents, and families. *Pediatrics, 127*(4), 800–804.

Pelling, E. L., & White, K. M. (2009). The theory of planned behavior applied to young people's use of social networking web sites. *CyberPsychology & Behavior, 12*(6), 755–759.

Perlman, D., & Peplau, L. A. (1981). Toward a social psychology of loneliness. *Personal Relationships, 3*, 31–56.

Peter, J., & Valkenburg, P. M. (2006). Adolescents' internet use: Testing the "disappearing digital divide" versus the "emerging digital differentiation" approach. *Poetics, 34*(4–5), 293–305.

Pickren, W., & Rutherford, A. (2010). *A history of modern psychology in context*. Wiley.

Pittman, M., & Reich, B. (2016). Social media and loneliness: Why an Instagram picture may be worth more than a thousand Twitter words. *Computers in Human Behavior, 62*, 155–167.

Przybylski, A. K., Murayama, K., DeHaan, C. R., & Gladwell, V. (2013). Motivational, emotional, and behavioral correlates of fear of missing out. *Computers in Human Behavior, 29*(4), 1841–1848.

Reid, D. J., & Reid, F. J. (2007). Text or talk? Social anxiety, loneliness, and divergent preferences for cell phone use. *CyberPsychology & Behavior, 10*(3), 424–435.

Rubin, K. H., Coplan, R. J., & Bowker, J. C. (2009). Social withdrawal in childhood. *Annual Review of Psychology, 60*, 141–171.

Scheufele, D. A., & Shah, D. V. (2000). Personality strength and social capital: The role of dispositional and informational variables in the production of civic participation. *Communication Research, 27*(2), 107–131.

Samaha, M., & Hawi, N. S. (2016). Relationships among smartphone addiction, stress, academic performance, and satisfaction with life. *Computers in Human Behavior, 57*, 321–325.

Shaw, L. H., & Gant, L. M. (2002). In defense of the internet: The relationship between Internet communication and depression, loneliness, self-esteem, and perceived social support. *Cyberpsychology and Behavior, 5*(2), 157–170.

Song, H., Zmyslinski-Seelig, A., Kim, J., Drent, A., Victor, A., Omori, K., & Allen, M. (2014). Does Facebook make you lonely? A meta-analysis. *Computers in Human Behavior, 36*, 446–452.

Skues, J. L., Williams, B., & Wise, L. (2012). The effects of personality traits, self-esteem, loneliness, and narcissism on Facebook use among university students. *Computers in Human Behavior, 28*(6), 2414–2419.

Steinfield, C., Ellison, N. B., Lampe, C., & Vitak, J. (2013). Online social network sites and the concept of social capital. In *Frontiers in new media research* (pp. 122–138). Routledge.

Stutzman, F., Vitak, J., Ellison, N. B., Gray, R., & Lampe, C. (2012, May). Privacy in interaction: Exploring disclosure and social capital in Facebook. In *Sixth international AAAI conference on weblogs and social media.*

Sundar, S. S., & Limperos, A. M. (2013). Uses and grats 2.0: New gratifications for new media. *Journal of Broadcasting & Electronic Media, 57*(4), 504–525.

Tosun, L. P. (2012). Motives for Facebook use and expressing "true self" on the Internet. *Computers in Human Behavior, 28*(4), 1510–1517.

Turel, O., & Serenko, A. (2012). The benefits and dangers of enjoyment with social networking websites. *European Journal of Information Systems, 21*(5), 512–528.

Underwood, H., & Findlay, B. (2004). Internet relationships and their impact on primary relationships. *Behaviour Change, 21*(2), 127.

Valkenburg, P. M., Peter, J., & Schouten, A. P. (2006). Friend networking sites and their relationship to adolescents' well-being and social self-esteem. *CyberPsychology & Behavior, 9*(5), 584–590.

Van Deursen, A. J. A. M., Bolle, C. L., Hegner, S. M., & Kommers, P. A. M. (2015). Modeling habitual and addictive smartphone behavior. *Computers in Human Behavior, 45*, 411–420.

Veenhoven, R. (1991). Is happiness relative? *Social Indicators Research, 24*(1), 1–34.

Verduyn, P., Lee, D. S., Park, J., Shablack, H., Orvell, A., Bayer, J., & Kross, E. (2015). Passive Facebook usage undermines affective well-being: Experimental and longitudinal evidence. *Journal of Experimental Psychology: General, 144*(2), 480.

Verduyn, P., Ybarra, O., Résibois, M., Jonides, J., & Kross, E. (2017). Do social network sites enhance or undermine subjective well-being? A critical review. *Social Issues and Policy Review, 11*(1), 274–330.

PART III

Disruptions Underneath Marketing

CHAPTER 7

How to Leverage Marketing to Build Sustainable Competitive Advantage: Insights from Leading Companies

Swaminathan Mani and Mridula Mishra

Introduction

As the marketplace gets crowded with too many me-too products competing for customers' attention and share of the wallet, creating and sustaining competitive advantage becomes a herculean although rewarding task for companies. Having a clear differentiation helps position the company as delivering superior value in customers' minds. This helps in top of the mind recall for the company's products, higher wallet shares and possibly a premium pricing resulting in higher profitability. Therefore, creating and sustaining a competitive advantage has several business

S. Mani (✉) · M. Mishra
Lovely Professional University, Phagwara, Punjab, India

M. Mishra
e-mail: mridula.mishra@lpu.co.in

Rajagopal and R. Behl (eds.), *Managing Disruptions in Business*, Palgrave Studies in Democracy, Innovation, and Entrepreneurship for Growth, https://doi.org/10.1007/978-3-030-79709-6_7

benefits that have been well documented in literature. However, companies are finding it challenging to find that unique value proposition, which is compelling and defend that position in the marketplace.

Traditionally companies have looked at several avenues to create competitive advantage—scale of production (Refineries, manufacturing plants), robust supply chain (FedEx), superior products (Apple), innovation and intellectual property creation (Microsoft, IBM), access to markets (Defense contracts), preferred landing slots (Airlines), design and aspiration (BMW), safety (Volvo and Qantas) and superior customer service (Taj Hotels). However, marketing can be a source of enduring competitive advantage if leveraged strategically. Three companies, which are in different sectors, have leveraged marketing to create and sustain differentiation for decades—Intel, Marriott International and Disney. These three firms are category leaders in their respective industry verticals; have been hugely successful for decades and have managed to reinvent frequently.

Intel which is traditionally in the B2B business (selling microprocessors to PC Manufacturers) decided to gain control of the purchase criteria in the PC market by converting themselves into a B2C company when it came to marketing spend. The 'Intel Inside' campaign catapulted the company into a world leader in the microprocessor industry leaving competitors like AMD far behind although AMD had technically similar capabilities and products. Similarly, Marriott International leveraged influencers marketing to connect, create and communicate value proposition with target customers and Disney leveraged marketing to communicate their theme of 'happiest place on earth' and established Disney as a fun place for family in minds of customers. Each of these three companies—Intel (Products Company), Marriott (Services Company) and Disney (that sells experience)—has used different components of marketing that aligned with their brand strength to communicate superior value. Given that these firms have been successful for over five decades, it is pertinent to evaluate their success using a marketing lens to understand the elements of their marketing strategy that enabled them to a leadership position. Practitioners in industry (irrespective whether marketing a product or services) can take advantage of the insights from these cases studies to build sustainable advantage for their company.

Insights From a Product Company: Case Study of Intel

Robert Noyce and Gordon Moore founded Intel in July of 1968 and Andy Grove (who subsequently went on to become the legendary CEO of Intel joined as an employee a year later). Intel's metal-oxide semiconductors (MOS) and later, silicon gate MOS chips, ushered the personal computer revolution. The three key inventions of transistors, Integrated circuits and microprocessors were some of the biggest inventions of the twentieth century. Intel was the world leader in microprocessor for the next 50 years. Intel competitors like AMD manufactured similar products from a technology capability perspective. However, Intel's cumulative profit between 1991 and 2015 was $ 140 billion, and AMD made a cumulative loss of $ 2 billion during the same period. Marketing and branding proved to be the biggest differentiator for Intel. Some of the key learning from Intel's success is given below:

Always have the end consumer in mind: while the customers of Intel microprocessors were the PC makers, Intel's most successful 'Intel Inside' campaign targeted the end users of the PC. Most of these consumers did not have an appreciation of the technological nuance and hardly got to observe the Intel microprocessor as it was inside the computer but felt reassured to see the 'Intel inside' logo on the PC which signaled high-quality product. This campaign built huge brand visibility for Intel and differentiation in the marketplace. PC makers wanted the logo 'Intel inside' on their computer as it fetched premium pricing in the market. Intel had transformed itself from an engineering firm to a consumer products firm.

Customer engagement: Intel engages with end consumers of PC across all ages through social media platforms and traditional platforms. Intel has trained its 80,000 employees (who are the brand ambassadors) to engage with consumer and actively listen to them. These do not just focus on technical specifications but build an emotional connection with users by building an active community of users.

Gain control of the purchase criteria in this market: Intel gained the control of the purchase criteria in the PC market which was the processor speed which kept increasing every passing year. The end consumer was conversant with the processor speed the same way they were conversant with the engine specifications of a car. However, Intel lost the control of purchase criteria in the mobile and tablet market to ARM and Qualcomm. Marketing can help set the narrative which can be used to build differentiation.

Simplify narrative: Intel did not undertake campaigns around long technical specification or technological nuances which most consumers don't understand or couldn't care less. Intel had multiple products (Chips, Microprocessors, Boards, Adapters, etc.) with varying specifications but kept the narrative simple—if there is 'intel inside' then product performances were guaranteed.

Experiential marketing: Intel conducts events (10–12% of marketing budget is spent on events) where it invites the decision makers and C-suites to come and experience Intel products. Ninety-five percent of public cloud runs on Intel architecture that has compelling business benefits across industry sectors and these used cases are demonstrated during the events so that potential customers can get hands-on experience of the technology.

Brand your products to avoid commoditization: Microprocessors could have easily become a commodity business when competing products were offering similar technical prowess and these products were largely hidden for the end consumer. But by relentless focus on branding and marketing these microprocessors, Intel ensured that they remain on the top of the mind recall for the end users when they are making a PC buying decision. Classic case of branding driving differentiation by elevating the narrative to emotional connects than just technical discussions.

Insights From a Services company: Case Study of Marriott Hotels

Marriott International, a diversified hospitality company, was founded in 1927 with two hotels then, is presently the largest hotel chain in the world by the number of available hotel rooms and lodging facilities (both owned and franchised)—over 1.4 million rooms operated by 30 brands, 7400 + properties across 131 countries and reported revenue of $ 20 billion for 2019. Another 500,000 rooms are under construction at the moment. Marketing of services is inherently challenging as there are too many moving parts in a 'formless' services business. Hotels business is inherently a 'perishable' commodity business (if the rooms remain vacant for the night it is a lost revenue opportunity), with diverse customer expectations (from basic bed and breakfast to full-suite services with pool, gym and party experience) and competition of all sizes (from five star hotels, Airbnb to small boutique single property motels) offering the core basic product. Despite the clutter, Marriott has managed to remain the numero uno player for over decades. Marriot's marketing strategy is based around the 3Cs—content, community and commerce.

Influencers marketing: One of the most important marketing strategies adopted by Marriott was marketing to key individuals who had the ability to influence the target market. Over 90% of people look at referral (travel sites like TripAdvisor are popular) before making decisions, conversion ratio is three to ten times for products endorsed by influencers and earns more for bang for the marketing buck. Marriott partnered with Jackson Harries from JacksGap with over four million followers to create short videos on Marriott destinations, collaborated with Snapchat, Shaun McBride and Casey Neistat to appeal to millennials (the target group of Marriott), worked with musicians to create the Navigator Live, a series of short videos that gives a sneak peek into the musicians who perform at Marriott hotels and finally created two short feature films that garnered over nine million views on YouTube. Getting the combination of content, messaging, influencer, channel and target audience right proved lucrative for Marriott and was their core marketing strategy.

Seamless marketing experience across channels: Customers interact with a firm through offline, online channels and would like to have a holistic experience without broken links. Marriott ensured that customer experience is consistent across channels by consolidating the teams handing customer experience into one unit. Earlier these units were silos which did not give a unified experience to customers. Not only the customers benefited from this seamless experience, Marriott benefitted it too as they were able to capture unique customer preferences better so that they can personalize the reach out strategy for them.

Leverage the power of category branding: In 2019, Marriott launched category marketing campaign called 'Room for possibility' targeted at longer stay travelers. The campaign features three brand properties—Residence Inn by Marriott, Element Hotels and TownePlace Suites by Marriott- offering the best of both worlds (the feel of home and the flexibility of being on the road). These properties offer dedicate living, working and bedrooms with a full-fledged kitchen and complimentary grocery delivery service.

Launching Marriott Bonvoy—loyalty program: Bonvoy which is shortened version of Bon voyage is a rebranded loyalty program that has

120 million members on it—the largest for a hotel. Using this loyalty program, Marriott hopes to keep the travelers updated about the latest news in an integrated manner so that the users will connect with all 30 branded properties of Marriott into one umbrella brand and experience. This will also set the tone for a massive multi- channel digital, social and media campaign that will span over 20 markets worldwide. The benefits of a robust, well-designed loyalty program and an integrated marketing campaign can become a force multiplier for Marriott.

Insights From a Company that Sells Experience: Case Study of Disney

In 1923 Walt Disney set up a studio to produce animated films and in 1928 launched the iconic character, Mickey Mouse. The animation became very successful that 50 years later it was the first cartoon character to receive a star on the sidewalk of Fame, in Hollywood. Disney land was established in 1955 and since properties have been established all over the world. The company reported revenue of almost $ 70 billion in 2019 with business interest in televisions, films, music, video games, amusement parks, broadcasting and sports network among others. Disney acquired Pixar and Marvel entertainment that has strengthened its overall portfolio by providing complementary skills in introducing newer heroic characters that can be monetized not only through the films but also through merchandising and animation skills. Disney is known for compelling storytelling—bringing many of its characters to life—superior customer experience, branding and marketing and an uncanny ability to cross-leverage its assets across group companies.

Compelling storytelling: Ability to tell an engaging story to capture the imagination of its target market is the biggest differentiation of Disney. These stories are inspiring and motivating which resonates with the customers. Time immemorial human civilization has progressed on the backdrop of stories of the times. Disney uses nostalgia (a powerful emotion) to establish and maintain customer loyalty (e.g., reviving old classics like the Jungle book which rakes in close to $ 1 billion in revenue) where the parents relive their earlier days all over again. Disney's ability to form an emotional and lasting connection with its customers through world-class narrative is at the core of its success.

Establish Disney land as destination theme parks: Disney has established 11 theme parks in major cities around the world and has branded them successfully as destination parks. So, a visit to Orlando, Hong Kong or Tokyo or Paris is incomplete without visiting Disney land. The rides and the various shows in the park are branded and marketed to bring them to life. Not only the theme parks bring in revenues but these larger-than-life characters also help in driving merchandising and licensing revenues as well.

Importance of branding: Disney has branded its products around the theme 'youthful', 'magical', 'family and fun'. There is something for everyone irrespective of their age (their intergenerational appeal is remarkable). Disney is known by its tagline 'the Happiest Place on Earth'—which many of their loyal customers agree with. Branding—whether a show or the rides, the characters or the theme park itself—has helped establish over 70% repeat customer visits—an indication of high customer satisfaction.

Marketing on wholesome user experience/map the user journey: Disney focuses on creating wholesome user experience—right from ticketing to schedule of shows, content (contemporary as well as nostalgic), themes parks, food courts and fireworks among others—and ensures that customers have wholesome fun with family. Data is collected on popular attractions and the schedule is tweaked accordingly. Newer content is continuously added to attract repeat visitors. Leveraging data, keep content fresh and focusing on the entire user journey makes Disney a destination of choice for families.

Counter-intuitive content marketing approach: Disney creates the story and builds the products around that story which is a counter-intuitive approach as other companies do the reverse (they create a product and build the story next). This content marketing approach is unique to Disney; it can differentiate itself from peers in an area of information overload. The content is designed to be exciting, personalized and fun. It has helped to transform a relatively undifferentiated product (spending time with family and there are many avenues for it) to a unique experience cherished by all family members for a long time.

Implications for Practitioners

These case studies pertained to three companies in three different industries—products, services and experience. All the three companies are category leaders in their respective sectors that have used, and continuing to use, the power of marketing to maintain their leadership positions.

While some of the strategies adopted by these firms may be unique to their business, there are also some common marketing strategies across categories. The key insights for marketing practitioners from the success of Intel, Marriott and Disney are below:

Compelling storytelling: Probably one of the most important of marketing for any firm would be to build and share compelling stories about the firm—stories that inspire or inform or engage the client. Stories are inherently emotional by nature and once audiences are hooked to the narrative, they will remember the content for a long time to come which is a premium in a cluttered world of information overload.

Branding for premium pricing and differentiation: Intel has shown that components that are not visible to end consumers can be branded to create differentiation and premium pricing. Similarly, Marriott has shown that branding can make a difference to an inherently commodity business. Disney has shown that something intangible like experience—which is unique to everyone—can be branded to create value.

Focus on customer experience end to end: Marketing needs to focus on end-to-end customer experience to identify what customers prefer and articulate value appropriately. Focusing on end-to-end customer experience will also reveal gaps in existing services that marketing can feed into those responsible for delivering those experiences.

Have end consumer of the products in the marketing radar: Marketing to customers' customer was a strategy that paid rich dividends to Intel. While the customer of Intel microprocessors were the PC manufacturers (which is a B2B market), Intel inside campaign focused on the ultimate buyers of the PC (converted it into a B2C market). This helped Intel to gain control of the purchase criteria in the PC market which catapulted it to a leadership position in the microprocessor industry for decades.

Simplify messaging: As companies grow, it spawns a plethora of products and brands that can overwhelm customers. Also, if there are multiple channels, that are disjointed, through which customers engage with the company it compounds the narrative. Therefore, it is marketing's job to simplify the narrative so that customers are able to appreciate the whole without getting overwhelmed.

Conclusion

As the three case examples from different industry sector show, marketing can be a force multiplier for business and can become a source of sustainable competitive advantage when leveraged appropriately. These companies used marketing tailored to their business demands, however, maintained the core of marketing—branding, compelling storytelling, unified customer engagement among others—to create sustainable competitive edge in the market. All the three firms—Intel, Marriott and Disney—have been the category leaders for decades thereby proving that the right ingredients of marketing working together can impact business metrics—revenue and profits—significantly over a long term. Many companies consider technology, technical know-how, manufacturing processes, access to scarce resources, access to markets, human capital and scale as source of enduring competitive advantage and treat marketing as a cost center. However, when used strategically, marketing can help build and sustain competitive edge as all these three firms have demonstrated in different sectors. Marketing practitioners can gain vastly by studying the strategies adopted by these firms.

References

Colon, G. (2016). *Disruptive marketing: What growth hackers, data punks, and other hybrid thinkers can teach us about navigating the new normal.* AMACOM.

Dawar, N. (2016). What Intel needs to remember about marketing. *Harvard Business Review.*

Gilmore, J. H., & Pine, B. J. (2002). *The experience is the marketing*. Brown Herron Publishing.

Grove, A. S. (1996). *Only the paranoid survive: How to exploit the crisis points that challenge every company and career*. Broadway Business.

Intel Corporation. https://www.intel.com. Accessed October 2020.

Kotler, P. (2004). *Ten deadly marketing sins: Signs and solutions*. Wiley.

Kotler, P., Kartajaya, H., & Setiawan, I. (2016). *Marketing 4.0: Moving from traditional to digital*. Wiley.

Malone, M. S. (2014). *The Intel Trinity: How Robert Noyce, Gordon Moore, and Andy Grove built the world's most important company*. Harper Collins.

Marriott International. https://www.marriott.com. Accessed October 2020.

Schickel, R. (2019). *The Disney version: The life, times, art and commerce of Walt Disney*. Simon & Schuster.

Thackray, A., Brock, D. C., & Jones, R. (2016). Moore's Law: The life of Gordon Moore, Silicon Valley's quiet revolutionary. *MRS BULLETIN, 41.*

The Walt Disney Company. https://thewaltdisneycompany.com. Accessed October 2020.

Wasko, J. (2020). *Understanding Disney: The manufacture of fantasy*. Wiley.

CHAPTER 8

Why Compromise? I Want the Extreme!

Pronobesh Banerjee

Past research shows when asked to make a choice from a set of three alternatives *x*, *y*, and *z*, which are described on two attributes, such that $x > y > z$ on one attribute, while $x < y < z$ on the other, consumers usually prefer the middle alternative, popularly known as compromise effect (Mao, 2016; Simonson, 1989; Wernerfelt, 1995). Arguably, choice sets, such as above, are designed in a way when the alternatives in a set lie on an equipreference contour, making them equally attractive. Thus, the question is, what justifies the choice of a middle alternative, which does not even have a high value on any of the given attributes but scores an average on both?

An underlying theme that guides such choice processes is preference uncertainty (Dhar & Simonson, 2003). For example, in situations such as above, when consumers do not have the option to defer choice, are not sure of attribute importance and the values that describes them (e.g. how does one choose among three options of laptops having hard drive

P. Banerjee (✉)
Indian Institute of Management Kozhikode, Kozhikode, Kerala, India
e-mail: pbanerjee@iimk.ac.in

Rajagopal and R. Behl (eds.), *Managing Disruptions in Business*, Palgrave Studies in Democracy, Innovation, and Entrepreneurship for Growth, https://doi.org/10.1007/978-3-030-79709-6_8

space, 750 GB, 1 TB and 1.5 TB, when one is under the impression that anything above 500 GB should be good enough for buying a laptop), they suffer from preference uncertainty. Given that they have to make a choice under conditions when uncertainty looms high, consumers assess attribute values within context and prefers the middle option, which has moderate values on both and is least likely to be criticized (Dhar & Simonson, 2003; Simonson, 1989). Thus, the choice of the middle alternative reflects a risk averse mindset of consumers—as one moves from the middle to the extremes, the comparative losses and gains in attribute values are less extreme compared to when one moves from one end to the other.

Recently, there has been a surge in describing *attribute values* on the same metric, for example, on a rating scale from 1 to 100 (Chernev, 2004). We argue that when attributes are rated such that one of the attributes has high values-lying towards one end of the scale, e.g. 90/100, while the other has comparatively low values-lying towards the other end of the scale, e.g. 30/100, contrary to compromise effect, an extreme alternative will be preferred. For example, if x, y and z are described on two attributes such that they have values, (100,10), (90,20) and (80,30), people would prefer z (80,30), an extreme alternative, though (90,20) is the compromise option.

The rest of the paper is organized as follows: first, I discuss the reasons behind compromise effect, second, I use findings from the numerical cognition literature to posit why consumers may prefer an extreme option, third, I report six studies, that support my theorization and finally, end with a general discussion and theoretical implications of our research.

Compromise Effect

When asked to make a choice, consumers often face a dilemma. How to choose? Suppose there are three laptops, which are described on two attributes, RAM and hard disc space, and are as follows: Laptop A, RAM 6 GB and hard disc space 1 Terabyte; Laptop B, RAM 8 GB and hard disk 750 GB, and Laptop C, RAM 10 GB and hard disk 500 GB. Although consumers may have some idea about attribute importance, RAM and hard disc space may turn out to be equally preferable while buying a laptop, but what about attribute values. For example, what is the meaning of having a laptop with a RAM of 10 GB versus 8 GB? More important, whether such numerical difference translates into any real value for the consumer. For example, if one goes from 6 to 8 GB RAM versus from 8 to 10 GB, will the difference in 2 GB be perceived differently when the point of comparison is 6 GB versus 8 GB? What about the attribute hard disc space? Does one really need a laptop with a one Terabyte hard disk space, when all through one has never bought a laptop with more than 500 GB space? More notably, what is the real differential advantage in buying a laptop with a one Terabyte hard disk space vis-a-vis one with 750 GB hard disc space? In addition, while making a choice, how will one compare an increase in value of one attribute with a concomitant decrease in the other, more so when the values are expressed in different units. For example, a 2 GB increase in RAM with a 250 GB decrease in hard drive space. Situations such as these are quite common when consumers are not only certain about attribute importance but also the values that describe them, leading to preference uncertainty (Dhar & Simonson, 2003; Sheng et al., 2005). If a consumer is still asked to make a choice, she essentially has two options: to defer choice or when forced to make a choice, look for reasons (Dhar & Simonson, 2003).

Unfortunately, she may not have the option to defer choice as is typically seen in most choice experiments. Under such circumstances of forced choice, what are the guiding factors that influence choice? At the least, a consumer should not feel bad about her choice that may negatively impact her self-esteem (Dhar & Simonson, 2003). In addition, she may think that she is under the radar and should not make a choice that may turn out to be foolish in the opinion of others (Janis & Mann, 1977). Given these motivations, consumers look for the best reason that favors a particular alternative (Dhar & Simonson, 2003). How may one decide on the best reason, when one is not only sure of attribute importance, but also is hesitant of the values that describe them? Past research shows under such situations, consumers tend to prefer the middle option that has moderate values on both, leading to compromise effect. Why?

If we consider the middle alternative as the reference point, and move back and forth from the extremes, it results in losses and gains that are moderate compared to when one moves from one extreme to the other. Since, losses loom larger than gains consumers settle for the safer middle option (moderate losses and gains), which reflects the risk averse mindset of the consumers (Tversky & Simonson, 1993). In fact, thought protocols of participants who choose the compromise alternative highlight the difficulty of making a decision and a tendency to settle for the safer middle option (Huber et al., 1982; Simonson, 1989). Moreover, the moderate option averts any regret from making a wrong choice, making it a safe choice (Dhar & Simonson, 2003). In addition, the choice of the middle option minimizes the maximum potential loss of an alternative if one is making a choice from a set of three alternatives none of which is dominating (Sheng et al., 2005), and therefore, is also in line with the risk averse mindset of the consumers.

In a similar vein, participants exhibit greater compromise effect when choosing for others (Chang et al., 2012). Arguably, it is safer to choose the middle option as the taste of others is unknown. Similarly, prevention-focused consumers exhibit a greater compromise effect, because choosing a middle option is more justifiable under prevention focus (Mourali et al., 2007). In the same way, choice maximisers are ones who look for the option that has the best value on both the attributes and not necessarily an option that satisfies the highest value on a particular attribute, opt for the compromise alternative (Mao, 2016).

While differing in their details, all these explanations are entrenched in "reason-based choice" (Shafir et al., 1993). Whether one is looking to avoid criticism, minimizing the disadvantages of that choice, or inferring the best choice from a given choice set, a decision-maker is looking for *reasons* to choose one option over another in face of uncertainty when one is not sure about her absolute preference.

Recent trend, especially in online websites, is to describe attribute values on a common scale from 1 to 100 (Chernev, 2004). For example, a three alternative set may be described as follows—(100,10), (90,20) and (80,30), where numbers in parentheses represents the rating of attribute values. Will consumers still prefer the middle option? Or are there reasons to believe that one may prefer to choose an extreme option in place of the safer middle option? One noticeable difference that distinguishes the above from the laptop example is that unlike the attribute values describing the laptop alternatives, both the attributes are rated on a common scale, making attribute comparisons feasible. We argue based on numerical cognition literature that making attribute comparisons possible shift the focus to the more discriminable attribute, second one in our case, making the choice on an extreme option (80,30), *reasonable*.

Numerical Cognition, Attribute Ratings and Choice

How does one process *numbers*? Past research shows that numbers are not only represented symbolically but also follows an analog representation. In other words, depiction of numbers follows semantic encoding where numbers are classified as small, medium and large on a mental number line (Dehaene et al., 1993, Feigenson et al., 2004). The most critical outcome of such representation of numbers is distance effect-numbers that are far apart (2, 9) that are more easily recognized compared to those which are neighbors (8, 9). For example, a typical distance effect experiment shows that when participants are asked to recognize which of the two is the highest, the responses take much longer when they are close together on the number line compared to when they are far apart (Feigenson et al., 2004). In addition, the two most used mathematical representation of number line—linear model with scalar variability and logarithmic model of fixed variability—show that large numbers overlap increasingly with nearby numbers compared to small numbers, where there is minimal overlap (Feigenson et al., 2004). In fact, adults respond more quickly when two numbers are small, 2 versus 3, compared to when they are large, 9 versus 10.

These two factors, distance effect and overlap of large numbers, essentially capture the gist of numerical cognition, which is popularly known as the ratio effect. In a similar vein, Rips (2013) shows that the accuracy in predicting the difference between small and large numbers produces a log like pattern such that relative to their true positions the small numbers fall slightly above the identity compared to large numbers, making the small numbers more distinct compared to large numbers. In addition, and as Aribarg et al. (2014) asserts, "Not only are large numbers compressed together, but there is diminishing sensitivity to the differences between those large numbers" (p. 281). In summary, research in numerical cognition shows that small numbers are more distinctly encoded compared to large numbers and more important, it follows a ratio effect where small numbers are more discriminable between their neighbors compared to the large numbers.

Now suppose consumers are asked to make a choice from a set of three alternatives whose attributes are rated as follows: attribute one, 100–90–80 and attribute two, 10–20–30. How will one make a choice? Following ratio effect, the discriminability of the attribute ratings will be very distinct when they lie toward the lower end of the scale. More important, discriminability of the numbers become more distinct when expressed in an expanded scale, 1–100, compared to a diminished scale, 1–10 (Aribarg et al., 2014). Thus, as one moves from 10 to 20 to 30 the discriminability among the numbers is perceptibly larger than when one moves from 80 to 90–100.

Presumably, when asked to make a choice the higher discriminability of the second attribute, makes the alternatives much more distinguishable, and consequently, gives a *reason* to depend primarily on the second attribute for making a choice. Moreover, focusing on the highly discriminable second attribute also help consumers to avoid some unfavorable situations. First, it gives them a way out of making cognitively challenging attribute trade-offs that underlies compromise effect (Dhar et al., 2000). Indeed, past research shows when consumers have an option to avoid trade-offs they prefer to do so (Hedgcock & Rao, 2009). Similarly, consumers prefer to avoid trade-offs as it turns out to be emotionally draining (Janis & Mann, 1977; Luce, 1998). And second, and as Shafir et al. (1993) assert, "First, a focus on reasons seems closer to the way we normally think and talk about choices. When facing a difficult choice (e.g. between schools, or jobs) we try to come up with reasons for and against each option - we do not normally attempt to estimate their overall values. Second, thinking of choice as guided by reasons provides a natural way to understand the conflict that characterizes the making of decisions. From the perspective of reason-based choice, conflict arises when the decision maker has good reasons for and against each option, or conflicting reasons for competing options. Unlike *numerical values, which are easy to compare*, conflicting reasons may be hard to reconcile." Presumably, the highly discriminable *numerical* values of the second attribute provide an enduring *reason* to focus on only the second attribute to make a choice, which helps to avert both emotionally draining and cognitively challenging attribute trade-offs, which is at the core of compromise effect. Thus, unlike situations that typically leads to the choice of the middle alternative, we contend that in situations such as above, an extreme alternative will be preferred.

In the next section, I report six studies that support my conjecture. Data was collected in Amazon Mechanical Turk. A nominal fee was paid to each online participant. Data was collected in trances.

A total of three hundred online subjects participated in study 1a–1f and made a total of nine hundred choices. The goal of study 1a is to show when attribute values are rated on a scale from 1 to 100, such that one of the attributes is rated higher than the other, 100–90–80 versus 10–20–30; consumers prefer the extreme instead of a safer middle alternative. Study 1b rules out attribute balance as an alternative explanation. Studies 1c to 1f provide further evidence of the underlying mechanism.

Study 1a

Participants were randomly assigned to two conditions. Condition one had three sets of two alternatives, each described on two attributes and coming from a different product category, mouthwash, mp3 player and grill (Please see Tables 8.1a and 8.1b), such that each participant makes a total of three choices (each from mouthwash, grills and mp3 player). Following which they rate attribute importance. For example, how important is cooking space/cooking speed in choosing a grill. We made sure that there is no difference in attribute importance, which may influence choice. The second condition had one more alternative added to each product category (Please see Tables 8.1a and 8.1b). All else remained same. In both the conditions the product categories were randomly presented.

Table 8.1a Two alternative conditions (Study 1a)

Grill brands		
Brands	Cooking space (Rated on a scale from 1 to 100)	Cooking speed (Rated on a scale from 1 to 100)
Brand x	100	30
Brand y	90	40
Mouthwash Brands		
Brands	Germ killing effectiveness (Rated on a scale from 1 to 100)	Decay prevention effectiveness (Rated on a scale from 1 to 100)
Brand a	100	10
Brand b	90	20
Mp3 Brands		
Brands	Features (Rated on a scale from 1 to 100)	Ease of use (Rated on a scale from 1 to 100)
Brand x	100	20
Brand y	90	30

Source Author

Table 8.1b Three alternative conditions (Study 1a)

Grill brands			
Brands		Cooking space (Rated on a scale from 1 to 100)	Cooking speed (Rated on a scale from 1 to 100)
Brand x		100	30
Brand y		90	40
Brand z		80	50
Mouthwash Brands			
Brands		Germ killing effectiveness (Rated on a scale from 1 to 100)	Decay prevention effectiveness (Rated on a scale from 1 to 100)
Brand a		100	10
Brand b		90	20
Brand c		80	30
Mp3 Brands			
Brands	Features (Rated on a scale from 1 to 100)		Ease of use (Rated on a scale from 1 to 100)
Brand x	100		20
Brand y	90		30
Brand z	80		40

Source Author

Results

There was no difference in attribute importance across conditions. In condition one, when only two alternatives were present, the share of the *first* alternative was 44% and that of the *second* was 56%. In condition two, when a third alternative was introduced, the choice shares was as follows: *first*, 22.85%; *second*, 29.52%; and *third*, 47.61% (extreme option). A chi-square test of goodness-of-fit is performed to see whether the alternatives are equally preferred. Preference for the three alternatives were not equally distributed ($\chi^2 = 10.34$, $p < 0.05$). Past research shows when a third alternative is introduced, there is a relative increase in share for the second alternative as also it garners the highest share in the set (Chernev, 2004), none of which is supported here. The middle option has a share of 29.52%, which is obviously not the highest share among the set of the three alternatives and also the relative share of the middle option is 56.36% (please see Chernev, 2004, for calculation of relative share), which is almost the same, 56%, as in the two-alternative condition. On the other hand, the third alternative garners the majority share as predicted ($M_{third} = 47.61\%$ versus $M_{first} = 22.85\%$, z is 3.75, $p < 0.05$, $M_{third} = 47.61\%$ versus $M_{second} = 29.52\%$, z is 2.69, $p < 0.05$). Thus, the results of study 1a supports our theorizing, when instead of the middle compromise alternative one chooses an extreme option.

Study 1b

Past research shows when attribute values are rated, the dispersion of attribute values from the midpoint acts as the reference point such that the least dispersed or the most balanced alternative garners the majority share (Chernev, 2004). If we consider (50,50) as the mid-point, the dispersion of the extreme alternative is the least compared to the other two. For example, the dispersion of (80,30) is much less compared to (100,10) and (90,20) and thus, makes it the most balanced alternative in the set. Thus, one may argue that the extreme option is chosen as it is the most balanced one.

To rule out this explanation, we collected data by reducing the attribute dispersion of the third alternative and making it more balanced (Please refer to Table 8.2). For example, (80,30) was made (70,40). Thus, if attribute balance is the reason for choice, the share of the extreme alternative should be higher in the set consisting of (100,10), (90,20) and (70,40) compared to (100,10), (90,20) and (80,30). On the other hand, if consumers focus on the second attribute then there should not be a difference between the two conditions.

Results

Each participant was randomly presented three choice sets (each containing three alternatives and coming from a different product category) and was asked to make a choice (Please refer to Table 8.2). A total of one hundred and eight choices were made. There was no significant difference in attribute importance. The share of the alternatives was as follows *first*, 25%, *second*, 27.78% and *third*, 47.22%. A chi-square test of goodness-of-fit is performed to see whether the alternatives are equally preferred. Preference for the three alternatives was not equally distributed ($\chi^2 = 9.5$, $p < 0.05$) and as expected the third alternative garners the maximum share ($M_{third} = 47.22\%$ versus $M_{first} = 25\%$, z is 3.39, $p <$

Table 8.2 Three alternative conditions (Study 1b)

Grill brands		
Brands	Cooking space (Rated on a scale from 1 to 100)	Cooking speed (Rated on a scale from 1 to 100)
Brand x	100	30
Brand y	90	40
Brand z	70	60
Mouthwash Brands		
Brands	Germ killing effectiveness (Rated on a scale from 1 to 100)	Decay prevention effectiveness (Rated on a scale from 1 to 100)
Brand a	100	10
Brand b	90	20
Brand c	70	40
Mp3 Brands		
Brands	Features (Rated on a scale from 1 to 100)	Ease of use (Rated on a scale from 1 to 100)
Brand x	100	20
Brand y	90	30
Brand z	80	50

Source Author

0.05, M_{third} = 47.22% versus M_{second} = 27.78%, *z* is 2.95, $p < 0.05$). However, the share of the third alternative, 47.22% was not significantly different from study 1a, 47.61% (*z* is 0.05). Thus, ruling out attribute balance as a reason of choice.

Study 1c

If participants *primarily* focus on the second attribute and makes a choice, the share of the third alternative should increase if we increase the relative discriminability of the second attribute with respect to the first. For example, in study 1a, the distribution of the second attribute was as follows: 10–20–30, 20–30–40 and 30–40–50, while that of the first attribute was, 100–90–80. If we change the distribution of the second attribute to: 10–30–50, 20–40–60 and 30–50–70, respectively (Please refer to Table 8.3), keeping that of the first attribute the same, the relative discriminability of the second attribute increases with respect to the first, enhancing the choice of the extreme option. Data was collected to test this.

Table 8.3 Three alternative conditions (Study 1c)

Grill brands		
Brands	Cooking space (Rated on a scale from 1 to 100)	Cooking speed (Rated on a scale from 1 to 100)
Brand x	100	30
Brand y	90	50
Brand z	80	70
Mouthwash Brands		
Brands	Germ killing effectiveness (Rated on a scale from 1 to 100)	Decay prevention effectiveness (Rated on a scale from 1 to 100)
Brand a	100	10
Brand b	90	30
Brand c	80	50
MP3 Brands		
Brands	Features (Rated on a scale from 1 to 100)	Ease of use (Rated on a scale from 1 to 100)
Brand x	100	20
Brand y	90	40
Brand z	80	60

Source Author

Results

Each participant was randomly presented three choice sets, each containing three alternatives, and was asked to make a choice. A total of ninety-six choices were made. There was no difference in attribute importance. The choice of the three alternatives was as follows: *first* 15.62%, *second* 27.08% and *third* 57.29%, with the extreme alternative gathering the maximum share. There is a gain in the share of the third alternative from 47.61% (study 1a) to 57.29% (study 1c), z is 1.37, $p < 0.08$. Thus, as theorized, the choice share of the extreme option increases with an increase in discriminability of the second attribute.

Study 1d

In a similar vein, if we bring the attribute ratings of the first attribute closer together it should simulate the effect of study 1c. Arguably, bringing the already high values of the first alternative closer together will make them look almost equal and at the same time increases the relative discriminability of the second attribute. For example, if we change

Table 8.4 Three alternative conditions (Study 1d)

Grill brands		
Brands	Cooking space (Rated on a scale from 1 to 100)	Cooking speed (Rated on a scale from 1 to 100)
Brand x	100	30
Brand y	95	40
Brand z	90	50
Mouthwash Brands		
Brands	Germ killing effectiveness (Rated on a scale from 1 to 100)	Decay prevention effectiveness (Rated on a scale from 1 to 100)
Brand a	100	10
Brand b	95	20
Brand c	90	30
Mp3 Brands		
Brands	Features (Rated on a scale from 1 to 100)	Ease of use (Rated on a scale from 1 to 100)
Brand x	100	20
Brand y	95	30
Brand z	90	40

Source Author

the attribute ratings of the first attribute from 100–90–80 (Study 1a) to 100–95–90 keeping that of the second attribute same (Please refer to Table 8.4), the share of the third alternative should increase compared to study 1a.

Results

Each participant was randomly presented three choice sets, each containing three alternatives, and was asked to make a choice (Please refer to Table 8.4). A total of one hundred and twenty-nine choices were made. There was no difference in attribute importance. The choice of the alternatives was as follows: *first* 15.50%, *second* 29.45% and *third* 55.03%. There is a directional gain in the share of the third alternative from 47.61% (study 1a) to 55.03% (study 1d), supporting the underling choice process.

Thus, the share of the third alternative increases if we either increase the discriminability of the second attribute (study 1c) or decrease the discriminability of the first attribute (study 1d), which in effect increases the relative discriminability of the second attribute with respect to the first, enhancing the focus on the second attribute. Consequently, the share of the third alternative increases compared to study 1a.

Study ie

If the focus on the second attribute increases the share of the third alternative, we may further amplify the effect by concurrently increasing the discriminability of the second attribute and decreasing the discriminability of the first (Please refer to Table 8.5). For example, from 100–90–80 to 100–95–90 for the first attribute and from 10–20–30 to 10–30–50 for the second attribute.

Results

Each participant was randomly presented three choice sets, each containing three alternatives, and was asked to make a choice (Please refer to Table 8.5). A total of one hundred and forty-four choices were made. There was no difference in attribute importance. The choice of the three

Table 8.5 Three alternative conditions (Study 1e)

Grill Brands		
Brands	Cooking space (Rated on a scale from 1 to 100)	Cooking speed (Rated on a scale from 1 to 100)
Brand x	100	30
Brand y	95	50
Brand z	90	70
Mouthwash Brands		
Brands	Germ killing effectiveness (Rated on a scale from 1 to 100)	Decay prevention effectiveness (Rated on a scale from 1 to 100)
Brand a	100	10
Brand b	95	30
Brand c	90	50
Mp3 Brands		
Brands	Features (Rated on a scale from 1 to 100)	Ease of use (Rated on a scale from 1 to 100)
Brand x	100	20
Brand y	95	40
Brand z	90	60

Source Author

alternatives was as follows: *first* 4.86%, *second* 15.97% and *third* 79.16%. As expected, the share of the third alternative is significantly higher than both studies 1c (z is 3.63, $p < 0.05$) and 1d (z is 4.25, $p < 0.05$), which supports our conjecture.

Study 1f

Past research shows when it is difficult to justify one's choice (e.g. compromise effect), given an option, one prefers to defer choice (Dhar & Simonson, 2003). For example, 26% of the consumers in the two-alternative condition and 23% in the three-alternative condition prefer to defer choice (Dhar & Simonson, 2003, Study 2).

Studies 1a–1d show that even under conditions that lead to compromise effect consumers prefer an extreme option. Moreover, and as argued in the paper the choice of the extreme option is influenced by the higher discriminability of the second attribute compared to the first, which provides a *reason* for choice. Thus, unlike past research, as the choice of the extreme option is backed by a justifiable reason, we expect the preference for the no choice option to be low compared to previous studies. Study 1f is designed to test this.

Results

The conditions were exactly similar to study 1a except we added a no-choice option: prefer to defer choice. There was no difference in attribute importance. A total of two hundred and nineteen choices were made and is as follows: two alternative conditions: *first* 34.67%, *second* 58.67% and *no choice* 6.67%; three alternative conditions, *first* 13.19%, *second* 36.80%, *third* 48.61% and *no choice*, 1.38%. Thus, compared to past research, the choice of the no choice option is low for both the two alternative (6.67% versus 26%) and three alternative conditions (1.38% versus 23%). This shows as consumers have a reason to make a choice the preference for the no-choice option is significantly lower than past research.

In the main the results of study one show that attribute discriminability impacts choice such that consumers depend on the more discriminable second attribute to make a choice, which also provides a reasonable justification why one chooses the extreme instead of the compromise alternative.

General Discussion

Past research shows when a third alternative is introduced to a choice set consisting of two, none of which is dominating, consumers prefer the safest middle alternative, which is popularly known as the compromise effect in the literature. One interesting finding that characterizes the choice of the middle option is not based on any well-grounded reasons but reveals a risk averse mind set of the consumers—when one chooses the middle option having moderate values on both, which is less likely to be criticized. Arguably, the alternatives lie on an equipreference contour, so there is no reason why one will predominantly choose the middle alternative over the other but for playing it safe.

My research shows that even under conditions that lead to compromise effect, consumers prefer an extreme alternative. I reason when attributes are rated on a common scale; rated on a scale from 1 to 100, they become easily comparable and consequently, shifts the focus of the consumers to the more discriminable attribute, which influences choice. For example, if there are three alternatives that are described on two attributes and have the following ratings—(100,10), (90,20) and (80,30), consumers prefer to choose an extreme option (80,30), which arguably has the highest value on the more discriminable second attribute, which guides choice.

Theoretical Contribution

Compromise effect is "... among the most important and robust phenomena documented in behavioral research in marketing" (Kivetz et al., 2004, p. 237). Similarly, a metanalysis of extremeness aversion research found compromise effect to be robust, which cannot be reduced to an experimental artifact but can reasonably be considered as an empirical generalization. In our research, we show that when attributes are rated on the same metric, consumers avoid the middle alternative and prefers an extreme. Thus, our research provides a moderator of compromise effect. To our mind this is the only study to report such an effect more so when the choice sits on one extreme.

Past research shows when attributes are rated consumers favor an alternative-based processing, when one moves from one attribute value to the other within an alternative, such that the least dispersed or the most-balanced alternative is chosen (Chernev, 2004). For example, in study 1a, (80,30) is the most balanced alternative out of the three—(100,10),

(90,20) and (80,30), as the distance of the attribute ratings from the mid-point (50,50) is the least. Thus, it may appear that the choice of the extreme alternative is an outcome of attribute balance. On the other hand, our research shows that even when attribute values are rated consumers may prefer an attribute-based processing—picking one attribute at a time and moving from one alternative to the other, as the results of the eye tracking study suggests. More important, the eye tracking study also shows that the frequency of attribute-based processing is higher along the more discriminable attribute. In the main, our research shows that attribute ratings may not always lead to alternative-based processing and more important, focus may shift to a single attribute, which influences choice. These findings are also in line with past research, which shows that consumers typically avert emotionally draining attribute trade-offs. Attribute discriminability offers such a possibility as reflected in the eye tracking study, when consumers primarily focus on the second attribute in making a choice.

References

Aribarg, A., Arora, N., Henderson, T., & Kim, Y. (2014). Private label imitation of a national brand: Implications for consumer choice and law. *Journal of Marketing Research, 51*(6), 657–675.

Chang, C.-C., Chuang, S.-C., Cheng, Y.-H., & Huang, T.-Y. (2012). The compromise effect in choosing for others. *Journal of Behavioral Decision Making, 25*(2), 109–122.

Chernev, A. (2004). Extremeness aversion and attribute-balance effects in choice. *Journal of Consumer Research, 31*(2), 249–263.

Dhar, R., Nowlis, S. M., & Sherman, S. J. (2000). Trying hard or hardly trying: An analysis of context effects in choice. *Journal of Consumer Psychology, 9*(4), 189–200.

Dhar, R., & Simonson, I. (2003). The effect of forced choice on choice. *Journal of Marketing Research, 40*(2), 146–160.

Feigenson, L., Dehaene, S., & Spelke, E. (2004). Core systems of number. *Trends in Cognitive Sciences, 8*(7), 307–314.

Hedgcock, W., & Rao, A. R. (2009). Trade-off aversion as an explanation for the attraction effect: A functional magnetic resonance imaging study. *Journal of Marketing Research, 46*(1), 1–13.

Huber, J., Payne, J. W., & Puto, C. (1982). Adding asymmetrically dominated alternatives: Violations of regularity and the similarity hypothesis. *Journal of Consumer Research, 9*(1), 90–98.

Janis, I. L., & Mann, L. (1977). *Decision making: A psychological analysis of conflict, choice, and commitment*. Free press.

Kivetz, R., Netzer, O., & Srinivasan, V. (2004). Alternative models for capturing the compromise effect. *Journal of Marketing Research, 41*(3), 237–257.

Luce, M. F. (1998). Choosing to avoid: Coping with negatively emotion-laden consumer decisions. *Journal of Consumer Research, 24*(4), 409–433.

Mao, W. (2016). When one desires too much of a good thing: The compromise effect under maximizing tendencies. *Journal of Consumer Psychology, 26*(1), 66–80.

Mourali, M., Bockenholt, U., & Laroche, M. (2007). Compromise and attraction effects under prevention and promotion motivations. *Journal of Consumer Research, 34*(2), 234–247.

Neumann, N., Böckenholt, U., & Sinha, A. (2016). A meta-analysis of extremeness aversion. *Journal of Consumer Psychology, 26*(2), 193–212.

Rips, L. J. (2013), How many is a zillion? Sources of number distortion, *Journal of Experimental Psychology: Learning, Memory, and Cognition, 39*(4), 1257–64.

Shafir, E., Simonson, I., & Tversky, A. (1993). Reason-based choice. *Cognition, 49*(1–2), 11–36.

Sheng, S., Parker, A. M., & Nakamoto, K. (2005). Understanding the mechanism and determinants of compromise effects. *Psychology & Marketing, 22*(7), 591–609.

Simonson, I. (1989). Choice based on reasons: The case of attraction and compromise effects. *Journal of Consumer Research, 16*(2), 158–174.

Tversky, A., & Simonson, I. (1993). Context-dependent preferences. *Management Science, 39*(10), 1179–1189.

Wernerfelt, B. (1995). A Rational reconstruction of the compromise effect: Using market data to infer utilities. *Journal of Consumer Research, 21*, 627–633.

CHAPTER 9

Consumer Paradox: A Manifestation of Self-Concept in Activism in Response to Supply Chain Practices

Andrée Marie López-Fernández

Introduction

There is no doubt that organizations' operations have a direct impact on society; their effects on business and social growth and development are customarily associated with their engagement, or lack thereof, in corporate social responsibility (CSR). The reality is that organizations' dynamics can either enhance or hinder social growth and development. In relation to supply chains, attention is usually placed on focal organizations, meaning those at the end of the supply chain that provide products and services to end consumers and have power and influence over the rest of the organizations in the chain (Wang & Wood, 2016). When focal organizations state to be engaged in CSR, their socially responsible actions, and declarations regarding the latter, tend to be assumed as guarantee that

A. M. López-Fernández (✉)
Universidad Panamericana, Mexico City, Mexico

Rajagopal and R. Behl (eds.), *Managing Disruptions in Business*, Palgrave Studies in Democracy, Innovation, and Entrepreneurship for Growth, https://doi.org/10.1007/978-3-030-79709-6_9

the rest of the supply chain's actions are well aligned. Consumption naturally, and perhaps unintendedly, perpetuates organizations' unethical and questionable practices; however, consumer behavior is what can ultimately sway organizational change; the latter reveals the consumer paradox which is influenced by both self-concept and supply chain practices.

Today, their behavior is particularly and constantly tweaked by the increasing bombardment of data and information regarding organizations' business practices, as well as those of their supply chain. Hyperconnectivity propelled by social media, as well as an increase in production and access to documentaries and docuseries, have had an important role in educating consumers on the reality of shocking and appalling conditions in which products and services are being produced, manufactured, distributed, and sold to them. A series of industries and sectors around the world, including textile, retail, agricultural, automotive, farming, food and beverage, pharmaceutical, music, and technology, among others, have been effectively put on blast, as their associated firms' unethical and illegal, if not immoral, practices have been exposed. Effects of the latter are visible in their impact on consumer behavior and their ultimate purchase decision-making.

The general objectives of the study were to understand the underlining effect of consumers' self-concept on consumer activism, and to evaluate the role of consumer awareness of organizations' global supply chain practices on the shaping of self-concept and consumer activism impacting purchase decision-making. In order to do so, a set of propositions were framed to describe theoretical findings, and a conceptual model developed in order to illustrate the association of variables, constructs, and propositions. The study contributes to the understanding of consumer behavior regarding their stance on ethical behavior, social responsibility, and sustainability for purchase decision-making.

Literature Review

Supply Chains

All organizations, regardless of size and line of business, have a supply chain. An organization's supply chain is the group of organizations that collaborate in a complex system (Serdarasan, 2013) to offer a product and/or service in a market. According to Beamon (1999), it is considered to be a "one-way, integrated manufacturing process wherein raw materials are converted into final products, then delivered to customers." It includes every actor that participates at any point in the creation, production, distribution, and selling of said product and/or service. Stevens (1989) defined the supply chain as "the connected series of activities which is concerned with planning, coordinating and controlling material, parts and finished goods from supplier to customer." Whether local or global, supply chains must be effectively managed by implementing techniques for continuous improvements, across the chain, and competitiveness (Albino et al., 2002; Hugos, 2018). As each supply chain is unique, decision-making should be carried out both individually and collectively (Hugos, 2018) to ensure that practices across the chain are aligned with previously agreed upon policies, norms, and standards of operation.

According to Chopra and Sodhi (2004) disruption may occur in supply chains due to "natural disasters, labor disputes, supplier bankruptcy, war and terrorism, dependency on a single source of supply as well as the capacity and responsiveness of alternative suppliers." And now, global health pandemic is also added to the list of possible disruptors. Therefore, their management is essential for a successful outcome. The effective management of supply chains is directly associated with the firm's performance and achievement of competitive advantage (Li et al., 2006), as it may impact lead times, costs, as well as quality (Talluri & Baker, 2002). Therefore, it is common for decision-makers to primarily focus on developing strategies for cost reduction and contract renegotiation; however, there are some organizational leaders who have opted for a socially responsible and sustainable supply chain. Their practices are aligned with social, environmental, and financial performance (Silvestre, 2015), and its management positively correlates with cost and environmental performance (Cousins et al., 2019). The reality is that even those firms stating to be and have a socially responsible supply chain are falling short in their engagement; in other words, they are not actually engaging in corporate social responsibility.

Focal firms are those that are at the far end of the supply chain (Frostenson & Prenkert, 2015), have direct contact with end consumers (Wang & Wood, 2016), and provide them with products and services. They are, therefore, the organizations in the supply chain that are visible to current and potential stakeholders, particularly to consumers. Further, they have the power and ability to influence practices, policies, and standards of the rest of the organizations in the chain (Wang & Wood, 2016). Focal firms set the tone, in that they indicate the manner in which the entire chain will operate and ought to act accordingly. So, technically, if they state to be engaged in corporate social responsibility, then, they and the rest of the chain should demonstrate zero tolerance for any unethical or questionable practices. Furthermore, the policies, actions, and results ought to be based on business strategies well aligned with socially responsible strategies.

Corporate Social Responsibility

Corporate social responsibility (CSR) is a mindset and holistic approach to business. It stems from the firm's corporate philosophy, which is informed by organizational culture (Schneider et al., 2013). It requires organizations to always operate in an ethical manner, with the intent of achieving positive effects on social, environmental, and financial performance. There are various advantages to firm engagement in CSR, including a positive association of the latter with collaborator commitment (Brammer et al., 2007), organizational performance (Margolis & Walsh, 2003), and competitive advantage (Porter & Kramer, 2006). CSR is also well associated with consumer satisfaction (Jermsittiparsert et al., 2019) and loyalty (Han et al., 2019), therefore, it is important for organizations to transparently share their socially responsible actions and results with current and potential stakeholders. Moreover, there are various reasons why firms should effectively engage in CSR, all which may be summed up as their accountability toward society, the environment, and the firm itself (such as internal and external stakeholders), as business operations are only feasible because of them and their effective management.

Firms proactively engaging in corporate social responsibility diligently ensure that all organizations in their supply chain are also socially responsible. Socially responsible supply chains are well associated with supply chain performance (Mani et al., 2018). To be clear, if any of the firms in the supply chain are engaging in questionable and/or unethical practices, then, the entire supply chain is rendered not socially responsible. It is common practice, for the focal companies that state to be socially responsible, to obtain socially responsible, environmentally friendly, and/or fair trade, certifications, labels, and marks to denote that they are doing good and well. However, these by no means ensure that the focal firm and the rest of the supply chain are, in fact, not engaging in any questionable or unethical practices.

Non-socially Responsible Supply Chains

There are many ways in which organizations across supply chains take part in unethical business dynamics. The latter include but are not limited to any type of discrimination, exploitation (human and environmental), violence, fraud, corruption, impunity, abuse, theft, as well as unfair and unequal wages, unsafe work conditions, microaggressions, among many others. One of the most pervasive forms of unethical behavior falls under the classification of modern slavery. Even though slavery has been abolished, the reality is that modern day slavery persists; in fact, there are currently about forty million people enslaved (Council on Foreign Relations, 2020) around the world. The U.S. Department of State (2020) affirms that slavery exists "any time a person has been recruited, transported, or compelled to work by force, fraud, or coercion." There are many types of modern slavery including: "sex trafficking, child sex trafficking, forced labor, bonded labor or debt bondage, domestic servitude, forced child labor, unlawful recruitment and use of child soldiers" (U.S. Department of State, 2020), as well as "human trafficking, descent-based slavery, forced and early marriage" (Anti-Slavery International, 2020).

According to Anti-Slavery International (2020), modern day slavery is defined as the "severe exploitation of other people for personal or commercial gain." Forced labor is a type of modern slavery and an appalling common practice in the private sector which, to be clear, includes organizations across supply chains. In 2016, the International Labor Organization (ILO) found that over 24 million people were in forced labor, of which about 64 percent are exploited within the private sector (Freedom United, 2020; ILO, 2017). That is, about 16 million people working for organizations in different stages of supply chains are being exploited. And, to add insult to injury, in 2019, "more than 630 million workers worldwide did not earn enough to lift themselves and their families out of extreme or moderate poverty" (ILO, 2020). To clarify, extreme poverty refers to people who are living with less than $1.90 per day (The World Bank, 2020).

The focal firm may be transparently sharing, for instance, "fair" wages within the firm and still willingly accept that at the other end of their supply chain workers are earning less than living wage, and in many cases less than minimum wage. Or boast about their secure, healthy, empowering working conditions, as a "great place to work" and accept that at the far end of the chain, workers are denied basic human rights. This is the case of the well-documented issues surrounding fast fashion; the year 2020 is about to end and sweatshops are still making headlines. Forbes has reported that these include garment workers in Los Angeles, California, working 12-hour shifts and earning about 3 cents apiece or 5 dollars an hour, substantially below the state's minimum wage (Meagher, 2020). And, even more enraging and disturbing, the ILO (2018) has reported that approximately 152 million children are forced into child labor worldwide. Children around the world are working at "all stages of the supply chain in the fashion industry: from the production of cotton seeds in Benin, harvesting in Uzbekistan, yarn spinning in India, right through to the different phases of putting garments together in factories across Bangladesh" (Moulds, 2017). As these are common practice across industries, it is not shocking that those consumers take a stance against the brands that are enabling this behavior.

Consumer Behavior

Basic economic principals of supply and demand dictate that an increase in demand causes an increase in supply. In a market with multiple competitors, demand is affected by a series of potential variables, such as price, quality, ease of use, convenience, among many others. In other words, organizations are faced with the need to constantly innovate their business strategies in order to add value to their products and services and appeal to their current and potential consumers. The most effective manner to achieve this is by understanding consumer behavior; that is to say, what motivates them, what influences and impacts their purchase decision-making, and what does their perception of added value entail, leading to their satisfaction and, ideally, their loyalty.

When considering consumer behavior generically, without doubt, price (Sinha & Batra, 1999) is and will probably remain one of the most important determinants in consumer purchase decision-making. However, the more variables considered, the finer the understanding; that is, organizational decision-makers are able to better appreciate the subtleties of consumer behavior toward a product/service and brand. There are certainly other factors which also play a significant role in consumerism, such as: personal values (Vinson et al., 1977), emotion (Richins, 1997), brand image (Zhang, 2015), culture (De Mooij & Hofstede, 2011), the environment, and sustainability (Dijksterhuis et al., 2005; Verbeke et al., 2007), among many others. Therefore, it is imperative to recognize the underlying variables that are providing context to consumer purchase decision-making to fully understand their process and, in turn, their impact on business growth and development.

Socially Responsible Consumer Behavior

It is fair to say that consumers are currently more vocal about their preference to associate with organizations that are responsive to stakeholders' needs and wants, conscious about the social issues that permeate society and are authentic, honest, and effective in their efforts to alleviate them. As ethical expectations (Whalen et al., 1991) are certainly a factor considered in decision-making, consumers are significantly comfortable with disseminating experiences and opinions they have of organizations' unethical practices on social media, particularly on Social Networking Sites (SNSs); meaning that, they further strengthen the awareness of other current and potential consumers about organizations' practices. According to (Amoako & Dartey-Baah, 2020), people have become more aware and interested in the impact of organization's actions on the environment and society, such as "environmental protection, employee protection, and customer convenience," and it is information of these practices that inform firm–stakeholder relationships. Thus, the correlation between ethics and consumer behavior (Bray et al., 2011), and socially responsible consumerism (Gonzalez et al., 2009) have gained special attention in the last decade, as they have become increasingly familiar in day-to-day conversations.

Ethical consumers demonstrate their stance on social issues, and the responsibility they feel toward them, by means of their purchases (De Pelsmacker et al., 2006). In other words, they relate what they purchase directly with a social matter (Shaw & Clarke, 1999) with which they are concerned. And, according to Roberts (1993), socially responsible consumers intend to positively impact social change by purchasing products and/or services that they consider to positively impact society and the environment. Webb et al. (2008) found that there are three key dimensions to socially responsible consumerism; these being, purchase decision-making based on an organization's CSR results and performance, proactive recycling, and avoiding the consumption of products that may have a negative impact on the environment. Lee and Cho (2019) affirmed that socially responsible consumption is related to consumers' value of self-transcendence. Therefore, socially responsible consumers' behavior is directly related to an issue that does or could potentially pervade and devastate society and the environment.

While CSR is the way organizations can tackle social and environmental issues, consumer activism is how consumers participate in the reduction and eradication of social and environmental issues. Although socially responsible consumerism has become mainstream, it is not a new concept and is certainly not a novel practice; in fact, according to Glickman (2004), American consumer activism can be traced back to the beginning of the nineteenth century and the abolitionist movement with the "free produce movement" which exhorted consumers to purchase free labor products, meaning, those not produced by slaves; further, it provided products for those consumers that were adamantly against slavery. And, in England, Elizabeth Heyrick who, in 1824, wrote the pamphlet "Immediate, not gradual Abolition: Or, an inquiry into the shortest, safest, and most effectual means of getting rid of West Indian slavery" (James & Shuttleworth, 2017), called for the boycott of products produced by means of slave labor. Therefore, as long as there has been firms engaging in questionable and unethical practices, there have been consumers unwilling to enable that behavior.

In relation to social responsibility, there are three types of consumers: activists, inactive, and conformist. Figure 9.1 depicts the three CSR-related types of consumers. An activist consumer diligently seeks information about the provenance of products, services, brands, and, in general, firm dynamics. They wish to be in the know and are engaged with at least one social and/or environmental issue that drives their purchase decision-making of products and services, and influences their word-of-mouth related to the brands offering the latter. A conformist consumer is aware of certain questionable or unethical practices and consciously decides to not take it into account for their purchase decision-making; the latter, however, does not impede them from sharing information about such practices. Also, the inactive consumer is unaware of firms' questionable or unethical practices and, therefore, do not influence their purchase decision-making. Hence,

P_1: Consumer unawareness of unethical or non-socially responsible supply chain practices leads to an inactive consumer behavior.

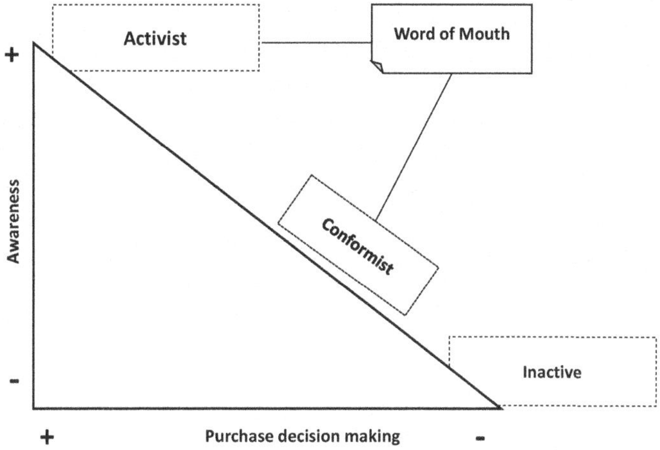

Fig. 9.1 Consumer taxonomy by corporate social responsibilities (*Source* Author)

Devinney et al. (2010) have posited that social consumerism is "embodied within and embodies general notions of corporate and consumer behavior coevolving to create, characterize, and police a marketplace." Further, according to Melé (2009), individuals have the power to direct decision-making, and policy-making, by means of their consumption; and, Vitell (2014) argues that if consumers demand socially responsible products and services, they can impact firm's engagement in CSR. Therefore, it makes sense that at least some consumers would use their power to influence a firm's business practices via their consumption.

Consumer Paradox

Bypassing the action and effects of actual consumption of a product and/or service, consumer decision-making is a paradox. We cannot negate the fact that our very existence on the planet correlates with the state of the environment. Human beings' actions certainly cause an effect on others and the environment, which can either be in the direction of improvement or deterioration; however, in many cases, the former and the latter occur simultaneously. Take, for example, a Penrose staircase which demonstrates a logical contradiction in action, whereby two-dimensional and logical elements are connected to generate a contradictory three-dimensional object. Something similar occurs with consumption. Consumer behavior, for all intents and purposes, perpetuates the vicious cycle of supply chains' unethical and questionable practices, particularly when referring to conformist consumers who are those that are aware of unethical and questionable practices yet purposefully dismiss them in favor of consumption. However, it is consumer purchase decision-making that can ultimately and effectively influence organizational change; hence, the consumer paradox is manifested.

Destruction and construction are both probable and simultaneous outcomes of consumption. In other words, the mere act of buying sets off a series of processes that inevitably harm the environment and, in most cases, interfere with society's well-being, restricting business and social growth and development. Nevertheless, with no intent to relieve firms from their responsibility, consumers have decisive power and influence to change organizational policies, standards, practices, and, ultimately, results. In other words, while consumption is associated with the destitution of the environment and modern-day slavery, it is also a significant means by which ethical and socially responsible behavior can be fueled. The question, then, is what sways some consumers in one direction and others in a completely opposite direction in terms of purchase decision-making? Or why do some consumers take the route of activism, while others choose to remain passive?

Self-Concept

Self-concept is the way an individual thinks about, perceives, and evaluates herself/himself. It is the "the totality of the individual's thoughts and feelings with reference to self as an object" (Rosenberg, 1989); therefore, it is a subjective perception of oneself (Zinkhan & Hong, 1991). It is both the "cognitive and affective understanding of who and what we are" (Schouten, 1991). The definition the self-concept is an ongoing process which begins in childhood and continues throughout adulthood, although it is less heightened in the latter. According to Slaninova and Stainerova (2015), the individual's experience with the environment is what shapes the self-concept; further, the environment as well as significant others are what influence how individuals form their self-concept. Therefore, it helps individuals understand and value themselves in terms of their relationships, role identities, and possessions (Schouten, 1991) among others.

Self-concept is relevant for consumer behavior understanding (Belk, 1988) as consumers' purchases aid in their definition of self-concept (Zinkhan & Hong, 1991), and they define others on the basis of their possessions (O'Cass & McEwen, 2004). Social identity theory (Hogg, 2018) describes the self-concept in terms of personal and social identity; in a sense, it is a manner in which individuals categorize and identify themselves in groups. As such, self-concept is well associated with brand perception and preference (Gonzalez-Jimenez, 2017; Ross, 1971), as they attribute certain personal traits to products, brands (also known as brand personality) (Schiffman & Kanuk, 2004), and services. Moreover, the ideal-self refers to the manner in which an individual would prefer to perceive her/himself, while the social-self denotes how the latter presents toward other individuals (Sirgy, 1982).

Self-image congruence relates to consumer behavior (Graeff, 1996) as it impacts their attitudes, preferences, and purchase intentions (Achouri & Bouslama, 2010), and it suggests that "people are what they buy" (Rodriguez, 2015); thus, consumerism occurs in the midst of the process of self-creation and self-improvement (Schouten, 1991). In reference to brand selection, Ilaw (2014) found that consumers prefer to purchase from organizations that demonstrate to be congruent with their self-image; moreover, consumers' self-concept is enhanced if this occurs and it is recognized by others (Grubb & Grathwohl, 1967).

It is consumers' self-concept that can drive activism; in fact, it is most likely the strongest mediator in consumer activism and purchase decision-making. However, while consumers' behavior is widely affected by the awareness and knowledge of, for instance, product attributes, it seems that mere awareness of unethical or questionable practices are not enough to sway all consumers to switch brands and/or engage in activism. This occurs because it may also solidify consumer behavior regarding conformism or inactivity as it depends on the individual's identity and how much the environment has influenced them. In other words, consumer behavior is not spontaneous or random rather, a consumer that categorizes and identifies her/himself as an ethical, socially responsible, and sustainable buyer further strengthens their self-concept as such with their purchase decision-making.

For instance, a consumer with a self-concept that drives activism will proactively seek to purchase from brands that execute strategies and have a firm stance on policies that ensure that practices, across their supply chains, are socially responsible. However, a conformist may be aware that the practices of organizations in the supply chain are not on the up and up, and still purchase from the brand. They may very well disagree with the practices; however, the awareness is not enough to deter their purchases. In other words, they present a higher degree of tolerance for unethical practices, particularly if they are occurring in the far end of a supply chain; therefore, the following propositions are formed:

P_{2a}: A consumer's self-concept impacted by awareness of unethical and non-socially responsible supply chain practices influence consumer activism.

P_{2b}: A consumer's self-concept not impacted by awareness of unethical and non-socially responsible supply chain practices influence their conformism.

P_3: Consumer activism derived from self-concept and awareness of supply chain practices, impacts purchase decision-making which directly impacts the firm.

P_4: Consumer conformism derived from self-concept and awareness of supply chain practices perpetuates the status quo of unethical and questionable business dynamics.

Consumers' Self-Concept Driving Change

It seems that mere awareness of unethical practices is insufficient to instigate change both by organizational leaders and consumers. As such, the self-concept element turns out to be highly relevant and discernable in activism. Activist consumers can drive organizational change by two general means: by avoiding consumption and by using their voice. As was stated earlier, understanding consumer behavior is elemental for supply and demand, and the latter can be a change-driving force. On one hand, by ceasing to demand a brand's products and/or services, which have been, for instance, performed by workers in forced labor, and/or manufactured by means of environmental destruction, consumer activists do not perpetuate the status quo and send a message of dissatisfaction. On the other hand, activist consumers' voices are significantly powerful; according to Hirschman (1970), voice is described as:

> *Any attempt at all to change, rather than to escape from, an objectionable state of affairs, whether through individual or collective petition to the management directly in charge, through appeal to a higher authority with the intention of forcing a change in management, or through various types of actions and protests, including those that are meant to mobilize public opinion.*

Therefore, consumers may use their voices to demand that firms change their current policies, standards, and norms for ethical ones and effectively engage in CSR. Currently, the most common forms of consumer voice include, but are not limited to, public shaming via social networking sites (Basak et al., 2019), as well as social media led boycotts, and call-out and cancel culture. The latter, in turn, can potentially influence business dynamics across supply chains; hence,

P_5: Consumer activist can dismantle the status quo of unethical and questionable business dynamics by demanding organizational policy change.

Model Analysis

Focal firms are those that are positioned at the end of the supply chain that have direct, or more direct, contact with end consumers and have power to influence policy-making across the supply chain. Too many focal companies claim CSR engagement, yet are permissive of non-socially responsible practices across their supply chains; therefore, for the study's purposes, the model contemplates unethical or questionable supply chain practices. Figure 9.2 depicts the conceptual model describing the effects of consumer awareness of supply chain practices and their self-concept on behavior.

Unaware consumers of unethical practices across the supply chain remain inactive in relation to firms' engagement in corporate social responsibility (P_1). Given their lack of awareness, their self-concept is not relevant for a socially responsible purchase decision-making. Individuals' self-concept and self-image impact their preferences and purchase intentions because the former indicates how they perceive themselves and the latter suggests that "people are what they buy" (Rodriguez, 2015). If their self-concept is strongly aligned with ethics and social responsibility, then, the awareness of unethical and non-socially responsible practices

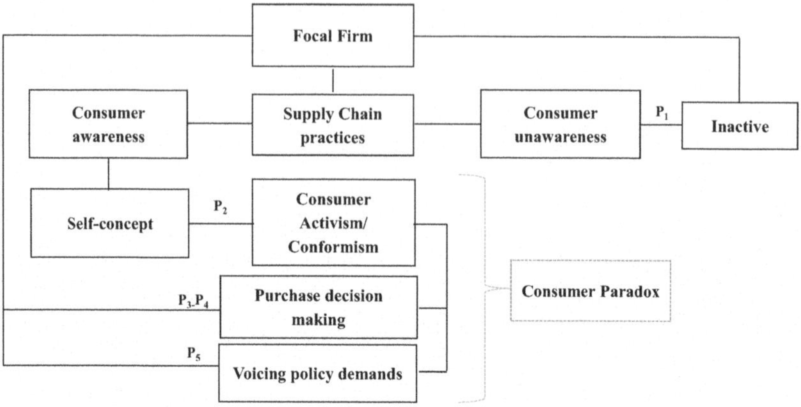

Fig. 9.2 Self-concept effect on consumer behavior in response to supply chain practices (*Source* Author)

across supply chains impacts self-concept and leads to the proactivity on consumer activism (P_{2a}) which, in turn, impacts their purchase decision-making (P_3); for instance, upon awareness, these consumers may decide to switch brands to another which is perceived to be engaging in CSR. Furthermore, given their power, they may use their voice to dismantle the status quo of unethical and questionable business dynamics by demanding that firms change their policies (P_5), actions and, ultimately, their results. However, if awareness of the unethical and non-socially responsible supply chain practices does not impact their self-concept, leading to consumers conformism (P_{2b}), purchase decision-making remains unaltered, further perpetuating the status quo of the firm's unethical and questionable business dynamics (P_4). In other words, they tolerate unethical practices, likely to satisfy a need that the product and/or service offers. Finally, the differences in dynamics of activist and conformist consumers illustrate the consumer paradox.

Concluding Remarks

Organizational culture, defined by the values that guide organizational dynamics (Schneider et al., 2013), is informed by the firm's engagement, or lack thereof, in corporate social responsibility. Therefore, there is a problematic dissonance between focal firm's statements of CSR engagement and the reality of supply chain actions. It is important to acknowledge that supply chains are not a cog in a machine; rather, they are a cog in society. As such, just like corporate social responsibility, they work through society, and for society. In the pursuit of executing strategies related to cost leadership, a series of alarming consequences are evidenced, across supply chains and industries, such as the unacceptable involvement of the private sector in the millions of workers in forced labor worldwide. Although malpractice, negligence, non-socially responsible, unethical, and illegal practices have been well documented, their awareness seems insufficient to drive change.

According to the International Labor Organization (ILO) (2016), decent and dignified work conditions are elemental to closing the poverty gap. In other words, illegal, degrading, and inappropriate working conditions have a direct correlation with a poverty-stricken population.

The latter seems to be no more than common sense; however, the reality is far from it. It should be clear that for activist consumers and firms engaged in CSR, a value chain is one that is ethical, sustainable, and socially responsible across the chain; in other words, it adds value in every stage of the chain by guaranteeing social well-being, and environmental protection. Moreover, as doing so will have a positive effect on financial performance, it is not only strategic, but also makes good business sense.

It may be argued that the current global health crisis has significantly disrupted, and in some cases devastated, global supply chains. Of course this has had a significant negative effect on the global economy; however, the somewhat more insidious part are the individuals that have been negatively impacted because of the supply chain breakdown. Yes, workers have lost their source of income because a part of the supply chain has stopped operations; however, they are being pushed into extreme poverty because the work conditions, pre-Covid-19, were already indignant. Therefore, it is no wonder consumers have been fighting for decades to end these practices by means of information dissemination and boycotting.

As consumers have substantial power to foster socially responsible actions, they can either be enablers or inhibitors of organization's active participation in, among other things, modern-day slavery. And, importantly, they and organizational leaders can take part in the co-creation of a truly socially responsible approach to doing business, rather than pursuing cost-effective, unethical, and irrational behavior, which has led to the hyper-normalization of abuse, extreme poverty, hunger, and inequality.

Future Research Directions

Future research could study the relation between conformists' self-concept and the thought process behind their purchase decision-making in order to understand the low impact of awareness of firms' unethical practices on their behavior. Also, future research could analyze different unethical practices across supply chains to determine if there are degrees of unethical behavior and if these have different effects on consumer purchase decision-making. Finally, it would be interesting to study potential differences of conformists' behavior in relation to different industries and cultures.

References

Achouri, M. A., & Bouslama, N. (2010). The effect of the congruence between brand personality and self-image on consumer's satisfaction and loyalty: A conceptual framework. *IBIMA Business Review, 2010*(627203), 1–16.

Albino, V., Izzo, C., & Kühtz, S. (2002, July). Input–output models for the analysis of a local/global supply chain. *International Journal of Production Economics, 78*(2), 119–131.

Amoako, G. K., & Dartey-Baah, K. (2020). Corporate social responsibility: Strategy for boosting brand perception and competitive advantage. In A. Kuna-Marszalek, & A. Klysik-Uryszek, *CSR and socially responsible investing strategies in transitioning and emerging economies* (pp. 65–78). IGI Global.

Anti-Slavery International. (2020). *What is modern slavery?* Retrieved October 21, 2020, from https://www.antislavery.org/slavery-today/modern-slavery/#:~:text=Modern%20slavery%20is%20the%20severe,as%20cooks%2C%20cleaners%20or%20nannies

Basak, R., Sural, S., Ganguly, N., & Soumya, K. G. (2019, April). Online public shaming on Twitter: Detection, analysis, and mitigation. *IEEE Transactions on Computational Social Systems, 2*(6), 208–220.

Beamon, B. M. (1999). Designing the green supply chain. *Logistics Information Management, 12*(4), 332–342.

Belk, R. W. (1988, September). Possessions and the extended self. *Journal of Consumer Research, 15*(2), 139–168.

Brammer, S., Millington, A., & Rayton, B. (2007). The contribution of corporate social responsibility to organizational commitment. *The International Journal of Human Resource Management, 18*(10), 1701–1719.

Bray, J., Johns, N., & Kilburn, D. (2011, February). An exploratory study into the factors impeding ethical consumption. *Journal of Business Ethics, 98*(4), 597–608.

Chopra, S., & Sodhi, M. S. (2004). Managing risk to avoid supply-chain breakdown. *MIT Sloan Management Review, Fall*, 53–61.

Council on Foreign Relations. (2020). *Modern Slavery*. Retrieved October 23, 2020, from https://www.cfr.org/interactives/modern-slavery/#!/section1/item-1

Cousins, P. D., Lawson, B., Petersen, K. J., & Fugate, B. B. (2019). Investigating green supply chain management practices and performance: The moderating roles of supply chain ecocentricity and traceability. *International Journal of Operations & Production Management, 39*(5), 767–786.

De Mooij, M., & Hofstede, G. (2011). Cross-cultural consumer behavior: A review of research findings. *Journal of International Consumer Marketing, 23*(3–4), 181–192.

De Pelsmacker, P., Driesen, L., & Rayp, G. (2006). Do consumers care about ethics? Willingness to pay for fair-trade coffee. *The Journal of Consumer Affairs, 39*(2), 363–385.

Devinney, T. M., Auger, P., & Eckhardt, G. M. (2010). *The myth of the ethical consumer*. Cambridge University Press.

Dijksterhuis, A., Smith, P. K., van Baaren, R. B., & Wigboldus, D. H. (2005). The unconscious consumer: Effects of environment on consumer behavior. *Journal of Consumer Psychology, 15*(3), 193–202.

Freedom United. (2020). *Freedom 101.* Retrieved October 9, 2020, from Learn: https://www.freedomunited.org/freedom-university/what-is-modern-slavery/

Frostenson, M., & Prenkert, F. (2015). November). Sustainable supply chain management when focal firms are complex: A network perspective. *Journal of Cleaner Production, 107*, 85–94.

Glickman, L. B. (2004, December). "Buy for the sake of the slave": Abolitionism and the origins of American consumer activism. *American Quarterly, 56*(4), 889–912.

Gonzalez, C., Korchia, M., Menuet, L., & Urbain, C. (2009, September). How do socially responsible consumers consider consumption? An approach with the free associations method. *Recherche et Applications en Marketing (English Edition), 24* (3), 25–41.

Gonzalez-Jimenez, H. (2017, June). The self-concept life cycle and brand perceptions: An interdisciplinary perspective. *AMS Review, 7*(1–2), 67–84.

Graeff, T. R. (1996, August). Image congruence effects on product evaluations: The role of self-monitoring and public/private consumption. *Psychology and Marketing, 13*(5), 481–499.

Grubb, E. L., & Grathwohl, H. L. (1967, October). Consumer self-concept, symbolism, and market behavior: A theoretical approach. *Journal of Marketing, 31*(4), 22–27.

Han, H., Yu, J., & Kim, W. (2019). Environmental corporate social responsibility and the strategy to boost the airline's image and customer loyalty intentions. *Journal of Travel & Tourism Marketing, 36*(3), 371–383.

Hirschman, A. O. (1970). *Exit, voice, and loyalty: Responses to decline in firms, organizations, and states*. Harvard University Press.

Hogg, M. A. (2018). Social identity theory. In P. J. Burke (Ed.), *Contemporary social psychological theories* (pp. 112–138). Stanford University Press.

Hugos, M. H. (2018). *Essentials of supply chain management* (4th ed.). Wiley.

Ilaw, M. A. (2014). Who you are affects what you buy: The influence of consumer identity on brand preference. *The Elon Journal of Undergraduate Research in Communications, 5*(2), 5–16.

ILO. (2016). *World employment and social outlook 2016: Transforming jobs to end poverty.* International Labour Office. Retrieved October 15, 2020, from https://www.ilo.org/wcmsp5/groups/public/---dgreports/---dcomm/---publ/documents/publication/wcms_481534.pdf

ILO. (2017). *Forced labour, modern slavery and human trafficking*. Retrieved October 9, 2020, from Topics: https://www.ilo.org/global/topics/forced-labour/lang--en/index.htm#:~:text=Out%20of%20the%2024.9%20million,labour%20imposed%20by%20state%20authorities

ILO. (2018). *Ending child labor by 2025: A review of policies and programmes.* Geneva: International Labour Organization. Retrieved October 10, 2020, from https://www.ilo.org/wcmsp5/groups/public/---ed_norm/---ipec/documents/publication/wcms_653987.pdf

ILO. (2020). *World employment and social outlook. Trends 2020.* Geneva: International Labour Office. Retrieved November 16, 2020, from https://www.ilo.org/wcmsp5/groups/public/---dgreports/---dcomm/---publ/documents/publication/wcms_734455.pdf

James, F., & Shuttleworth, R. (2017). Chapter Three Susanna Watts and Elizabeth Heyrick: Collaborative campaigning in the Midlands, 1820–34. In A. O. Winckles, A. Rehbein, T. Fulford, & A. Vardy (Eds.), *Women's literary networks and romanticism: "A tribe of authoresses"* (pp. 47–72). Liverpool University Press.

Jermsittiparsert, K., Siam, M. R., Issa, M. R., Ahmed, U., & Pahi, M. (2019). Do consumers expect companies to be socially responsible? The impact of corporate social responsibility on buying behavior. *Uncertain Suppy Chain Management, 7*(4), 741–752.

Lee, J., & Cho, M. (2019, March). New insights into socially responsible consumers: The role of personal values. *International Journal of Consumer Studies, 43*(2), 123–133.

Li, S., Ragu-Nathan, B., Ragu-Nathan, T. S., & Subba Rao, S. (2006, April). The impact of supply chain management practices on competitive advantage and organizational performance. *Omega, 34*(2), 107–124.

Mani, V., Gunasekaran, A., & Delgado, C. (2018). Enhancing supply chain performance through supplier social sustainability: An emerging economy perspective. *International Journal of Production Economics, 195*(C), 259–272.
Margolis, J. D., & Walsh, J. P. (2003). Misery loves companies: Rethinking social initiatives by business. *Administrative Science Quarterly, 48*(2), 268–305.
Meagher, S. (2020, February 5). *The not-so-hidden ethical cost of fast fashion: Sneaky sweatshops in our own backyard.* Retrieved October 9, 2020, from Retail: https://www.forbes.com/sites/syamameagher/2020/02/05/the-not-so-hidden-ethical-cost-of-fast-fashion-sneaky-sweatshops-in-our-own-backyard/?sh=1d13844f25d1
Melé, J. A. (2009). *Dinero y conciencia. ¿A quién sirve mi dinero?* Plataforma Editorial.
Moulds, J. (2017). *Child labour in the fashion supply chain. Where, why and what can be done* (T. Guardian, Ed.). Retrieved October 10, 2020, from Child Labor: https://labs.theguardian.com/unicef-child-labour/
O'Cass, A., & McEwen, H. (2004, September). Exploring consumer status and conspicuous consumption. *Journal of Consumer Behavior, 4*(1), 25–39.
Porter, M. E., & Kramer, M. R. (2006, December). Strategy and society. The link between competitive advantage and corporate social responsibility. *Harvard Business Review, 84*(12), 78–92.
Richins, M. L. (1997, September). Measuring emotions in the consumption experience. *Journal of Consumer Research, 24*, 127–146.
Roberts, J. A. (1993). Sex differences in socially responsible consumers' behavior. *Psychological Reports, 73*(1), 139–148.
Rodriguez, A. A. (2015). The image congruence hypothesis: A meta-analytic review. In H. E. Spotts, *Marketing, technology and customer commitment in the new economy. Developments in marketing science: Proceedings of the Academy of Marketing* (p. 173). Springer.
Rosenberg, M. (1989, September). Self-concept research: A historical overview. *Social Forces, 68*(1), 34–44.
Ross, I. (1971, January). Self-concept and brand preference. *The Journal of Business, 44*(1), 38–50.
Schiffman, L. G., & Kanuk, L. L. (2004). *Consumer behaviour*. Prentice Hall.
Schneider, B., Ehrhart, M. G., & Macey, W. H. (2013). January). Organizational climate and culture. *Annual Review of Psychology, 64*, 361–388.
Schouten, J. (1991, March). Selves in transition: Symbolic consumption in personal rites of passage and identity reconstruction. *Journal of Consumer Research, 17*(4), 412–425.
Serdarasan, S. (2013, November). A review of supply chain complexity drivers. *Computers & Industrial Engineering, 66*(3), 533–540.

Shaw, D., & Clarke, I. (1999). Belief formation in ethical consumer groups: An exploratory study. *Marketing Intelligence & Planning, 17*(2), 109–119.

Silvestre, B. S. (2015, June). A hard nut to crack! Implementing supply chain sustainability in an emerging economy. *Journal of Cleaner Production, 96*, 171–181.

Sinha, I., & Batra, R. (1999, September). The effect of consumer price consciousness on private label purchase. *International Journal of Research in Marketing, 16*(3), 237–251.

Sirgy, M. J. (1982, December). Self-concept in consumer behavior: A critical review. *Journal of Consumer Research, 9*(3), 287–300.

Slaninova, G., & Stainerova, M. (2015, January). The Self-concept of Students—Formation and its Changes. *Procedia—Social and Behavioral Sciences, 171*, 257–262.

Stevens, G. C. (1989). Integrating the supply chain. *International Journal of Physical Distribution & Materials Management, 19*(8), 3–8.

Talluri, S., & Baker, R. C. (2002, September). A multi-phase mathematical programming approach for effective supply chain design. *European Journal of Operational Research, 141*(3), 544–558.

The World Bank. (2020). *Poverty*. Retrieved November 9, 2020, from Unerstanding poverty: https://www.worldbank.org/en/topic/poverty

U.S. Department of State. (2020). *What is Modern Slavery?* Retrieved October 19, 2020, from Office to Monitor and combat trafficking in persons: https://www.state.gov/what-is-modern-slavery/

Verbeke, W., Vanhonacker, F., Sioen, I., Van Camp, J., & De Henauw, S. (2007, November). Perceived importance of sustainability and ethics related to fish: A consumer behavior perspective. *AMBIO: A Journal of the Human Environment, 36*(7), 580–585.

Vinson, D. E., Scott, J. E., & Lamont, L. M. (1977, April). The role of personal values in marketing and consumer behavior. *Journal of Marketing, 41*(2), 44–50.

Vitell, S. J. (2014). A case for consumer social responsibility (CnSR): Including a selected review of consumer ethics/social responsibility. *Journal of Business Ethics, 130*(4), 767–774.

Wang, X., & Wood, L. C. (2016). The influence of supply chain sustainability practices on suppliers. In B. Christiansen, *Handbook of research on global supply chain management* (pp. 531–544). IGI Global.

Webb, D. J., Mohr, L. A., & Harris, K. E. (2008, February). A re-examination of socially responsible consumption and its measurement. *Journal of Business Research, 61*(2), 91–98.

Whalen, J., Pitts, R. E., & Wong, J. K. (1991). Exploring the structure of ethical attributions as a component of the consumer decision model: The vicarious versus personal perspective. *Journal of Business Ethics, 10*, 285–293.

Zhang, Y. (2015). The impact of brand image on consumer behavior: A literature review. *Open Journal of Business and Management, 3*(1), 58–62.
Zinkhan, G. M., & Hong, J. W. (1991). Self-concept and advertising effectiveness: A conceptual model of congruency conspicuousness and response mode. *Advances in Consumer Research, 18*, 348–354.

CHAPTER 10

Framework of Design-to-Market Business Modeling for Frugal Entrepreneurial Products

Ananya Rajagopal

Introduction

The dynamic nature of the markets determines their entrepreneurial orientation, value proposition, and growth strategies. The business model of a firm helps in building organizational structure and drives the firm's performance and growth. Frugal innovation, which emphasizes low-cost technology-oriented products, has emerged as a contemporary style of innovation in Asia and the countries in the global south to provide value added benefit to the customers. The major challenge in promoting frugal innovation is to provide need-based solutions and inculcate high perceived value among consumers. The principal value creators include

A. Rajagopal (✉)
Department of Business and Economics, Universidad
Anahuac Mexico, Mexico City, Mexico
e-mail: ananya.rajagopal@anahuac.mx

Rajagopal and R. Behl (eds.), *Managing Disruptions in Business*, Palgrave Studies in Democracy, Innovation, and Entrepreneurship for Growth, https://doi.org/10.1007/978-3-030-79709-6_10

low price products, robust, contemporary technology, easy-to-use, and value for money. Frugal innovation has a growth potential within the niche market that focuses on targeted large populations in developing economies (Hossain, 2021). The frugal solutions are locally developed and initially tested with local lead users who attract early adapters within the market proximities and explore larger markets in collaboration with the sponsoring companies. Strategic alliance with sponsoring companies has a major challenge of commercializing local innovations and upscaling them to fit to the demand in mass markets. Consequently, most frugal innovations in association with large companies tend to develop a commercial brand, and strategically fit it to a hybrid model embedded with marketing technology, enhanced capital resources, and media propagation, to scale up the innovations to match the requirements in the competitive marketplace. The frugal innovations are founded on the factors including cost, growing demand, sustainability, value perceptions, output demonstration, channelization, and effective leadership between the niche and upstream market players (Soman et al., 2012).

With advancements in technology, public policies, and public–private partnerships, frugal innovations have surged in consumer and industrial products in the newly targeted markets such as renewable energy products, consumer electronics and robotics, agriculture, and in the products of social health sectors. Frugal entrepreneurs develop such products in the resource-limitation environment by using appropriate bricolage strategies that ensures austerity to overcome the resource constraints. Consequently, the frugal innovation is nurtured in a resource-scarce environment by ensuring quality solutions at relatively lower prices than the commonly available products (Zeschky et al., 2014). There is an increasing consensus among entrepreneurs that frugal innovation needs to be promoted as an alternate stream of production to supplement the commercial innovation and provide value to the customers at the bottom-of-the-pyramid. Despite the social consciousness about frugal innovations, the major underlying challenge is of developing suitable market for them and their commercialization. The social dimensions of frugal innovations include collective intelligence, crowdfunding, and social governance perspectives, which focus on acquisition of technologies, developing innovation process, and promoting user-oriented product designs (Seles et al., 2019). Frugal innovation initiatives are based on the philosophy of providing customer-oriented services to enhance trust, loyalty, and differentiation to effectively position the brand in the marketplace.

Most research studies focus on developing frugal innovation in emerging economies, which has been conceived as an essential socio-economic productivity stream seeing the resource shortages, environmental damages, and plethora of entrepreneurial limitations. Consequently, the low-cost innovation using intermediate (homegrown) technologies have been the foundation of frugal concepts in product and services innovation. As such innovations aim to override high-value commercial innovations, they embed disruptive attributes with social value-generation perspectives (Bucherer et al., 2012). Sometimes, low-cost disruptive innovations compliment to new technologies that make the consumers adapt frugal innovations to derive value-added benefits. Such innovations, supported by the commercialization strategies, help in combining high-end products with design-to-market architecture helping frugal innovation to roll into mass markets. The sponsorship of large companies to commercialize frugal innovations transforms them from the stationary mode of marketing to dynamic business models considering the disruption as a competitive leverage (Soni & Krishnan, 2014). Frugal innovations, in collaboration with large companies, often transform into reverse innovation, which refers to market expansion rather than product penetration, with the purpose of enhancing the customer outreach and marketability of products. Consumers with conscious consumption value frugal lifestyle as a socio-economic attitude. The increasing trend of customers towards consumption of low-budget innovative products has persuaded entrepreneurs to engage in frugal innovations in developing markets (Hossain, 2018).

Developing frugal innovations in the social and economic context requires adapting to systems thinking approach, which integrates social, economic, and technological systems into entrepreneurial productivity. Systems thinking helps in enhancing innovation process by maximizing the effectiveness of resource utilization and marketability. The systems thinking approach explains networking of socio-economic attributes with business models to systematically measure the consumer needs, competitive advantages, and profitability (Nakata & Hwang, 2020). The local entrepreneurial practices with variability in the non-standardized product architectures and processes often obstruct the market performance of frugal innovation products. Therefore, entrepreneurial complexity, resource utilization, and design thinking can be synchronized through systems thinking approaches that can reduce the divergence of the product attributes. In addition, systems thinking reduces the extent of passive acceptance of frugal innovation products in larger markets across socio-demographic segments, and streamlines the performance of perceived use value towards the low-cost technology products (Carayon et al., 2015). Systems thinking in entrepreneurship leads to design thinking process, which is based on the approach towards solving socio-economic problems and creating need for affordable innovations. The design thinking is associated with development of new products and services bridging the knowledge gaps, customer needs, and perceived use value for low-cost technology-oriented products. Therefore, the design thinking broadly encompasses a triadic design perspective comprising design-to-market, design-to-society, and design-to-value (Gruber et al., 2015).

The design-to-market strategy is based on the holistic approach to market integrating the strategies to optimize the values associated with customers, suppliers, and retailers. The design-to-market strategy is focused on end-to-end market designing, which requires systems approach and strategies to manage major externalities, technology change, and manufacturer-customer-retailer interface. The key challenge in developing and implementing design-to-market strategy is towards convergence of customer solutions and price–quality relationship to gain competitive leverage. In the absence of appropriate design-to-market strategy, the entrepreneurial products often fail in the competitive markets and are downplayed by the suppliers. Consequently, this strategy helps in integrating the backward and forward linkages, and enhancing customer value by providing affordable frugal solutions. Markets with major externalities pose higher threats to frugal innovation as changes in technology and market designs both cause value deteriorations among consumers for frugal products and services. Consequently, frugal innovations are confined to niche markets and face widespread failures in larger markets due to the lack of appropriate market design focused on end users. The design-to-market strategy focuses on enhancing end-user satisfaction and achieving competitive leverage to expand market outreach of frugal innovation products. This is an upthrust strategy for low-cost technology products to experience out-of-niche leap against commercially competing brands in larger markets (Labbe et al., 2015). In view of the above discussion, this chapter illustrates the attributes of frugal innovation, marketability, and entrepreneurial competitiveness in the dynamic marketplace. Converging the systems thinking approach with frugal innovation practices under the socio-economic ecosystem, this chapter emphasizes design perspectives to marketing strategy. The strategic alliances of low-cost technology-oriented enterprises with large companies to push frugal innovations in upstream markets constitute the core discussions of this chapter. Broadly, this chapter lays foundation on the framework of design-to-market business modeling for frugal entrepreneurial products.

Market Competition

Large companies focus on outperforming their rivals by developing identical or similar products to gain market competitiveness by implementing marketing strategies for each element of marketing-mix. These companies intend to enhance their market share by developing brand loyalty. However, market competition also infuses the behavior of brand defection among consumers, which throws a more rigorous challenge to the firms. The market competition largely induces incremental improvements in cost and quality management besides providing fringe benefits to customers on marginal reduction in prices and increase in promotional benefits. Nonetheless, frugal innovations developed by small and medium enterprises fail to acquire a safe space to market their innovative products and grow consistently in the competitive marketplace. The frugal enterprises are often unable to break the competitive labyrinth in the marketplace as the frugal innovative products lack secured marketspace to create value among the niche consumer segments. Consequently, small and medium enterprises engaged in developing frugal innovations are pushed back to niche market environment. Such situations often drive these enterprises to cocoon their growth perspectives unless the commercialization of frugal innovations is supported by large companies. This path of entrepreneurial evolution requires both competitive and collaborative mindset to systematically develop alliances with large firms and explore opportunities. Taking frugal innovations to competitive markets with such alliances have a bidirectional effect on design and productivity, and development of markets with commercial branding. By doing so, the frugal innovative products can find liberal territories (non-competitive) that represent consumer preferences towards cost, quality, and value perspectives (Kim & Mauborgne, 1999).

The rise of small and medium enterprises (SMEs) engaged in developing low-cost innovation and technology products is often stimulated by public policies and social consciousness, which support resources and internal capabilities of firms. The cost-subsidies and tax holidays provided under public policies in developing economies give a quick boost to the products of small and medium enterprises. Such support from public policies enables these enterprises to develop consortium of frugal innovative products and penetrate the competitive marketplace through umbrella branding initiative. These attributes require transformation, as the global dynamics on low-cost innovative products within the affordable brackets of consumers is rapidly changing. Large companies are fragmenting their brands categorically for upstream and downstream markets to compete with the frugal innovation products of SMEs. In pharmaceutical industry, most multi-national companies, like Pfizer, have fragmented their brands for many essential pharmaceutical products as Vitales (Mexico) to compete with the generic interchange (GI) pharmaceutical products. Therefore, SMEs are focusing their strategies on the value for money segment along with the strategies of brand enhancement to compete with multi-national companies and gain competitive leverage (Ramamurti & Willamson, 2019).

The market competition today is characterized with ultra-low-cost operations, speed of processing and delivery, flexibility, and customization of products and services. Social marketing strategy is followed in mobilizing frugal innovation products in their home markets (Ruz-Mendoza et al., 2021). The products developed in home grown markets require modifications to match with the customer needs in larger markets. SMEs need to periodically strengthen their technology and innovation capabilities in domestic research and development centers to increase their risk-absorbing capacity and develop markets in cutting-edge customer segments. In addition, brand development needs to be undertaken in market events and trade shows to educate customers and inculcate top-of-the-mind brand manifestation. Therefore, investment in brand building through periodical campaigns is an uphill challenge for the enterprises, which operate in low resources. The value for money concept helps in improving the scope of mass retailing in developing economies where frugal innovative products address to the bottom-of-the-pyramid market segment. However, it is essential to learn from mistakes in cross-market (upstream and downstream) management and integrate customization in deliverables to the customers (Santos & Williamson, 2015).

The major challenge for SMEs to compete in the competitive marketplace is to protect their customer niche against the large companies. The SMEs are characterized with disruptive and low-cost innovation products, and they try to play with pricing tactics to attract customers. However, large companies downplay the marketing strategies of low-cost innovators and focus on omnichannel strategy to serve the predetermined target customers, which raises barriers for frugal innovation enterprises to penetrate the marketspace. The low-cost innovation enterprises need to focus on single consumer segment, deliver basic products, and provide the bottom-line benefits to support their low prices. Nonetheless, these strategies may not provide an opportunity for SMEs to sustain the business competition of branded products promoted by large companies. Eventually, large companies push back to eliminate the price rivals from the entire market segments. Since SMEs cannot sustain the price-war by lowering the profits, it would be a difficult proposition for frugal-innovation products to face the marketplace studded with the large companies with branded products. However, the low-price product enterprises constitute the market at the bottom-of-the-pyramid segment, which always provides scope of business for both low-cost and value-added players. The customer preferences and strategies of traditional businesses deploy transformational synergies for the enterprises engaged in manufacturing and marketing of low-cost and value-driven products in the bottom-of-the-pyramid market segment. The attributes of market competition in the context of market players and customer segments are exhibited in Fig. 10.1, which illustrates the strategy perspectives in convergence with the core attributes.

Market competition is a major concern for SMEs to grow against the large companies carrying out business with commercial brands. Consequently, the strategy foundation of these firms is laid on weak strategy canvas, which affects their market share and profitability. Although the competition-oriented theories suggest that market competition provides scope for improving efficiency and discouraging the managerial slackness, conventional thinking, and near negative effects. Figure 10.1 illustrates various dimensions of market competition on a comparative platform for SMEs and large companies including public enterprises.

The major challenges with SMEs are resource limitation and organizational practices of ownership control and conventional leadership. The large companies plan high investments through own resources or in combination with public equity to encourage research and development, and the approaches to commercialize innovation. The SMEs largely depend on crowdfunding, government finance, or subsidies. Such orientation of SMEs drives strategies towards maintaining low-profile business and gaining creditworthiness to strengthen quick payback possibilities

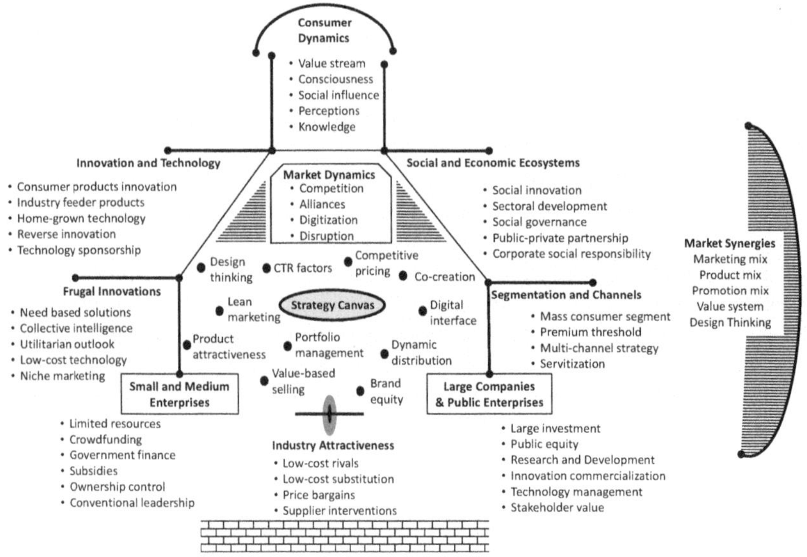

Fig. 10.1 Market dynamics and strategy canvas (*Source* Author)

(Pacheco et al., 2018). Consequently, these enterprises deviate from enhancing the stakeholder value as compared to the large firms, which have effective strategies to increase value propositions among the market players. However, industry attractiveness matters for both types of enterprises (SMEs and Large firms) to sustain industry competition and pave path to business growth and expansion. The low-cost rivals are not only sensitive to the bottom-of-the-pyramid consumer segment, but also have potential to alter the consumption behavior towards frugal innovative products over time. In addition, low-price substitutions, price bargain with customers and suppliers, and inflow of disruptive products constitute *halo effect*[1] in business performance, growth, and expansion.

SMEs focus on frugal innovations and low-cost technologies, while the large companies aim at technology management contextual to social and economic systems and its commercialization by structuring appropriate

[1] Halo effect refers to the tendency of impression created in one area to influence opinion in another area. Halo effect can be explained also in the context of butterfly effect.

segments and multi-channel marketing strategies. Frugal innovations are developed on utilitarian outlook by screening collective intelligence to provide need-based solutions within niche markets. In transitional economies, most SMEs are growing as suppliers of industrial feeder products than customer-centric product innovators. These enterprises use home-grown or intermediate technology, and intend to seek sponsorship of large companies to uplift the reverse innovations as commercial brands and operate beyond niche market scenarios. Large companies and public enterprises focus on social innovation through public–private partnership and corporate social responsibility. Large firms in competitive markets tend to exhibit value-based social performance to gain high corporate profile as profit-oriented competitive strategies often reduce social concerns. The competitive pressures force firms to increase their social innovation and development actions through corporate social responsibility within industry specification. Social performance of companies is a multi-dimensional strategy, which converges society and business relationships to achieve consistent business growth by improving social performance and socio-economic order of corporate ventures (Leong & Yang, 2020).

Consumer dynamics and market dynamics help in structuring market competition within the market ecosystem. Consumer dynamics incorporates value stream management, perceptions, knowledge, and behavioral perspectives within social consciousness and influence. Market competition, strategic alliances, technology and digitization, and disruptive practices drive market dynamics. By mapping consumer dynamics and market dynamics, strategy canvas can be designed using design thinking, lean marketing strategies, co-creation, and digital interface to develop synergy among market players in the competitive business environment (Buhl et al., 2019. In addition, the strategies on product attractiveness, portfolio management, dynamic distribution, price competitiveness, brand equity management, and value-based selling approaches constitute the front-end of strategy canvas. The cost, time, and risk factors play critical role at the backend of the canvas.

Strategy canvas for SMEs involves design thinking and value-based portfolio management along with creative selling and brand equity. However, these companies face a major challenge in developing competitiveness in the dynamic market space, and create collective value for innovations. As most products of SMEs emerge out of frugal innovation process, the competitive differentiation and creating mindset of customers becomes methodically difficult due to unfamiliar brands and trade-off between substitute products with synchronized price-quality. Such entrepreneurial problems often remain obscure during the growth of SMEs in offering frugal products and services and breaking the function-emotional cognitive niche (Kim & Mauborgne, 1999). To overcome the challenges of marketplace competition, SMEs should create a positioning map of various factorial combinations such as price-benefit, product-value, and brand-quality. The positioning map can be created along with the following steps by:

- Defining the market holistically
- Understanding customer preferences on competing products and substitutes
- Tracking price-benefit stimulus to identify the primary and secondary benefits of the product
- Enhancing product attributes to justify variance in price and quality against the substitution products
- Mapping value perceptions of customers perceived on the product utilization and value-for-money
- Developing an attractive brand suitable to within the competitive landscape of given market and establishing the quality parameters to endorse brand value
- Highlighting price-premium in primary and secondary benefits on the product to generate customer value with an objective to achieve higher market share
- Building customers as referrals and gatekeepers to support continuous growth of the brand in competitive marketplace by optimizing price-benefit experience.

There are many ways to develop competitive maps using the above points of benefit to exhibit brand personality of frugal innovative products and position them in unoccupied or less crowded market spaces to stimulate protective growth. SMEs can identify virgin opportunities by locating the less competitive markets, and establish their market position by understanding the contextual attributes as discussed above to counter rival strategies and safeguard their market niche (D'Aveni, 2007). The nature of marketplace competition has changed from brick and mortar retailing to virtual departmental stores which are allowing the products and services without prejudice of brand and size of the firm. The virtual competition is creating fierce fights across frugal brands of emerging companies including SMEs, start-up enterprises, and contract manufacturers. Many large companies have also drawn their products to the battlefield, which were developed as reverse innovation products with global–local strategic alliances. Consequently, the global marketplace for frugal innovative products is observing rapid movements in creating value through co-designing of products, and building agile marketing strategies including customization, delivery options, and post-sales services (Tang et al., 2021). In addition, the low-cost technology aims at enhancing customer leverage towards buying and adaptation of frugal innovation products. The agility in marketing strategies become a critical factor in managing the increasing competition among frugal innovation products developed by SMEs, start-up enterprises, and large firms. However, successful low-cost innovative products make headway in competitive marketplace following the triadic combination of rapid movements, agility in marketing strategies, and creating value. The combination of such strategies can be explained with a biomimicry illustration as Gannets' strategy, which explains the precise and powerful action of sea diving birds in catching fish.

Most SMEs are unable to create blue ocean strategy with the pursuit of differentiation and low-cost to open new market space and create new demand because these companies enter into the red ocean full of competition and face complexities to survive (Kim & Mauborgne, 2005). Nonetheless, some frugal innovative products that are capable to adapt to Gannets' strategy are able to survive the red oceans.

Design-to-Market

Developing marketing strategies by integrating functional market players, customers, and stakeholders is broadly considered as design-to-market philosophy. However, systems thinking is an organization-wide concept that embeds design thinking to enhance organizational performance and market competitiveness. Broadly, systems consist of people (customers, stakeholders, and front liners including sales and customer relation employees), technologies (low-cost, high-value, and hybrid technologies), organizational structures (vertical, horizontal, and team based), and processes (paper-based, seamless, and hybrid). These systems exhibit integrated functionality to make the business organizations viable and achieve high competitiveness in the marketplace. Systems thinking approach has evolved within the operations research design by converging the design and management attributes (Norton, 2010). This approach has been extended to enhance organizational performance by involving stakeholders and customers. The systems thinking aims at understanding customer choices within the social and ecological ecosystems that establish a balance between business and marketing in competitive marketplace. Therefore, this approach is considered as a continuous learning stream for organizations to streamline the design thinking process and develop products and services within the broad framework of customer preferences. Systems thinking, combined with design thinking process, has been adapted by the organizational members of the society for organizational learning (SOL) since 1990s. The SOL members include Shell, Harley Davidson, Hewlett Packard, Xerox, and Nike along with others have initiated series of actions to find collaborative solutions to variety of sustainable issues that affect consumer preferences, social values, and corporate reputation. Consequently, design thinking is blended with corporate philosophy and collective intelligence driven from social resources. The systems thinking leads to design thinking process connecting conceptual, relational, and action-oriented systematic change in business (Senge et al., 2007).

Design thinking is an outgrowth of systems thinking, which has gained extensive attention in business, technology, and marketing management. The design-to-market approach is a recent sprout in dynamic global marketplace that tends to converge customer preferences, technology, innovations, and disruptions to develop an integrated market structure. The implementation of design-to-market approaches are sensitive to cost, time, adaptability, values, and revenue streams, measuring the competitive benchmarks, market share, and consistent profitability within the market and industry. Consequently, the design-to-market approaches are largely customized and may not fit all organizations varying in size of business and geographic expansion of markets. Nonetheless, this approach can be well nurtured right from the initial stages of business operations concentrating on providing customer solutions following contemporary management insights. The agile business frameworks, lean start-ups, and social innovations that are initiated by micro or large enterprises streamlining the scientific management methods like Six-Sigma, critical thinking, and Logical Framework Analysis help enterprises in administering the design-to-market strategy. This linear path to design-to-market strategy assimilates the fundamentals of Six-Sigma (define, measure, analyze, implement, and control) leads to examine the voice-of-customers, critical to quality, design functions, and Quality Function Deployment (Beckman, 2020). Systems thinking must put forward new solutions to challenge market competition, customer values, and underlying social perspectives. This requires developing a multi-quadrant map comprising competition attributes, business influencers, innovation management, technology ecosystem, social diagnostics, and customer perceived value. In addition, transparency in communication in explaining the causes and effects of each quadrant of design-to-market strategy from the perspective of functional determinants (product, price, place, promotion, pace, performance, people, and psychodynamics) needs to be considered by the companies during the process of implementation. The attributes of design-to-market approach converging ecosystems and order of evolution of markets have been explained in Fig. 10.2.

Frugal innovations in the contemporary business environment are re-defined as low-cost innovations targeted for the unserved, lower end of the mass market (ULM). These innovations have grown from simplified form, which were initially focused on social consumption, to multi-dimensional markets with relatively complex designs embedding technology and augmented stakeholder values. Frugal innovations have moved out of the niche market today, carrying societal values to develop multi-dimensional and multi-utilitarian designs through low-cost and green architectural aspects (Hall & Vredenburg, 2003). Consequently, these aspects have shown strong growth in large emerging

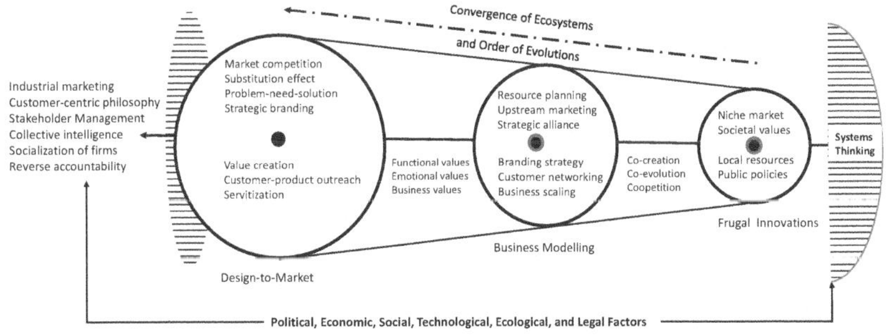

Fig. 10.2 Design-to-market business modeling: Evolution and ecosystem (*Source* Author)

economies including China and India in penetrating the mass consumer market with upscaling of business and collective recognition to the low-cost innovative products. The steep growth in low-cost mobile phone market in the communication industrial segment in India and China has established the social value of frugal products over the economic leverages and market competitiveness. Such shift has been stimulated by the social marketing model of low-cost innovative products through digital consumer communities and networking practices. Experience sharing and competitive benchmarking among customers have provided opportunities to the frugal companies to offer innovative solutions in the ULM by shifting the demand from large markets to the middle market segments (Govindrajan & Trimble, 2012).

The attributes of frugal innovation have been exhibited in Fig. 10.2, which illustrates the new dimensions of low-cost innovation supported by public policies and societal values despite resource limitations. The frugal innovations have rapidly reformed to new designs through co-creation, co-evolution, and coopetition (cooperative competition). These factors integrate systems thinking as an organizational tool in the process of developing frugal innovations, which stimulates business modeling and design-to-market approaches, as the frugal enterprises eventually switch from niche to larger operations (Guo et al., 2016). The business modeling for frugal innovative products is re-oriented towards upstream markets using business scaling, branding strategy, and customer networking. In addition, enterprises managing low-cost innovations explore strategic alliances with large companies to integrate production and marketing process with commercialization strategies. Such alliances also ease the resource limitations and help in restructuring of the production process. The convergence of business modelling with design-to-market approach is driven by functional, emotional, and embedded business values of the collaborating organizations. These values significantly contribute to design solutions and in creating inclusive markets. The transformation of frugal innovations from niche to broader markets enhances the scope of consumer economies spanning over the middle class and bottom-of-the-pyramid consumers. Consequently, the enhanced marketing opportunities help in creating inclusive growth by attracting large number of potential customers to the lower end of the market. The inclusive approach to frugal innovation has the attributes of overriding the social and economic constraints, bridging access to customers and markets, and implementing upscale business models (Lim & Fujimoto, 2019).

Design-to-market approach for frugal innovation products encompasses flexibility in product attributes, value propositions, and competitive benchmarks. These innovative products are set through the transition process from niche to larger markets through the stakeholder push (referrals) and pull (value for money propositions) strategies. However, it is often difficult for frugal innovative products to breathe through the multi-brand congestion in upstream markets causing structural setbacks within the enterprises. The design-to-market approach is substantially backed by digital marketing strategies, which are cost effective and are supported by AATAR model (Awareness, Attributes, Trial, Availability, and Repeat buying). Customers are attracted to launch-trials of low-cost technology products as the return policies support the customer perception on experimentation. The players in virtual retail marketplace like Amazon have encouraged low-cost technology products in an ULM segment by guaranteeing the return policy and safeguarding customer interest. The design-to-market approach protects frugal innovation products from dynamic fluctuations in the market competition and the substitution effect, as these products are oriented towards offering need-based solution with servitization approach. Consequently, the low-cost technology products are able to create socio-economic and personal values (self-esteem and self-actualization) among customers (Goldfarb & Tucker, 2019). However, the major challenge among frugal enterprises is to sustain profound impacts of changing customer preferences and hybrid technologies to protect the innovation value and create trade-offs between price-quality measures. Most enterprises tend to enter a new marketplace at low cost to ensure profitability and perceive high market share. This strategy reduces the firm's reputation in the competitive marketplace, which affects customer value and market competitiveness of the low-cost innovative products (Chen & Zhang, 2018).

Frugal innovations, business modeling, and design-to-market approaches are supported by systems thinking, which focuses on customer centric philosophy, collective intelligence, and socialization of firms. The stakeholder management is one of the major attributes of customer-centric philosophy, which empowers customers not only to offer new ideas in designing business models, but also to exercise reverse accountability. In successful frugal innovation enterprises, the stakeholders control the production and marketing process of customer-centric designed products. The stakeholders intervene in the business-process improvement and question the leadership output. This process is identified as reverse accountability, which has become popular as a part of systems thinking approach and adapted by the large companies as well (Tetlock et al., 2013).

Design-to-market approach is evolved around design thinking consciousness in large private and public sector firms including not-to-profit organizations. The design thinking is largely dependent on the critical leadership ideas and organizational work culture, which encourages team culture and workplace autonomy. The design thinking methods are associated with cognitive ergonomics, emotions, and diligence. Design thinking requires cost savings, comprehensive project charter, clear deliverables, and value perceptions in developing a customer centric prototype and documenting the customer experiences and values associated with the innovative product. Consequently, the design thinking process needs to be familiarized within market players, stakeholders, and employees of the organization to synchronize the success through design-to-market philosophy (Bason & Austin, 2019). Design-to-market strategy has become an upstream approach in making new products aesthetically attractive by enhancing brand perceptions through SMART (Strategic, Measurable, Analytical, Responsive, and Timely) and stimulating communications. The design thinking, in association with design-to-market approach, focuses on the needs and desires of stakeholders in a technologically feasible and strategically viable business model. The design thinking process is not always smooth, as it is influenced by growth in technology, organizational cultures, and market trends. Therefore, brainstorming and consistency in prototyping are the major challenges to streamline the design-to-market strategies for low-cost innovative products. However, radical shifts emerging from market trends need to have smooth transition in the design thinking and design-to-market processes. The design-to-market strategy stimulates co-evolution of small entrepreneurial firms with large business organizations on various strategic alliances, which explains the double helix effect in exploring new opportunities, decision-making, and developing a synchronized design thinking process (Rajagopal, 2021).

General Discussion

The schematic discussion on design-to-market concepts explains that the characteristics of frugal innovation taking into consideration the acceptance of innovation-led products and services in the marketplace. Products and services based on frugal innovation enhance market competitiveness leading to entrepreneurial growth and performance. Market competition drives the firm's ability to respond to the changing market and consumer needs through effective management of constrained resources, competitive drivers, and inculcating hedonic vs utilitarian values. The emergence of consumer participation in the designing and evolution of innovative products and services leads to co-creation, which is implemented by many frugal innovation-led emerging enterprises. Consumers are being more conscious in their consumption patterns, where they lay importance not only social and environmental impact of their consumption habits, but also on the production process being sustainable. The frugal grassroot entrepreneurship is founded on co-creation, crowdfunding, and open technology platforms changing the market dynamics towards offering innovative, cost-effective, and readily available products and services (Prabhu, 2017). This chapter also outline strategies used for converging various approaches within the socio-economic ecosystem. Such strategies emphasize on the design-to-market and design-to-society perspectives in order to gain access to consumer's needs and preferences. While the implementation of such strategies is challenging, frugal innovation-led firms also face limitations in making the products and services cost-effective. The emerging economies and SMEs need to adopt bottom-up organizational models to implement a systemic change. Discussions on the design-to-market concept also highlights the importance of strategic alliances in large companies with emerging companies in order to establish frugal innovation-led products and services in upstream marketplace.

Limitations and Future Research Perspectives

The limitations of this study open more avenues for future research, which have been discussed in this section. The study presents a conceptual framework, which can be analyzed using empirical research methods to gain in-depth comprehension of the design-to-market strategies for frugal innovation-led enterprises. The study discusses the design-to-market approach for frugal innovative products based on the systems thinking approach. However, considering a design thinking approach will not only provide structured tasks for innovation-led new product development and services. In future, research may focus on considering design thinking approach based on the dynamic nature of consumer mindset leading to acceptance and promotion of innovation-led products and services. In view of the discussions in this study, the pursuit of sustainable growth by the frugal innovation-led enterprises induces challenges such as innovation scope definition, adequate stakeholder management, and implementation of consumer need-based approach. Future studies may focus on identification of consumer-centric and consumer need-based approach to confront complexities in the changing consumer needs.

References

Bason, C., & Austin, R. D. (2019). *The right way to lead design thinking*. Harvard Business School Press.

Beckman, S. L. (2020). To frame or reframe: Where might design thinking research go next? *California Management Review, 64*(2), 144–162.

Bucherer, E., Eisert, U., & Gassmann, O. (2012). Towards systematic business model innovation: Lessons from product innovation management. *Creative Innovation and Management, 21*(2), 183–198.

Buhl, A., Schmidt-Keilich, M., Muster, V., Blazejewski, S., Schrader, U., Harrach, C., Schäfer, M., & Süßbauer, M. (2019). Design thinking for sustainability: Why and how design thinking can foster sustainability-oriented innovation development. *Journal of Cleaner Production, 231*, 1248–1257.

Carayon, P., Hancock, P., Leveson, N., Noy, I., Sznelwar, L., & Van Hootegem, G. (2015). Advancing a sociotechnical systems approach to workplace safety – Developing the conceptual framework. *Ergonomics, 58*(4), 548–564.

Chen, Y., & Zhang, T. (2018). Intermediaries and consumer search. *International Journal of Industrial Organization, 57*, 255–277.

D'Aveni, R. A. (2007). Mapping your competitive position. *Harvard Business Review, 85*(11), 110–120.

Goldfarb, A., & Tucker, C. (2019). Digital economics. *Journal of Economic Literature, 57*(1), 3–43.

Govindarajan, V., & Trimble, C. (2012). *Reverse innovation: Create far from home, win everywhere*. Harvard Business Review Press.

Gruber, M., de Leon, N., George, G., & Thompson, P. (2015). From the editors: Managing by design. *Academy of Management Journal, 58*(1), 1–7.

Guo, J., Tan, R., Sun, J., Cao, G., & Zhang, L. (2016). An approach for generating design scheme of new market disruptive products driven by function differentiation. *Computers & Industrial Engineering, 102*, 302–315.

Hall, J., & Vredenburg, H. (2003). The challenges of innovating for sustainable development. *MIT Sloan Management Review, 45*(1), 61–68.

Hossain, M. (2018). Frugal innovation: A review and a research agenda. *Journal of Cleaner Production, 182*, 926–936.

Hossain, M. (2021). Frugal innovation and sustainable business models. *Technology in Society*, 64. https://doi.org/10.1016/j.techsoc.2020.101508

Kim, W. C., & Mauborgne, R. A. (1999). Creating new market space. *Harvard Business Review, 77*(1), 83–93.

Kim, W. C., & Mauborgne, R. A. (2005). Blue ocean strategy: From theory to practice. *California Management Review, 47*(3), 105–121.

Labbe, D., Ferrage, A., Rytz, A., Pace, J., & Martin, N. (2015). Pleasantness, emotions and perceptions induced by coffee beverage experience depend on the consumption motivation (hedonic or utilitarian). *Food Quality and Preference, 44*(1), 56–61.

Leong, C. K., & Yang, Y. C. (2020). Market competition and firms' social performance. *Economic Modelling, 91*, 601–612.

Lim, C., & Fujimoto, T. (2019). Frugal innovation and design changes expanding the cost-performance frontier: A Schumpeterian approach. *Research Policy, 48*(4), 1016–1029.

Nakata, C., & Hwang, J. (2020). Design thinking for innovation: Composition, consequence, and contingency. *Journal of Business Research, 118*(1), 117–128.

Norton, D. P. (2010). *A platform for strategy management*. Harvard Business School Publishing.

Pacheco, D. A., Schwengber ten Caten, C., Jung, C. F., Navas, H. V. G., & Cruz-Machado, V. A. (2018). Eco-innovation determinants in manufacturing SMEs from emerging markets: Systematic literature review and challenges. *Journal of Engineering and Technology Management, 48*(1), 44–63.

Prabhu, J. (2017). Frugal innovation: Doing more with less for more. *Philosophical Translations of the Royal Society A*, 375. https://doi.org/10.1098/rsta.2016.0372

Rajagopal. (2021). *Entrepreneurship, Education, and Economics: A Helix Effect on Business Growth*. In Rajagopal, & R. Behl (Eds.), Entrepreneurship and regional development: Analyzing growth models in emerging markets (pp. 3–24). Palgrave Macmillan.

Ramamurti, R., & Williamson, P. J. (2019). Rivalry between emerging-market MNEs and developed-country MNEs: Capability holes and the race to the future. *Business Horizons, 62*(2), 157–169.

Ruz-Mendoza, M. A., Trifu, A., Cambra-Fierro, J., & Melero-Polo, I. (2021). Standardized vs. customized firm-initiated interactions: Their effect on

customer gratitude and performance in a B2B context. *Journal of Business Research, 133*, 341–353.
Santos, J. F., & Williamson, P. J. (2015). The new mission for multinationals. *MIT Sloan Management Review, 56*(4), 45–55.
Senge, P. M., Lichtenstein, B. B., Kaeufer, K., Bradbury, H., & Carroll, J. S. (2007). Collaborating for systemic change. *MIT Sloan Management Review, 48*(2), 44–53.
Seles, B.M.R.P., de Sousa Jabbour A.B.L., Jabbour, C.J.C., Latan, H., and Roubaud D. (2019). Do environmental practices improve business performance even in an economic crisis? Extending the win-win perspective. *Ecological Economics, 163*(C), 189–204.
Soman, D., Kumar, V., Metcalfe, M., & Wong, J. (2012). *Beyond great ideas: A framework for scaling local innovations*. University of Toronto.
Soni, P., & Krishnan, R. T. (2014). Frugal innovation: Aligning theory, practice, and public policy. *Journal of Indian Business Research, 6*(1), 29–47.
Tang, Y., Zhang, S., & Peng, J. (2021). The value of marketing innovation: Market-driven versus market-driving. *Journal of Business Research, 126*(1), 88–98.
Tetlock, P. E., Vieider, F. M., Patil, S. V., & Grant, A. M. (2013). Accountability and ideology: When left looks right and right looks left. *Organizational Behavior and Human Decision Processes, 122*(1), 22–35.
Zeschky, M. B., Winterhalter, S., & Gassmann, O. (2014). From cost to frugal and reverse innovation: Mapping the field and implications for global competitiveness. *Research-Technology Management, 57*(4), 20–27.

CHAPTER 11

The Role of Digital Citizenship Behavior on Digital Marketing and Consumer Buying Behavior

Subhasish Das and Manit Mishra

Introduction

The world has progressed from the industrial to the information epochs. The way people get information has changed as a result of recent technological advancements (1). While developing technologies have sped up the process of getting information, they have also increased the risk of data being misused and abused. Copyright infringement, unauthorized access, plagiarism, and intimidation have all been documented as a result of technological advancements (Coster & Sigalas, 2017). As a result,

S. Das (✉)
GIET University, Gunupur, Odisha, India
e-mail: subhasish@giet.edu

M. Mishra
IMI, Bhubaneswar, Odisha, India
e-mail: manit.mishra@imibh.edu.in

Rajagopal and R. Behl (eds.), *Managing Disruptions in Business*, Palgrave Studies in Democracy, Innovation, and Entrepreneurship for Growth, https://doi.org/10.1007/978-3-030-79709-6_11

numerous researchers have recently focused on digital citizenship. Since the mid-1990s, the United Kingdom has been promoting digital citizenship. Digital citizenship entails more than just avoiding online dangers; it also entails creating a safe environment for online communities (Ribble & Bailey, 2007).

Digital marketing is a very vast concept and includes email marketing, mobile marketing, content marketing, social media marketing, search engine optimization, etc. It facilitates generation of leads, customer acquisition, customer engagement, improving brand awareness and, web user experience (Omar & Atteya, 2020). It uses digital channels to communicate directly to potential customers. Email, digital TV, and mobile phones have made this activity easy. The effect of digital channels on consumer behavior is still developing. Email has been a good channel for digital marketing (Dwivedi et al., 2020).

Consumers while buying engage in a series of steps such as problem recognition, information search, alternative evaluation, purchase decision, and post purchase behavior. It is essential to understand how components of digital marketing influence on the consumer buying behavior.

Consumer decision-making process is heavily affected by the customer's engagement on social networks. The rise of net platforms has accelerated the customers' behavioral changes related to information search and decision-making. Now the corporate has wide range of options to influence the customer like e-advertisement, social media marketing, etc. Therefore the corporate must change their approach of marketing. Therefore the corporate must focus on digital marketing to understand and influence netizens (Tiago & Veríssimo, 2014). But this focus would be appropriate only when the corporate know how and when digital marketing affects consumer buying behavior (Powers et al., 2012). This paper tries to explain this problem statement by examining the effect of digital marketing on customer buying decision process and understanding the role of digital citizenship behavior.

Literature Review

Digital citizenship is defined by Ribble, Bailey, and Ross as "the rules of behaviour with reference to technology use." Digital access, digital commerce, digital communication, digital literacy, digital etiquette, digital law, digital rights and responsibilities, digital health and wellbeing, and digital security were listed as nine elements of digital citizenship

(Coster, & Sigalas, 2017; Hollandsworth et al., 2011; Milenkova et al., 2020; Mossberger et al., 2007; Ribble, 2011; Ribble & Bailey, 2007; Ribble & Miller, 2013; Shelley et al., 2004). Digital citizenship refers to the use of the Internet and technology as rules, appropriate behavior, and participation in an online society (Choi, 2016). Ribble et al. (2004) define digital citizenship as the ethical, social, and cultural knowledge of concerns associated to technology use. This encompasses acceptable norms as well as the consequences of actively employing technology (Ribble et al., 2004).

Gazi (2016), Ohler (2011), Ribble and Bailey (2007), Ribble (2011, 2015), and Ribble and Miller, (2013) defined Digital citizenship as having appropriate online behavior, standards or codes of online actions, and responsible technology use. "Digital citizenship reflects our quest to help netizens, as well as ourselves, develop the skills and perspectives necessary to live a digital lifestyle that is safe, ethical, and responsible, as well as inspired," according to the white paper "Digital Citizenship: A Holistic Primer," coauthored by Impero Software and the directors of the Digital Citizenship Institute, Curran, Ribble, and Ohler (Impero Software & Digital Citizenship Institute, 2016, p. 2). The authors' goal in producing this article was to "assist schools in better understanding and teaching digital citizenship" (p. 1). Digital citizenship is not a technological trend or a term for online-behavior rules; rather, it is a set of real-world challenges that affect all technology users, regardless of age or status (Snyder, 2016). Positive and poor online behavior are highlighted by nine elements (Ribble, 2011). Because of the maturity level required to participate with Web 2.0 tools, netizens are maturing at a faster rate than past generations (Ribble & Miller, 2013). As a result, all references to digital citizenship in this literature review will relate to an individual's acceptable, ethical, and responsible use of technology in all elements of device use, websites, open-education resources, and document creation. This definition resulted from a review and combination of prior scholars' definitions. To understand how education may decrease negative consequences and produce a better-rounded netizens. Junko and Ananou (2015) detailed the social, emotional, ethical, and cognitive influence technology has had on today's learners. Netizens engage in proper online-behavior practises when educators stress digital citizenship in the educational setting (Chou et al., 2012). As a result, it is critical for educators to not only understand digital citizenship but also to incorporate sound practises into their technological training.

Digital access, digital commerce, digital communication, digital literacy, digital etiquette, digital law, digital rights and responsibilities, digital health and well-being, and digital security (and safety) are the nine characteristics of digital citizenship identified by Ribble (2011, 2015). Use of the Internet: The term "digital access" refers to having equal access to technical resources in order to fully participate in society, which includes making adjustments for those with disabilities. In the classroom, digital access can be used to assist netizens with impairments in accessing traditional curricular materials. Many studies, according to Choi's (2016) concept analysis, attribute access to digital resources, also known as the digital divide, as a barrier to developing media and information literacy abilities as a citizen. Commerce on the Internet: The ability to acquire and sell goods online to encourage a globalized market for items is known as digital commerce (Curran & Ribble, 2017; Ribble, 2015). Netizens should be informed about the expenses of purchasing products online, such as more coins for a game or a new tablet application (Curran & Ribble, 2017).

Furthermore, when making online transactions, netizens must be aware of how their personal information might be compromised by using unsecure websites (Curran & Ribble, 2017). The way people connect through digital methods, as well as the flow and interaction of information received through technology, is referred to as digital communication. People who are lifelong learners, according to Uzunboylu and Hürsen (2011), change their behavior as a result of events in their personal and professional lives. Being a lifelong learner entails mastering skills like knowledge retrieval and knowing how to interact intelligently, appropriately, and efficiently utilizing technology like email and cell phones (Ozdamli & Ozdal, 2015). It may be more beneficial to focus on the desired message before selecting a tool to convey it via text, email, and social media applications like SnapChat and Twitter, or face-to-face (Curran & Ribble, 2017). Literacy in the Digital Age Digital literacy, also known as new literacies, media literacies, or information literacies, is an individual's basic comprehension of computer functions and technology use, as well as their ability to apply digital skills to specific situations in order to participate in the online world (Curran & Ribble, 2017). For digital citizenship, new literacy skills are required (Simsek & Simsek, 2013).

The emergence of new literacy has improved access to reliable and creditable information, boosting one's ability to share, compare, and contextualize information through gaining new abilities (Simsek & Simsek, 2013, p. 133). Users' confidence in utilizing the Internet to access and assess information, as well as cooperate, collaborate, and interact with others, improves their self-efficacy with technology use (Aesaert et al., 2014; Simsek & Simsek, 2013). Digital etiquette is sometimes known as "netiquette," which refers to recognized rules for online behavior. Netiquette is a term that refers to online morals and ethics (Park et al., 2014). Cyberspace has its own set of rules that distinguish it from the real world and assist users in identifying what is and is not appropriate behavior when engaging in online activities (Park et al., 2014).

Organizations must have Acceptable Use Policies (AUPs), and people must understand when it is appropriate to use specific technology and gadgets in their personal and professional lives (Ribble, 2015). Understanding what constitutes unacceptable behavior and what constitutes a violation of actual laws is central to digital law, which is closely tied to concerns of intellectual property and copyright (Curran & Ribble, 2017). Furthermore, adopting a code of conduct for fair access, sharing, downloading, changing, or reusing digitally distributed material is part of digital law. Laws were enacted to ensure that people's rights were safeguarded and that those who behaved badly in digital environments were held accountable. Inappropriate online behavior includes developing and sharing computer viruses or hacking protocols, plagiarizing and distributing other people's work while claiming it as one's own, sharing files that should be paid for before use, creating and distributing unacceptable media such as child pornography, and actively pursuing and invading an individual's privacy. (Known as Internet stalking; Ribble, 2015).

Digital Well-Being and Health Digital health and well-being refers to an individual's ability to preserve physical and mental health while engaging in digital activities, as well as the recognition and acceptance that one can misuse technology vs the ability to strike a balance between online and offline lives. The disadvantage of this factor stems from the amount of time people spend staring at displays rather than moving around (Curran & Ribble, 2017). 65 percent of Americans use social media on a regular basis (Pew Research Center, 2015). With the widespread use of online platforms for amusement and connection, it is important to teach kids how to create good interpersonal relationships through digital communication and face-to-face encounters (Curran & Ribble, 2017).

Individuals utilize digital security methods, rules, and processes to guarantee that their Internet use does not negatively affect other elements of their lives. This section emphasizes the need for people to take precautions in order to protect themselves. Ensure that personal information is not compromised or stolen as a result of online interactions. People who practice good digital safety and security have habits and practices such as purchasing and installing virus protection on their computers, creating backup systems for valuable documents using external hard drives or cloud storage, and only sharing sensitive and personal information on sites with clear safety protocols (Ribble, 2015). Teachers must have specific computer security knowledge and expertise in order to understand and pass on unique computer security behaviors (Jagasia et al., 2015). Through the application of Ribble's (2015) Educators, netizens, parents, and legislators can develop knowledge of ethical, acceptable, and responsible usage of technology by using the nine principles of digital citizenship. Stakeholders can also determine what types of technology are unwanted, substandard, or unlawful in educational settings as well as in the larger, more open, networked, and globalized world. By focusing on key areas of technology use and integration, the nine factors give a framework for addressing difficulties. These elements should be taught throughout a Netizens's education to ensure that developmentally appropriate topics are presented at critical points in a Netizens's use of technology (Ribble, 2015). Many dangers exist through Internet access (Shillair et al., 2015); individuals should learn safe online behaviors at younger ages than ever before.

Internet safety education activities grew swiftly in response to public concern about the threats that adolescents confront while using new technology, but the direction of youth education in this area is changing as more is learned about young behavior and experiences. Digital citizenship includes three key online dimensions: higher pay (because of digital abilities), democratic engagement, and improved communication options. The term "digital citizenship" was first used to refer to internet access (e.g., "raising the number of teenage digital citizens") but it is now more commonly used to refer to safe and responsible online activity. of duty, rights, safety, and security (Hollandsworth et al., 2011). Others call it "proper technology usage" and "making safe, responsible, and respectful online choices." Digital citizenship education has been translated into curricula on the following topics: Internet safety, privacy and security, relationships and communication, cyber bullying, digital footprints, reputation, self-image and identity, information literacy, and creative credit and copyright by a media education program. However, if digital citizenship is to become a new educational focus that is sold to schools, a lot of conceptual and evaluative work is required to ensure that its aims are well-defined and that its outcomes are successfully attained. Computer technology serves as a platform for content creation and delivery, allowing for faster creation and distribution of processing data (Ribble & Miller, 2013).

Digital marketing communicates information to the targeted customers through personal computers, mobile phones, and game consoles precisely (Jobber & Ellis-Chadwik, 2013). Not only for precise communication, is digital marketing also known for ease, convenience, appearance of variety of products, etc. The growing popularity and efficacy of e-marketing has attracted marketers toward digital marketing (Afzal & Khan, 2015). It is majorly supported by the social networking platforms.

Email is another tool of digital marketing, known for customized and timely reach ability to customer (Scharl et al., 2005). Email is quick and adjustable for various clients and is easily measurable (Davis, 2010). But email marketing also has a drawback of getting ignored by the recipient if the sender is unknown. Mobile marketing has evolved as a better media of marketing in the last decade. It is true to say that mobile has become an important gadget for everyone due to its multi-utility features (Haghirian et al., 2005). It is the interactive digital media of sending customized, location sensitive product information through customer-glued ubiquitous network (Kaplan, 2012). It is a set activity enabling organizations to communicate with the targeted customers in an interactive manner.

Mobile marketing facilitates organizations to target and retarget potential customers by influencing their decision-making process through customized product suggestions (Li et al., 2013). Cookie-based browsing data and server log files enable marketers to send more customized messages ever before (Trusov et al., 2016). The visitors of a website are labeled with cookies and the cookies are used for targeting or retargeting those visitors with customer product information. This has allowed marketers to send relevant real-time product information (Yaniv, 2008). On the other hand, consumer decision-making is one of the most dynamic process in marketing. Marketers often fail to understand it as understanding the customer decision process just like hitting the bulls eye (Kotler & Keller, 2012). The traditional consumer decision-making model identifies need recognition, information search, evaluation of alternatives, and purchase and post purchase decision as the five stages of making decisions.

The need can be physical and psychological (Michael, 2006) and they can be divided into physiological, safety, social, esteem, and self-actualization (Maslow, 1954). Once the need is identified the customer searches information related to the need. In this process they get influenced by their own experience or external sources (Oliver et al., 2011). Customers look for information that provides options for solving or extra insights related to the product (Punj & Moore, 2009). The information so collected is assessed for its appropriateness, and evaluates the product on the basis of their hard and soft parameters. The hard parameters are attributes and the soft are the characteristics (Hallaq & Pettit, 1983). The evaluation process also gets influenced by the tangible and intangible benefits of the product (Ha, 2010). Once the information is evaluated the customer moves towards making decision for purchase. While deciding for purchase customers look at supplier with current real market prices (Palos-Sanchez & Saura, 2018). This is the stage where the customer performs a transaction on the planned product and supplier. But sometimes the customer end up with the unplanned purchase which is due to an impulse buy or a temping deal (Inman et al., 2009). The purchase stage is widely affected by accessibility of the information related to product and supplier (Hoyer & Macinnis, 2008). At last the customer tries to assess, whether the purchase satisfied the need or solved the problem they begun with. When the product meets the need of the customer it affects the brand loyalty (Ofir & Simonson, 2005).

Hypothesis of the Study

H1: Digital marketing affects consumer buying decision process.

H2: Digital citizenship behavior mediates the relationship between digital marketing and consumer buying decision process.

H3: Digital citizenship behavior moderates the relationship between digital marketing and consumer buying decision process.

Table 11.1 Demographical profile

Gender	*Frequency*	*Percent*
Male	63	65.6
Female	33	34.4
Total	96	100

Table 11.2 Age

Age	*Frequency*	*Percent*
Age (≤29)	31	32.2
Age (30–39)	22	23
Age (40–49)	29	30
Age (≥50)	14	14.8
Total	96	100

Table 11.3 Construct validity

Constructs	*CR*	*AVE*	*MSV*
DM	0.89	0.85	0.61
DCB	0.83	0.91	0.348
CBB	0.91	0.8	0.233

Research Methodology

This is a descriptive study. The respondents of the study are the netizens and 96 responses are complete in all aspects. Therefore sample size of the study is 96. Out of the 96 respondents 65 percent are male and rests are female. The respondents below 30 years of age are 31 percent, between 30 to 39 years of age is 22 percent, between 40 to 49 years of age is 29 percent and above 50 years of age is 14 percent (Tables 11.1, 11.2, 11.3).

Construct Validity

The study measures construct such as digital marketing, consumer buying behavior, and digital citizenship behavior and are measured on the basis of scales developed by Khan and Jan (2019) respectively. The construct validity is measured on the basis of convergent and discriminant validity. Convergent validity is measured on the basis of composite reliability, internal consistency, and average variance extracted (AVE). The values of composite reliability are found in between 0.89 and 0.91, and the internal consistency is found in between 0.85 to 0.93 and the values of AVE are found to be between 0.82 and 0.87. The discriminant validity is measured on the basis of cross loadings, AVE > MSV (maximum shared variance) criteria and Heterotrait and Monotrait ratio HTMT. It is observed from the analysis that, there were no cross loadings and the values of AVEs are greater than the MSV and the value of HTMT is 0.56 which is below the recommended value of 0.85 (Henseler et al., 2015).

Structural Model

Smart PLS is used to analyze the structural model which is a robust technique for analyzing complex structural models as well as in analyzing the mediation and moderation effects (Ringle et al., 2005. The fitness of the model is checked from the values of SRMR and NFI and Table 11.4 clearly indicates that they both are below the cut of ranges. Therefore the model is fit.

The path coefficients of the structural model and the bootstrapping results indicate that there is a significant positive effect of digital marketing on consumer buying behavior and digital citizenship behavior. The digital marketing has an effect of 0.579 behaviors on consumer buying behavior, Digital citizenship behavior has an effect of 0.42 on consumer buying behavior and digital marketing has an effect of 0.453 on digital citizenship behavior which is very much evident from Table 11.5.

The bootstrapping results from Table 11.6 indicate that digital citizenship behavior is only mediating not moderating the relationship between digital marketing.

Table 11.4 Model fitness

Fit indices	*Obtained*	*Standards*
SRMR	0.047	< 0.06
NFI	0.96	> 090

Table 11.5 Path model

Relationship	*Path coefficients*	*P-value*
DM → CBB	0.579	0.000
DCB → CBB	0.42	0.000
DM → DCB	0.453	0.000

Table 11.6 Mediation and moderation

Relationship	*Original sample*	*Sample mean*	*SD*	*T Statistics*	*P value*	*Interpretation*
DM → CBB	0.475	0.474	0.089	5.324	0.000	Accepted
DM → DCB	0.402	0.414	0.113	3.558	0.000	Accepted
DCB → CBB	0.397	0.406	0.083	4.78	0.000	Accepted
Mediation (DM → DCB → CBB)	0.160	0.168	0.059	2.726	0.0007	Accepted
Moderation	0.046	0.046	0.048	0.952	0.342	Rejected

Conclusion

The study concludes that digital marketing has a significant positive effect on consumer buying behavior and digital citizenship behavior. And digital citizenship behavior is mediating the relationship between digital marketing and consumer buying behavior. The study could not establish the moderation effect. Digital marketing has the highest effect of 0.579 on consumer buying behavior. It is evident from the study that digital marketing affects digital citizenship behavior and digital citizenship behavior in turn affects consumer buying behavior. The study establishes and accepts the hypotheses H1, H2 and could not establish H3. Marketers must consider digital citizenship behavior of netizens while planning and assessing the effect of digital marketing on consumer buying behavior as digital mediates the effect. Therefore, the marketers must know the psychology of the consumers especially towards digital citizenship and also focus on the change in their buying behavior to influence them through digital marketing. The netizens should also be made more aware of the need of being appropriate i.e., showing appropriate behavior while being online. They must act responsibly. The digitalization is capable of bringing positive change in behavior of consumers. The greater the involvement of online customer greater change can be seen in their consumer buying behavior.

References

Aesaert, K., Van Nijlen, D., Vanderlinde, R., & van Braak, J. (2014). Direct measures of digital information processing and communication skills in primary education: Using item response theory for the development and validation of an ICT competence scale. *Computers & Education, 76*, 168–181. https://doi.org/10.1016/j.compedu.2014.03.013

Afzal, S., & Khan, J. R. (2015). Impact of online and conventional advertisement on consumer buying behaviour of branded garments. *Asian Journal of Management Sciences & Education, 4*, 125–135.

Choi, M. (2016). A concept analysis of digital citizenship for democratic citizenship education in the Internet age. *Theory and Research in Social Education, 44*, 565–607. https://doi.org/10.1080/00933104.2016.1210549

Chou, C. C., Block, L., & Jesness, R. (2012). A case study of mobile learning pilot project in K-12 schools. *Journal of Educational Technology Development and Exchange, 5*, 11–26. https://doi.org/10.18784/jetde.0502.02

Curran, Marialice B. F. X., & Ribble, M. (2017). P-20 model of digital citizenship. *New Directions for Student Leadership, 2017*(153), 35–46. https://doi.org/10.1002/yd.2022

Davis, J. A. (2010). *Competitive success, how branding adds value*. John Wiley and Sons.

De Coster, I.; Sigalas, E. (2017). *Citizenship Education at School in Europe, Eurydice Brief*. Education, Audiovisual and Culture Executive Agency; European Commission.

Dwivedi, Y. K., Ismagilova, E., Hughes, D. L., Carlson, J., Filieri, R., Jacobson, J., ... & Wang, Y. (2020). Setting the future of digital and social media marketing research: Perspectives and research propositions. *International Journal of Information Management, 59*, 102168. https://doi.org/10.1016/j.ijinfomgt.2020.102168

Ha, J. (2010). Perceived values, satisfaction, and behavioral intentions: The role of familiarity in Korean restaurants. *International Journal of Hospitality Management, 29*(1), 2–13.https://doi.org/10.1016/j.ijhm.2009.03.009

Haghirian, P., Madlberger, M., & Tanuskova, A. (2005). Increasing advertising value of mobile marketing - An empirical study of antecedents. In *Proceedings of the 38th Annual Hawaii International Conference on System Sciences* (pp. 32–32). IEEE. https://doi.org/10.1109/HICSS.2005.311

Hallaq, J., & Pettit, K. (1983). The relationship of product type, perceived evaluative criteria, and the order of consumption of the evaluation of consumer products. *Advances in Consumer Research, 6*(4), 600–604.

Henseler, J., Ringle, C. M., & Sarstedt, M. (2015). A new criterion for assessing discriminant validity in variance-based structural equation modelling. *Journal of Academy of Market Science, 43*(1), 115–135.

Hollandsworth, R., Dowdy, L., & Donovan, J. (2011). Digital citizenship in K-12: It takes a village. *TechTrends, 55*(4), 37–47. https://doi.org/10.1007/s11528-011-0510-z

Hoyer, W. D., & MacInnis, D. H. (2008). *Consumer behavior* (5th ed.). Cengage Learning.

Inman, J. J., Winer, R. S., & Ferraro, R. (2009). The interplay among category characteristics, customer characteristics, and customer activities on in-store decision making. *Journal of Marketing, 73*(5), 19–29. https://doi.org/10.1509/jmkg.73.5.19

Gazi, Z. A. (2016). Internalization of digital citizenship for the future of all levels of education. *Egitim ve Bilim, 41*(186), 137–148. Retrieved August 10, 2020 from http://egitimvebilim.ted.org.tr/index.php/EB/article/viewFile/4533/2471

Jagasia, J., Baul, U., & Mallik, D. (2015). A framework for communities of practice in learning organizations. *Business Perspectives & Research, 3*, 1–20. https://doi.org/10.1177/2278533714551861

Jobber, D., & Ellis-Chadwick, F. (2013). *Principles and practice of marketing* (7th ed.). McGraw-Hill Education.

Junko, Y., & Ananou, S. (2015). Humanity in the digital Age: Cognitive, social, emotional, and ethical implications. *Contemporary Educational Technology, 6*, 1–18. Retrieved from ERIC database (EJ1105609)

Kaplan, A. M. (2012). If you love something, let it go mobile: Mobile marketing and mobile social media 4x4. *Business Horizons, 55*(2), 129–139. https://doi.org/10.1016/j.bushor.2011.10.009

Khan, M. F., & Jan, A. (2019). A measure of social media marketing: Scale development and validation. *Jindal Journal of Business Research, 8*(2), 158–168.

Kotler, P., & Keller, K. L. (2012). *Marketing Management* (14th ed.), Pearson Education.

Li, H., Xhang, S., & Wang, X. (2013). A personalization recommendation algorithm for E-commerce. *Journal of Software, 8*(1), 176–183. https://doi.org/10.4304/jsw.8.1.176-183

Maslow, A. H. (1954). *Motivation and personality*. Harper.

Michael, S. (2006). *Consumer behavior – A European Perspective*. Financial Times, Prentice-Hall.

Milenkova, V., Keranova, D., Peicheva, D. (2020). Digital Skills, New Media and Information Literacy as a Conditions of Digitization. In *Applied Human Factors and Ergonomics (AHFEE 2019)* (pp. 65–72). Springer.

Mossberger, K., Tolbert, C. J., & McNeal, R. S. (2007). *Excerpts from digital citizenship: The internet, society, and participation*. MIT Press.
Ofir, C., & Simonson, I. (2005). The effect of stating expectations on customer satisfaction and shopping experience. *Stanford, Graduate School of Business*. https://doi.org/10.2139/ssrn.678382
Ohler, J. (2011). Character education for the digital age. *Educational Leadership, 68*(5). Retrieved from http://www.ascd.org/publications/educational-leadership/feb11/vol68/num05/Character-Education-for-the-Digital-Age.aspx
Oliver, H., Volschenk, J., & Smit, E. (2011). Residential consumers in the Cape Peninsula's willingness to pay for premium-priced green electricity. *Energy Policy, 39*, 544–550. https://doi.org/10.1016/j.enpol.2010.10.012
Omar, A. M., & Atteya, N. (2020). The impact of digital marketing on consumer buying decision process in the Egyptian market. *International Journal of Biometrics, 15*, 120.
Ozdamli, F., & Ozdal, H. (2015). Life-long learning competence perceptions of the teachers and abilities in using information-communication technologies. *Procedia-Social and Behavioral Sciences, 182*, 718–725. https://doi.org/10.1016/j.sbspro.2015.04.819
Palos-Sanchez, P., & Saura, J. R. (2018). The effect of internet searches on forestation: The case of a green search engine. *Forests, 9*, 51. https://doi.org/10.3390/f9020051
Park, S., Na, E., & Kim, E. (2014). The relationship between online activities, netiquette and cyberbullying. *Children and Youth Services Review*, 4274–4281. https://doi.org/10.1016/j.childyouth.2014.04.002
Powers, T., Advincula, D., Austin, M. S., Graiko, S., & Snyder, J. (2012). Digital and social media in the purchase decision process. *Journal of Advertising Research, 52*(4), 479–489. https://doi.org/10.2501/JAR-52-4-479-489
Punj, G., & Moore, R. (2009). Information search and consideration set formation in a web-based store environment. *Journal of Business Research, 62*(6), 644–650. https://doi.org/10.1016/j.jbusres.2007.04.013
Ribble, M. (2011). *Digital citizenship in schools* (2nd ed.). International Society for Technology in Education.
Ribble, M. (2012). Digital citizenship for educational change. *Kappa Delta Pi Record, 48*, 148–151. https://doi.org/10.1080/00228958.2012.73401
Ribble, M. (2015). *Digital citizenship in schools: Nine elements all students should know* (3rd ed.). International Society of Technology in Education.
Ribble, M. S., Bailey, G. D., & Ross, T. W. (2004). Digital citizenship: Addressing appropriate technology behavior. *Learning & Leading with Technology, 32*(1), 6–12. Retrieved by ERIC database (EJ695788).
Ribble, M., & Bailey, G. (2007). *Digital citizenship in schools*. Technology in Education.

Ribble, M., & Miller, T. N. (2013). Educational leadership in an online world: Connecting netizens to technology responsibly, safely, and ethically. *Journal of Asynchronous Learning Networks, 17*, 137–145.

Ringle CM, Wende S, Will A 2005 SmartPLS 2.0 M3. www.smartpls.de

rran, M. X., & Ribble, M. (2017). P-20 model of digital citizenship. *New Directions for Netizens Leadership, 2017*(153), 35–46. https://doi.org/10.1002/yd.20228

Scharl, A., Dickinger, A., & Murphy, J. (2005). Diffusion and success factors of mobile marketing. *Electronic Commerce Research and Applications, 4*(2), 159–173.

Shelley, M., Thrane, L., Shulman, S., Lang, E., Beisser, S., Larson, T., & Mutiti, J. (2004). Digital citizenship. *Social Science Computer Review, 22*, 256–269.

Shillair, R., Cotten, S., Tsai, H., Alhabash, S., LaRose, R., & Rifon, N. (2015). July). Online safety begins with you and me: Convincing Internet users to protect themselves. *Computers in Human Behavior, 48*, 199–207. https://doi.org/10.1016/j.chb.2015.01.046

Simsek, E., & Simsek, A. (2013). New literacies for digital citizenship. *Contemporary Educational Technology, 4*, 126–137. Retrieved from ERIC database (EJ1105529).

Tiago, M. T. P. M. B., & Veríssimo, J. M. C. (2014). Digital marketing and social media: Why bother? *Business Horizons, 57*(6), 703–708. https://doi.org/10.1016/j.bushor.2014.07.002

Trusov, M., Ma, L., & Jamal, Z. (2016). Crumbs of the cookie: User profiling in customer-base analysis and behavioral targeting. *Marketing Science, 35*(3), 405–426. https://doi.org/10.1287/mksc.2015.0956

Uzunboylu, H., & Hürsen, C. (2011). Lifelong learning competence scale (LLLCS): The study of validity and reliability. *Hacettepe University Journal of Education, 41*, 449–460.

Ververidis, C., & Polyzos, G. C. (2002). Mobile marketing using a location-based service. In *Proceedings of the First International Conference on Mobile Business*. Prentice-Hall.

Yaniv, G. (2008). Sold on mobile marketing: Effective wireless carrier mobile advertising and how to make it even more so. *International Journal of Mobile Marketing, 3*(2), 86–91.

CHAPTER 12

Repulsion Effect: An Eye-Tracking Study

Pronobesh Banerjee, Promothesh Chatterjee, and Tamara Masters

Consumers often make trade-offs in their choices. For example, when choosing among two grills, Option A and Option B, a consumer may need to trade-off between cooking speed and cooking area. If both attributes are equally important and Option A is superior on cooking speed while Option B is superior on cooking area, the consumer encounters a choice conflict. If another Option C (decoy) is introduced in

P. Banerjee (✉)
Indian Institute of Management Kozhikode, Kozhikode, India
e-mail: pbanerjee@iimk.ac.in

P. Chatterjee · T. Masters
Department of Marketing, University of Utah, SFEBB 7103,
Spencer Fox Eccles Business Building, 1655 East Campus Center Drive, Salt Lake City, UT, USA
e-mail: promothesh@eccles.utah.edu

T. Masters
e-mail: tamara.masters@eccles.utah.edu

Rajagopal and R. Behl (eds.), *Managing Disruptions in Business*, Palgrave Studies in Democracy, Innovation, and Entrepreneurship for Growth, https://doi.org/10.1007/978-3-030-79709-6_12

the set, and C is asymmetrically dominated by A (i.e., A is better on one attribute and at least as good on the other attribute) but not B (competitor), the consumer will tend to choose the dominating Option A (target). This finding, called the attraction effect (AE), is one of the most explored issues in the field of marketing. Studies have reported the AE in a large variety of substantive domains and with different methodological designs (e.g., Dhar & Simonson, 2003; Huber & Puto, 1983; Huber et al., 1982; Lehmann & Pan, 1994; Simonson & Tversky, 1992; Sivakumar & Cherian, 1995; Wedell & Pettibone, 1996). For example, research documents the AE in consumers' reactions to advertisements (Moran & Meyer, 2006), in supermarkets (Doyle et al., 1999), in general elections (Hedgcock & Rao, 2009; Pan et al., 1995), in lottery choices (Herne, 1999; Wedell, 1991), and in simple perceptual decision tasks (Trueblood et al., 2013). The AE also occurs with birds (e.g., starlings, hummingbirds, gray jays) and honeybees in their foraging and food consumption decisions (Bateson et al., 2002; Schuck-Paim et al., 2004; Shafir et al., 2002).

In contrast with these studies, we explore a certain condition in which the presence of an *asymmetrically dominated decoy increases the choice share of the competitor*—that is, the repulsion effect (see Huber et al., 2014; Simonson, 2014). Despite repeated research attempts throughout the years, the repulsion effect has proved elusive to find systematically (Simonson, 2014). The objective of the current study is to demonstrate the repulsion effect in a consistent and systematic manner. We show that for products with skewed attribute values (i.e., products that are rated exceptional on one attribute and mediocre on another, such as when Product A is rated exceptional on Attribute 1 and mediocre on Attribute 2 and Product B is rated slightly less exceptional than option A on Attribute 1 and slightly less mediocre on Attribute 2), the presence of an extreme asymmetrically dominated decoy favoring the target (i.e., Product C is rated exceptional on Attribute 1 but extremely poor on Attribute 2) results in the repulsion effect instead of the AE. We explicate this finding using numerical cognition research.

Next, we briefly review the AE literature (for recent reviews on the latest developments in AE literature, see Lichters et al., 2015; Sivakumar, 2016). Then, we elaborate on numerical cognition and investigate how numerical values of attributes may influence the repulsion effect. Finally, we report an eye-tracking study and conclude with a general discussion.

Literature Review

Attraction Effect

Research evidence suggests that consumer judgment and decision-making are context dependent (e.g., Huber et al., 1982; Mellers & Cooke, 1994; Simonson & Tversky, 1992). One of the most extensively studied context effects is the asymmetrically dominated decoy effect (Huber et al., 1982) or the attraction effect (AE). Consider two products, A (target) and B (competitor) with attributes A_1, A_2 and B_1, B_2, respectively. If A_1 is superior to B_1 (e.g., 70/100 vs. 50/100) but A_2 is inferior to B_2 (e.g., 50/100 vs. 70/100), consumers have no clear reason to choose either option, especially if both attributes are equally important. However, introducing a third alternative (decoy) with attributes C_1, C_2 (e.g., 70/100, 40/100), such that it is dominated by the target but not the competitor, enhances the attractiveness of the target, and increases the target's choice share.

Although research has employed different theoretical accounts to explain the AE, Wedell and Pettibone (1996) subsume the explanations under three categories: (1) weight-change, (2) value-shift, and (3) value-added models. The weight-change model suggests that the weights assigned to the attributes change when a decoy is introduced but that the attribute values are not affected. The value-shift model argues that subjective values, or the attractiveness of the attribute values, are affected by the decoy but that the weights assigned to the attributes are not. Last, the value-added model suggests that the inferiority of the decoy to the target allows consumers to justify their choice.

Huber et al. (1982) explicate the value-shift model by using Parducci's (1974) range-frequency theory. Range-frequency theory proposes that the judgment of a stimulus's attribute values depends on its contextual distribution. Using their contextual position in the attribute space, research has examined three categories of decoys—range (R), frequency (F), and range–frequency (RF) (Fig. 12.1). The R decoy extends the range on the attribute on which the target is weak, while the F decoy increases the differences in ranks on which the target is superior. The RF decoy combines both aspects to manipulate the range and rank differences. R* and F* are extreme extensions of the R and F decoys. Extant literature has mixed empirical evidence about the efficacy of these decoys in attraction effect.

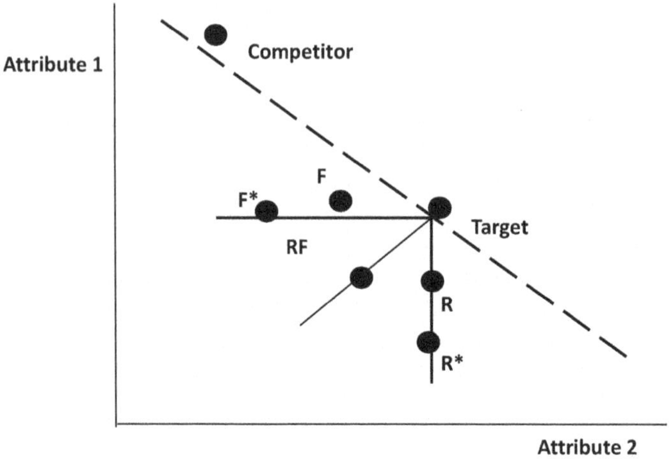

Fig. 12.1 Nomenclature of decoys used in studies

The Repulsion Effect, Numerical Cognition, and Attribute Values

As we noted previously, the AE is robust and has been demonstrated across various domains in the nearly four decades years since its discovery. However, recently Frederick et al. (2014) and Yang and Lynn (2014) have questioned the generalizability of the AE to real life situations, even finding evidence of a repulsion effect with some of their stimuli. While the idea that the asymmetrically dominated decoy might increase the choice share of a competitor instead of the target is intriguing, why this should happen is unclear. Simonson (2014) argues that a repulsion effect might occur is that the decoy taints that particular region of the attribute space, causing consumers to choose the competitor. However, researchers have been unable to find the repulsion effect consistently. An empirical issue that perhaps has made the repulsion effect elusive is that in designing the choice configuration, the choice shares in the control condition were so overwhelmingly in favor of the competitor that the introduction of the decoy did not change the distribution. To address this issue, we fine-tuned our choice set configuration on the basis of the findings from numerical cognition.

Numerical cognition examines the cognitive, developmental, and neural bases of numbers and mathematics. An important finding is that consumers perceive a numeric magnitude inexactly (Dehaene, 2011). Numerical cognition research has argued for an analog mental representation of the numbers, such that the magnitude of numbers is classified as small, medium, or large on a mental number line (Dehaene, 2011). Possibly the strongest indication of a mental representation of numbers as magnitudes comes from the number comparison task. In their study, Moyer and Landauer (1967) argue that the response time participants take to discriminate between two numbers decreases with the numerical distance between them. For example, numbers that are far apart (e.g., 2 and 9) are more easily discriminated than adjoining numbers (e.g., 8 and 9). Consumers also display an effect of size, such that their discrimination of magnitudes at a fixed numerical distance (e.g., 10 and 20 vs. 90 and 100) reduces curvilinearly with increases in magnitude (Parkman, 1971). In other words, discrimination of magnitudes is more precise for smaller numbers but imprecision increases for larger numbers on the mental number line (e.g., Feigenson & Carey, 2005; Lipton & Spelke, 2004). These discriminability issues presumably arise from the imprecision in internal representations of numeric magnitude relative to the symbolic numbers (Izard & Dehaene, 2008; Rips, 2013). Several models exist to explain these phenomena, including the accumulator model (Gallistel & Gelman, 2000), the compressed-number-line model (Dehaene, 1992), and the numerosity-code model (Butterworth, 2011), and they make similar predictions about behavioral outcomes.

To summarize, extant research in numerical cognition suggests that (a) distant numbers are discriminated more easily compared to overlapping numbers, and (b) discrimination of magnitude of fixed numeric distance reduces with increase in magnitudes. Next, we extrapolate these findings to make specific predictions about the repulsion effect.

Conceptualization

While studies on numerical cognition involve magnitude judgments on a single dimension, AE studies typically involve numeric values of two attributes. Furthermore, AE studies have a control condition in which one option is numerically superior to the other option on one attribute but inferior on the other attribute (i.e., neither option dominates the other). The experimental condition has an additional inferior option (decoy) with two attributes. Consumer decision-making in the control condition involves making a trade-off between the two options; the presence of the asymmetrically dominated decoy in the experimental condition affects this trade-off. To maximize our chances of finding repulsion effect, we consider products with skewed attribute values (vs. balanced attribute values; Chernev, 2005)—that is, products rated as exceptional on one attribute and mediocre/poor on the other attribute. Our aim in choosing products with skewed attribute values is to reduce the role of trade-offs in consumer decision-making so that choice is heavily influenced by one attribute as findings from numerical cognition can be applied along a single dimension.

Consider, for example, a mouthwash with two attributes: germ-killing and decay-prevention effectiveness. Target A has superior germ-killing effectiveness (rated 10/10) but inferior decay-prevention effectiveness (4/10), while competitor B has inferior germ-killing effectiveness (9/10) but superior decay-prevention effectiveness (5/10). Note that the choice task involves resolving a one-point rating superiority of A on germ-killing effectiveness versus a one-point rating superiority of B on decay-prevention effectiveness. This trade-off between A and B is systematically affected by the introduction of an asymmetrically dominated decoy C, with the same germ-killing effectiveness rating (10/10) as A but a much inferior decay-prevention decay ability (1/10). Previous AE studies would suggest that this choice configuration would result in an attraction effect, such that the introduction of the decoy C would enhance the choice share of target A. However, in this research, based-on rationale from numerical cognition literature, we show that this type of choice configuration results in the repulsion effect.

Consider the attribute germ-killing effectiveness that has high ratings for all the products in the experimental condition: A has attribute rating 10/10, B has attribute rating 9/10, and C has attribute rating 10/10. Numerical cognition literature would suggest that as one goes further on the number line, the mental representation of larger numbers such as 9 and 10 has overlapping representation, and therefore the two would have low discriminability. Low discriminability across the ratings on this attribute (germ-killing effectiveness) does not help consumers in their decision-making (in both the control and experimental conditions) because both have excellent ratings (9 and 10). This situation would result in consumers ignoring this attribute in their decision-making. Now consider the second attribute, decay-prevention effectiveness, that has lower ratings for all products: A has 4/10, B has 5/10, and C has 1/10. In the control condition, participants compare just two values 4 and

5, and because their decision would be based largely on values of this attribute, many would choose Option B. In the experimental condition, consumers' decision would be based on three attribute values: 4, 5, and 1 for products A, B, and C, respectively. For the repulsion effect to occur, the choice share of B should be significantly higher in the experimental condition than in the control condition. We argue that the decoy acts as the point of reference and the perceived difference between the attribute ratings of 4 and 5 is enhanced compared with the control condition.

We adopt Holyoak's (1978) reference point model of subjective magnitude comparison to elaborate on how consumers process number triplets (as is the case if they focus only on one attribute). Holyoak's model suggests three processing stages for such comparisons (in addition to encoding and responses). In the first stage, consumers identify whether triplets are unilateral (i.e., all numbers in the comparison task are less than or greater than the reference point) or bilateral (i.e., one number is greater than the reference point, and one number is less than the reference point), as the distance estimation procedure from the reference point to these numbers depends on this conclusion. The second stage entails assessing the distance from each comparison digit to the reference point. In the third stage, the two derived distances are compared. In the illustration, the consumer will assess the triplets (e.g., 4, 5, and 1) as unilateral. In the second stage, the distances between the digits 4 and 5 from the reference point value 1 are computed, giving 3 and 4 as the answer. In the third stage, 4 is clearly identified as the greater of the two numbers. Recall that numerical cognition literature suggests that smaller numbers such as 3 and 4 have greater discriminability than more distant numbers such as 4 and 5. In other words, the presence of a low rating 1 in the set of attribute ratings (1, 4, and 5) affects the discriminability among the numbers. In the control condition, the difference is between 4 and 5, while in the experimental condition, because of the presence of the decoy as a reference point, the difference is between 3 (i.e., 4–1) and 4 (i.e., 5–1). Therefore, whenever an extremely poor decoy is introduced, the discriminability between the target and competitor is enhanced compared to control condition on the second attribute. Thus, the presence of the decoy results in greater discriminability (smaller numbers have greater discriminability) between the inferior attribute values and favors the competitor attribute rating (i.e., 5), resulting in increased choice share of the competitor (the repulsion effect) compared with the control condition.

Repulsion Effect and Eye Tracking

In our numerical cognition-based explanation, we argue that participants ignore attribute 1 because of high values and focus on attribute 2. Furthermore, the extremely low value of decoy on the inferior attribute acts as a reference point and enhances the discriminability between target and competitor. Finally, because of enhanced discriminability competitor is chosen as it has the greater inferior attribute value. Thus, the aim of the eye-tracking study is to investigate the differences in cognitive processing as measured by eye tracking through gaze patterns. Gaze patterns, also known as saccades, are the rapid jumps of the pupils from one point to another. Saccades can provide information on whether attention is shifting from one area of interest to another and provide insight into the decision process (Kimchi et al., 2016; Krol & Krol, 2019; Yu et al., 2015). For example, in this study saccades can take three directions. First, horizontal movement between areas of interest would signify that the participant is comparing different attributes within a brand. Second, saccades that display vertical movement between areas of interest would indicate that the participant is comparing a given attribute between brands. This vertical movement should be the predominant pattern based on our categorization-based theorizing. The third possibility of diagonal movement between areas of interest would mean that the participant is moving between one brand-attribute combination to a different brand-attribute combination in a diagonal pattern. A dominance in one saccade pattern would provide information about the type of processing in which the person is engaging (Shi et al., 2013). We expect in the no decoy condition, due to the high values of attribute 1, the participants will move their attention to attribute 2 for decision-making which will result in more eye movement on attribute 2 than attribute 1. With the introduction of a decoy, participants will be expected to give more attention to the values in attribute 2 than attribute 1. Additionally, based on our proposed mechanism we expect in the presence of a decoy, participants will give more attention to attribute 2 of the competitor brand y compared to brand x and brand z (decoy). With this in mind, we investigated the differential impact of attention as measured by saccade patterns.

Method

Three hundred and eight undergraduate students took part in this study for partial course credit. Participant were of age 18–35 years (M = 22.6 years), and 61% were male. We collected the data using a high-frequency (120 Hz) eye tracker (Tobii T120) that collected raw eye-movement data points every 8.3 ms. The eye tracker is integrated into a 17-inch monitor wand with no visible eye-tracking devise that might affect a participant's behavior. The eye tracker uses near infrared illumination to create reflection patterns on the viewer's cornea and pupil with two image sensors that capture images of the eyes. Participants came individually to the lab every ten minutes. After a calibration procedure, the eye-tracking recording began. The study was a 2 (choice: no decoy vs. decoy) × 2 (product: cell phone and laptop) mixed design. Choice was between-subjects, and products were within-subject. These products were chosen based on a pretest of products our test population were familiar with. As in the previous studies, the participants were randomly assigned to one of the conditions: with decoy or without decoy. The product had one superior attribute and one inferior attribute. Participants were asked to indicate their choice among brand x, brand y, or brand z (the decoy in the with-decoy condition). Attention check and demographic information were then collected.

Results and Discussion

Data came from 304 participants, 152 in the no-decoy condition and 152 in the decoy-present condition. All participants passed the attention check; however, the eye-tracking data were not fully recorded for all the participants who took part in the study, leading us to exclude 7 participants from the analysis. One participant chose the decoy for cell phones and two chose the decoy for laptops and were not included in the percentage computations of choice patterns. Repulsion was evident, with a significant increase in the choice of brand y in the decoy condition (55.8%) compared with the no decoy condition (34.5%; $z = 5.13$, $p < 0.0001$).

For the eye-tracking data, we defined non-overlapping areas of interest to regions of the choice table. We used areas of interest to determine eye-gaze movement (saccades). We coded and counted saccades in terms of whether the participant looked between products (vertical movement between rows) and attributes (horizontal movement between columns) or moved from one product–attribute mix to a different product–attribute mix (diagonal movement to a different column and row). As expected in the no decoy condition, participants fixated more on attribute 2 than attribute 1 across the two brands x and y for both product categories. This is consistent with our argument that because of the presence of high values in attribute 1, decision-making is based primarily on attribute 2.

Difference in Saccades (Eye Movement Between Areas of Interest)

We compared saccades (eye movements) of participants who saw the decoy (three brands) versus no decoy (two brands). The pattern of saccades provides a glimpse into the comparative cognitive processing that precede choice. We analyzed the number of saccades and direction of movement between these fixations. Nine participants were eliminated from this analysis due to incomplete saccade data capture resulting in 283 participants in this analysis. Based on our proposed mechanism we predict that greater comparison and thus saccades will occur in attribute 2 compared to attribute 1. As predicted there was a significant difference between the decoy and no-decoy condition in the number of vertical saccades as participants compared a given attribute between different products. In the vertical saccades, pupil fixation moved vertically between rows more when a decoy was present than when it was not present ($M_{\text{decoy}} = 4.15$, $M_{\text{no decoy}} = 3.26$; $F(1, 282) = 5.06$, $p = 0.03$). This suggests that the presence of decoy encourages an attribute-based processing than a product-based processing. When we analyze the change in attention (saccades) within a given attribute we found significantly more vertical saccades along attribute 2 for those exposed to a decoy ($M_{\text{decoy}} = 2.35$) than those not exposed to a decoy ($M_{\text{no decoy}} = 1.81$; $t(283) = 4.22$, $p < 0.001$), this is in line with our proposed mechanism of the decisional comparisons occurring within attribute 2. Also, of note, comparison of the number of saccades between attributes (between columns horizontally) in the decoy versus no-decoy condition yielded no significance ($M_{\text{decoy}} = 3.34$, $M_{\text{no decoy}} = 3.27$; $F(1, 282) = 0.024$, $p = 0.88$). This is consistent with a lack of product-based processing. The increase in saccades vertically along attribute 2 with the introduction of a decoy illustrates our proposed reference point model for the repulsion effect. In the decoy condition, participants' eyes shifted their attention vertically more along attribute 2 (M_{decoy} = 2.35) than attribute 1 (M_{decoy} = 1.80; $t(283) = 4.45$, $p < 0.001$) as they compared the values of brand x and y. This pattern of attribute-based processing is consistent with our conceptualization that decision-making occurs primarily on attribute 2.

In summary, eye tracking revealed a difference in attention as measured by gaze patterns in the areas of interest and the shift of attention to attribute 2 as measured by saccades in the presence of a decoy. Saccade analysis revealed more saccades (attention changes) up and down attribute 2 as participants looked back and forth between the different values of the target brand (*x*) and competitor brand (*y*) in the presence of a decoy. The change in attention illustrates our proposed categorization model, which predicts a difference in decision-making that resulted in a shift in preference from brand x for the competitor brand *y* (repulsion effect). As fixed attention and saccades increased, participants nominally ruled out the decoy and assessed the distance from each comparison digit as they looked up and down within a given attribute, which favored the competitor (brand y) attribute, resulting in the repulsion effect. This eye-tracker study provided evidence of the proposed mechanism of the repulsion effect.

General Discussion

In this study, we examine the elusive repulsion effect and provide evidence in support of the numerical cognition-based theorizing. Fredrick et al. (2014) note the lack of experimental research on the repulsion effect; however, over the years, several researchers have tried to systemati cally investigate the hypothesized repulsion effect, with limited success (Simonson, 2014). The reason the repulsion effect might be expected is that the added inferior option taints that region of the attribute space, making it repulsive and leading consumers to choose the other extreme. For example, an added cheap option of poor quality may lead consumers to opt for quality over price (triggering the rule "You get what you pay for"), though such theorizing is speculative without any experimental results to support it. Recent research has examined this tainting hypothesis in a perceptual decision-making task and demonstrated the repulsion effect with stimulus that assesses size of rectangles (Spektor et al., 2018). They find that both task complexity and arrangement of options on screen determine the nature of the context effect. While the tainting hypothesis necessitates higher level reasoning processes, in rectangle size tasks decision-making is obviously based on perceptual processes. Furthermore, the perceptual context effects strongly differ from the choice context effects (Dutilh & Rieskamp, 2016; Trueblood & Pettibone, 2017), thus it seems unlikely that the processes underlying repulsion effect in perceptual tasks and choice are same.

Theoretical Contribution and Implications

We build on the huge literature that has examined consumer choice processes, by introducing the role of attribute values using numerical cognition findings. This is especially important for context effect research because some theories (e.g., Parducci's [1974] range-frequency theory) have specified how different attribute values affect consumer judgment and decision-making. Consider, for example, the range decoy R (Fig. 12.1), which extends the range of the values on which the target is inferior, making the target look better and increasing its choice. Consequently, the extreme range decoy R* should result in even higher choice share, but empirical research often does not find this. Perhaps the answer lies in the numerical discriminability of the attribute values as the higher adjoining attribute values have lower discriminability.

This research has certain limitations. A common criticism of most context effect research is that the products are not actually available and are often described only on two or three simple attributes with no identifying brand names (Fredrick et al., 2014). This criticism is applicable to our research as well. However, the objective of our research was such that we were forced to use such stimuli. Overall, we demonstrate the elusive repulsion effect using findings from a novel stream of literature (numerical cognition) that has hitherto not been explored in consumer choice literature.

References

Bateson, M., Healy, S. D., & Andrew Hurly, T. (2002). Irrational choices in hummingbird foraging behaviour. *Animal Behaviour, 63*(3), 587–596.

Butterworth, B. (2011). Foundational numerical capacities and the origins of Dyscalculia. In *Space, Time and Number in the Brain* (pp. 249–265). Academic Press.

Chernev, A. (2005). Context effects without a context: attribute balance as a reason for choice. *Journal of Consumer Research, 32*(2), 213–223.

Dehaene, S. (1992). Varieties of numerical abilities. *Cognition, 44*(1–2), 1–42.

Dehaene, S. (2011). *The Number Sense: How the Mind Creates Mathematics*. OUP USA.

Dhar, R., & Simonson, I. (2003). The effect of forced choice on choice. *Journal of Marketing Research, 40*(2), 146–160.

Doyle, J. R., O'Connor, D. J., Reynolds, G. M., & Bottomley, P. A. (1999). The robustness of the asymmetrically dominated effect: Buying frames, phantom alternatives, and in-store purchases. *Psychology & Marketing, 16*(3), 225–243.

Dutilh, G., & Rieskamp, J. (2016). Comparing perceptual and preferential decision making. *Psychonomic Bulletin & Review, 23*(3), 723–737.

Feigenson, L., & Carey, S. (2005). On the limits of infants' quantification of small object arrays. *Cognition, 97*(3), 295–313.

Frederick, S., Lee, L., & Baskin, E. (2014). The limits of attraction. *Journal of Marketing Research, 51*(4), 487–507.

Gallistel, C. R., & Gelman, R. (2000). Non-verbal numerical cognition: From reals to integers. *Trends in Cognitive Sciences, 4*(2), 59–65.

Hedgcock, W., & Rao, A. R. (2009). Trade-Off aversion as an explanation for the attraction effect: A functional magnetic resonance imaging study. *Journal of Marketing Research, 46*(1), 1–13.

Herne, K. (1999). The effects of decoy gambles on individual choice. *Experimental Economics, 2*(1), 31–40.

Holyoak, K. J. (1978). Comparative judgments with numerical reference points. *Cognitive Psychology, 10*(2), 203–243.

Huber, J., Payne, J. W., & Puto, C. (1982). Adding asymmetrically dominated alternatives: Violations of regularity and the similarity hypothesis. *Journal of Consumer Research, 9*(1), 90–98.

Huber, J., Payne, J. W., & Puto, C. P. (2014). Let's be honest about the attraction effect. *Journal of Marketing Research, 51*(4), 520–525.

Huber, J., & Puto, C. (1983). Market boundaries and product choice: Illustrating attraction and substitution effects. *Journal of Consumer Research, 10*(1), 31–44.

Izard, V., & Dehaene, S. (2008). Calibrating the mental number line. *Cognition, 106*(3), 1221–1247.

Kimchi, R., Yeshurun, Y., Spehar, B., & Pirkner, Y. (2016). Perceptual organization visual attention and objecthood. *Vision Research, 126*, 34–51.

Krol, M., & Krol, M. (2019). Inferiority, not similarity of the decoy to target, is what drives the transfer of attention underlying the attraction effect: Evidence from an eye-tracking study with real choices. *Working Paper*.

Lehmann, D. R., & Pan, Y. (1994). Context effects, new brand entry, and consideration sets. *Journal of Marketing Research, 31*(3), 364–374.

Lichters, M., Sarstedt, M., & Vogt, B. (2015). On the practical relevance of the attraction effect: A cautionary note and guidelines for context effect experiments. *AMS Review, 5*(1–2), 1–19.
Lichters, M., Bengart, P., Sarstedt, M., & Vogt, B. (2017). What really matters in attraction effect research: When choices have economic consequences. *Marketing Letters, 28*(1), 127–138.
Lipton, J. S., & Spelke, E. S. (2004). Discrimination of large and small numerosities by human infants. *Infancy, 5*(3), 271–290.
Mellers, B. A., & Cooke, A. D. J. (1994). Trade-offs depend on attribute range. *Journal of Experimental Psychology: Human Perception and Performance, 20*(5), 1055–1067.
Moran, S., & Meyer, J. (2006). Using context effects to increase a leader's advantage: What set of alternatives should be included in the comparison set? *International Journal of Research in Marketing, 23*(2), 141–154.
Moyer, R. S., & Landauer, T. K. (1967). Time required for judgements of numerical inequality. *Nature, 215*(5109), 1519.
Pan, Y., O'Curry, S., & Pitts, R. (1995). The attraction effect and political choice in two elections. *Journal of Consumer Psychology, 4*(1), 85–101.
Parducci, A. (1974). Contextual effects: A range-frequency analysis. *Handbook of Perception, 2*, 127–141.
Parkman, J. M. (1971). Temporal aspects of digit and letter inequality judgments. *Journal of Experimental Psychology, 91*(2), 191–205.
Rips, L. J. (2013). How many is a zillion? Sources of number distortion. *Journal of Experimental Psychology: Learning, Memory, and Cognition, 39*(4), 1257–1264.
Schuck-Paim, C., Pompilio, L., & Kacelnik, A. (2004). State-dependent decisions cause apparent violations of rationality in animal choice. *PLoS Biology, 2*(12), e402.
Shafir, S., Waite, T. A., & Smith, B. H. (2002). Context-dependent violations of rational choice in honeybees (*Apis mellifera*) and gray jays (*Perisoreus canadensis*). *Behavioral Ecology and Sociobiology, 51*(2), 180–187.
Shi, S. W., Wedel, M., & Pieters, F. G. M. (2013). Information acquisition during online decision making: A model-based exploration using eye-tracking data. *Management Science, 59*(5), 1009–1026.
Simonson, I. (2014). Vices and virtues of misguided replications: The case of asymmetric dominance. *Journal of Marketing Research, 51*(4), 514–519.
Simonson, I., & Tversky, A. (1992). Choice in context: Tradeoff contrast and extremeness aversion. *Journal of Marketing Research, 29*(3), 281–295.
Sivakumar, K., & Cherian, J. (1995). Role of product entry and exit on the attraction effect. *Marketing Letters, 6*(1), 45–51.
Sivakumar, K. (2016). A unified conceptualization of the attraction effect. *AMS Review, 6*(1–2), 39–58.

Spektor, M. S., Kellen, D., & Hotaling, J. M. (2018). When the good looks bad: An experimental exploration of the repulsion effect. *Psychological Science, 29*(8), 1309–1320.

Trueblood, J. S., Brown, S. D., Heathcote, A., & Busemeyer, J. R. (2013). Not just for consumers: Context effects are fundamental to decision making. *Psychological Science, 24*(6), 901–908.

Trueblood, J. S., & Pettibone, J. C. (2017). The phantom decoy effect in perceptual decision making. *Journal of Behavioral Decision Making, 30*(2), 157–167.

Wedell, D. H. (1991). Distinguishing among models of contextually induced preference reversals. *Journal of Experimental Psychology: Learning, Memory, and Cognition, 17*(4), 767–778.

Wedell, D. H., & Pettibone, J. C. (1996). Using judgments to understand decoy effects in choice. *Organizational Behavior and Human Decision Processes, 67*(3), 326–344.

Yang, S., & Lynn, M. (2014). More evidence challenging the robustness and usefulness of the attraction effect. *Journal of Marketing Research, 51*(4), 508–513.

Yu, G., Xu, B., Zhao, Y., Zhang, B., Yang, M., Kan, J. Y. Y. Milstein, D. M., Thevarajah, D., & Dorris, M. C. (2015). Microsaccade direction reflects the economic value of potential saccade goals and predicts saccade choice. *Journal of neurophysiology, 115*(2), 741–751.

CHAPTER 13

A Study on the Impact of Case Study-Based Teaching Pedagogy in Marketing Education: An Analytic Hierarchy Process Approach

Subhajit Bhattacharya and Rohit Vishal Kumar

Introduction

Management education can be seen as a combined and integrated learning arena wherein the management graduates acquire a set of knowledge or information, skills or abilities, and ethics that they implement in their professional life. To create budding management professionals the main requirement is to reduce the gap between the theoretical knowledge and applied know-how (or between knowing and doing). Management

S. Bhattacharya (✉)
XIM University, Bhubaneswar, India
e-mail: subhajit@xim.edu.in

R. V. Kumar
International Management Institute, Bhubaneswar, India
e-mail: rvkumar@imibh.ed

Rajagopal and R. Behl (eds.), *Managing Disruptions in Business*, Palgrave Studies in Democracy, Innovation, and Entrepreneurship for Growth, https://doi.org/10.1007/978-3-030-79709-6_13

schooling assists in snowballing the relevant potential skill set, problem-solving abilities, and performance aptitudes (Gersel & Thaning, 2020; Ungaretti et al., 2015) that help future managers to be more capable of performing in today's volatile, uncertain, complex, and ambiguous (VUCA) business ecosystem (Horney et al., 2010; Popova et al., 2018; Sarkar, 2016; Schoemaker et al., 2018).

Business Schools are continuously performing a great role to impart the relevant technical and behavioral knowledge to craft the future business and management professionals, but it also can be seen that many B-Schools are not able to match up to the obligations of the contemporary complex business world (Elmuti, 2004). With the rapidly changing time, business situations are becoming even more complex. In this context, the business wisdom, decision-making ability, and creativity approach can be useful to decode the complexity of the contemporary business environment to generate meaningful solutions. Thus, management and business education are transformed into a sought-after knowledge creation and decimation platform to be relevant in this competitive marketplace (Datare et al., 2011). The Graduate Management Admission Council, in their Global Management Education Graduate Survey (2015), has critically established that some skills are becoming indispensable to be more employable as future managers are "*Decision-Making Ability, Analytical Skill, Problem Solving Skill,* and *Creativity*", which has also been validated by Bloomberg Job Skills Report (2015). Marketing as a subject is very much practice-oriented wherein product decisions, branding, consumer insights, pricing, sales, and customer relations are based on various theories, the outcome orientation and reality is a pivotal aspect to it (Borin et al., 2008). Young (2002) defined "hands-on" and "minds-on" knowledge are extremely vital elements in the domain of the marketing professions. Therefore, all the B-schools engaged in imparting marketing management education must focus on augmenting the students' capability in this changing marketing environment.

Across continents, the different premier B-Schools are constantly researching how to link the marketing acumen to give it a practical perspective. The pedagogy is thus oriented in different forms in which case study, simulation, role play, and experiential learning is utilized to engage the young minds and catalyze their professional learning outcomes with higher students' engagement (Albert & Grzeda, 2015; Bakhru, 2018). The need for students' engagement is getting higher priority in the education sector (Langendahl et al., 2017; Singh et al., 2015; Sunley et al., 2019). Search for the same case study is being used in marketing courses by premier business schools as an integral part of their teaching pedagogy since Harvard started with the same in the 1920s. The Case Study created teaching method helps in the long-term holding of knowledge of the theoretical concepts and its applications in generating the best solutions by addressing the case dilemma in connection with actual business decision seeking context (Bhattacharya & Chattopadhyay, 2019; Christensen & Carlile, 2009; Corey, 1998; Greenberg et al., 2017; Jain, 2005; Konst & Kairisto-Mertanen, 2020; Mesny, 2013).

The established and upcoming business schools in India too are increasingly adapting to the case teaching pedagogy for enhanced learning outcomes (Mukherjee, 2015, 2018; Roy & Banerjee, 2012; Tripathy, 2008). Case study development is not restricted to the analysis of the realistic situation the organization is going through but acts as an impetus to vivid research in the field of marketing. With the help of case teaching pedagogy, the B-Schools are trying to bridge the theories with the proper context and its relevance to the same (Bhattacharya & Chattopadhyay, 2019; Christensen & Carlile, 2009; Dixit et al., 2005; Matthew et al., 2019; Mesny, 2013; Matthews et al., 2011; Roy & Banerjee, 2012; Tripathy, 2008). The time is ripe to analyze the relevance of case teaching pedagogy in the marketing domain and its impact on the takers (Goebel & Humphreys, 2014; Koh, 2014; Shapiro et al., 2021; Sudhir & Unnithan, 2018). This has played an important role and motivated us to find out how the case study is used as a teaching pedagogy that evokes the response of the stakeholders (Mukherjee, 2015, 2018; Tripathy, 2008). Reputed Business Schools orient and brand the same toward simulating the practice behind the theory, thus discussion of the fundamentals is restricted and the application of the subject of discussion is considered relevant with the help of comprehensive teaching pedagogy.

The present study focuses on the benefits of case study teaching as pedagogy and the marketing acumen derived therein in an Indian context. This paper is an in-depth study on the same as the adoption of case-based teaching pedagogy is toward the practical orientation of management education and needs a comprehensive understanding of the fundamentals of the theory on which it is based. To validate our research, we have thought of the process to analyze the contribution of the case-based teaching methods with the help of empirical data in this age of complex and changing business ecosystems to create budding marketing professionals.

Literature Review

The researchers in the domain of marketing education have argued that marketing skills or acumen depend on knowledge diversity and practical exposures along with experience and encounter with real-time problems relating to the marketing environment (Albert & Grzeda, 2015; Ellis & Waller, 2017). Marketing schooling as one of the important verticals in the domain of management education is extremely applied and very dynamic too (Albert & Grzeda, 2015; Ellis & Waller, 2017; Harrison & Ajjan, 2019; Madhavaram & Laverie, 2010; Rivera & Alarcón, 2018). Morgan and McCabe (2012, p. 142) have highlighted that "learning by doing" along with understating consumers' buying behavior, as well as experience related to complex marketing procedures in the present situation, can significantly boost the marketing skills or acumen.

Eminent academic researchers have put their true effort into investigating the pedagogical challenges and issues to help the domain of management education and its learning outcomes. Some of the scholars have highlighted that the lecture-based pedagogy is one of the unsurpassed ways to distribute knowledge among the students (Burkill et al., 2008; Churchill and John, 1958; Griffin & Cashin, 1989; Roy & Banerjee, 2012), but some social scientists have demonstrated the faith that lecture-based pedagogy is the old schools of concept but learning by doing is the better approach in this complex learning environment to generate a higher learning outcome (Bauer et al., 2011; Fry, 2014; Gibbs, 1988; Joyce, 2012; Kolb & Kolb, 2009; Zhao & Jiang, 2009). In today's teaching and learning environment outcome-based education is getting popular day by day (Borin et al., 2008; Davis, 2003; Kaliannan & Suseela, 2012; Saiful & Puteh, 2011). This is an alternative belief that problem-based education can boost the functional working knowledge and justify the relevance of the theoretical concepts pertaining to practical context (Hallinger and Jiafang, 2011; Brownell & Daphne, 2004; Carriger, 2015; Anderson & Lawton, 2005; Roh & Kim, 2015). But the case-based education pedagogy is serving the purpose of generating the linkage between decision-making skills, practical insights, and theoretical concepts along with long-term retention of knowledge of the ideas that are shared in class (Bhattacharya & Chattopadhyay, 2019; Christensen & Carlile, 2009; Dixit et al., 2005; Matthew et al., 2019; Mesny, 2013; Matthews et al., 2011; Roy & Banerjee, 2012; Tripathy, 2008; Goebel & Humphreys, 2014; Koh, 2014; Shapiro et al., 2021; Sudhir & Unnithan,

2018). This also motivates the students to develop a habit to see any particular problems with multiple perspectives to formulate a prudent decision related to the real-life business situation (Jain, 2005; Berrell et al., 2001; Dixit et al., 2005; Christensen & Carlile, 2009; Mesny, 2013). Case-based teaching pedagogy encourages critical thinking that can be considered as an effective method of marketing class instruction to improve in-depth thoughtful insight in marketing knowledge (Albert & Grzeda, 2015; Bhattacharya & Chattopadhyay, 2019; Mukherjee, 2018; Raya, 2017; Tripathy, 2008).

In today's marketing education some business schools in India already have started simulation-based teaching to help the students to comprehend the rational headway process to analyze problem-solving effectively by creating a replicated virtual condition (Farrell, 2020; Gundala & Singh, 2016; Tingley & Vrooman, 2020; Vos, 2015). But simulation and management simulation games as teaching pedagogy is a costly affair (Boet et al., 2013; Perry et al., 2011; Teng et al., 2019). Considering the cost aspect and technical aspect many business schools emphasize upon case teaching pedagogy to make the marketing education so relevant (Mukherjee, 2018; Neely & Tucker, 2013; Perry et al., 2011; Vos, 2014, 2015). Case study pedagogy can be very much useful in generating the decision-making skill abilities within the management students (Neely & Tucker, 2013; Novák et al., 2017; Peden & Eisenhart, 2010). Managerial Efficiency of the managers can be understood as the output and efficiency, that requires being conscious about the targets and determining a proper process to attain the target. In marketing, this is considered one of the main traits of any manager. Case study as the teaching pedagogy can boost the students to understand the different aspects of understanding the goal orientation and solution generation capabilities to be relevant with the marketing or sales targets (Christensen & Hansen, 1987; Jain, 2005; Shivakumar, 2012).

In this VUCA world, the role of business foresight of the business professionals can minimize the risk of uncertainties. The predictive analysis is always not true but the situation analysis and rational thinking can create a perspective of the situation analysis to deal with the current and future problems with the logical progression that can help managers to see the future on the base of the current market behavior (Kepner & Tregoe, 1976). The beauty of case study pedagogy is that future managers can grow with the right attitudes toward data (both numerical and behavioral) analysis. Most of the modern marketing cases come with data interpretation part; this data analysis skills help them to see the business future by using the current situation. This habit grows with the interpretation of facts and figures discussed in any case to address the problem in the case (Gupta & Bharadwaj, 2013; Jackson, 2011; Jain, 2005; Matthew et al., 2019).

Analytical ability is another skill that is highly supported by case study pedagogy by finding the root cause of the actual problem from the different dimensions based on the business circumstances and available data related to the case. This analytical ability is one of the core skills needed within any potential manager (Bridgman et al., 2018; Brownell & Daphne, 2004; Hallinger & Lu, 2011). Regarding the concept of self-efficacy, Bandura (1982) has stated in research that "how well one can execute courses of action required to deal with prospective situations" indicates the individual strong perception related to job and commitment to perform within any organization. When the management students continuously solve numerous cases then they get the exposures to the many protagonist and leaders and their activities and commitments related to the organization success, which then consciously or unconsciously imbibes the skill of self-efficacy that grows with the individual's commitment, that is, they learn the dos and don'ts that is considered as the typical exception of any business organizations (Bonney, 2015; Mukherjee, 2015, 2018; Tripathy, 2008; Yoon et al., 2006).

Problem-solving aptitude is one of the minimum requirements of any potential manager that has been voiced by Bloomberg Job Skills Report (2015). In the case-study analysis, students do focus on one of the widely used approaches to problem-solving which is SA-PA-DA-PPA (i.e., Situation Analysis, Problem Analysis, Decision Analysis, and Potential Problem Analysis) for deeper introspection of the problem domain to generate possible solutions (Kepner & Tregoe, 1976). The case-study teaching pedagogy tunes the students with the diverse problem areas of business that in turn motivates the students to generate the solutions. These exercises can be very useful to inculcate the problem-solving aptitude within the marketing management students (Gupta & Bharadwaj, 2013; Jackson, 2011; Jain, 2005; Mukherjee, 2018; Rennick & McKay, 2018; VanderZanden et al., 2008; Warnock & Mohammadi-Aragh, 2016). Creativity is another very essential ability of the new age managers which helps the managers to generate a unique approach to explain business situations and execute the prudent action points for business success.

Case study discussion in the classroom sessions motivate the students to produce creative solutions, and this nurtures the creative skill of the management students (Bhattacharya & Chattopadhyay, 2019; Mukherjee, 2018; Raya, 2017; Selkrig & Keamy, 2017; Xunyu, 2017).

Outlook India (2016) in their article "Are you Industry Ready?", have critically pronounced a case study-based teaching approach that can link the theoretical concepts with the application relevance is considered a good step to make the students' industry ready and job fit, which has also been supported by another article published in Times of India (2019) named "How does a B-school make students industry-ready?" Industry readiness is the amalgamation of all the different skills such as those the recruiters expect within the potential management graduate. The management students should exhibit decision-making ability, analytical skill, problem-solving skills, and creativity at the time of the job interview; case study pedagogy can help the management students to imbibe the aforesaid skills in tandem with each other (Bhattacharya & Chattopadhyay, 2019; Christensen & Carlile, 2009; Corey, 1998; Jackson, 2011; Mukherjee, 2018; Neely & Tucker, 2013).

The different scholarly studies in the domain of management education have tried to unfold the contributions of different management education pedagogy and their challenges too. Most of the studies have been done so far either based on the students' responses or the teachers' responses. The researchers have restricted their studies within few angles to it in an unintegrated way, and ranking of the learning outcomes is also rare. But our research is a bit different, which have thoughtfully attempted to unfold the different learning outcome in an integrated manner. This article has also tried to incorporate the opinion of marketing management students along with the voice of marketing management faculty members by using the analytical hierarchy process (AHP).

Analytic Hierarchy Process (AHP)

AHP, since it was first introduced as one of the efficient research tools, has been an effective way to process the data to generate multiple-criteria decision-making. This method was propagated by Thomas L. Saaty (1980) became very popular in scientific research. But in the domain of social science different researchers have started applying this tool for its simplicity and efficiency (Omkarprasad & Kumar, 2006). Many extraordinary research studies have been done in the domain of social science by following the AHP; in marketing research the application of AHP is few but a growing phenomenon. AHP modeling can also be considered as a measurement procedure (Saaty, 1980, 1990) that constructs any compound, multi-periodical, multi-attribute, and multi-criterion into a structure hierarchical outcome to check the contribution of the different criteria or the attributes. In the AHP process relative priority scale is being used to capture the data on how one attribute or criteria is preferred over the other attribute or criteria by the responders and based on the responses, a matrix is formed to find the weights and sequence by following rules of normalization. AHP can deliver an organized framework and process to validate the weights and sequence for better decision-making and factfinding for any strategic marketing decision-making. In data capturing a different scale is being used (1–9 point scale/relative scale) which is as follows:

Attribute 1	9	8	7	6	5	4	3	2	1	2	3	4	5	6	7	8	9	Attribute 2
Attribute 2																		Attribute 3
Attribute 3																		Attribute 1

The interpretation of the scale is as illustrated in Table 13.1.

Research Objectives

The present study focuses on the benefits of case study teaching as pedagogy and the marketing acumen derived therein. The paper is an in-depth study on the same as the adoption of case-based teaching pedagogy is toward the practical orientation of management education and needs a comprehensive understanding of the fundamentals of the theory on which it is based. This study had intended to analyze how different B-schools in India are meaningfully using the case-based teaching pedagogy in producing high-impact skills within the potential marketing professionals. Another objective of this study was to see the need to focus on the different important learning outcomes that must be highlighted to generate a higher learning outcome in the domain of marketing education when the case study teaching pedagogy is a concern. To do that ranking of the different learning outcomes and skill set is essential, and the current study has tried to systematically analyze the empirical responses with a hierarchy process with a strong statistical model.

Table 13.1 Interpretations to the attributes of the scale

Intensity of importance	*Definition*	*Explanation*
1	Equal importance	Two activities contribute equally to the objective
3	Weak importance of one over another	Experience and judgement slightly favor one activity over another
5	Essential or strong importance	Experience and judgement strongly favor one activity over another
7	Demonstrated importance	An activity is strongly favored and its dominance is demonstrated in practice
9	Absolute importance	The evidence favoring one activity over another is of the highest possible order of affirmation
2,4,6,8	Intermediate values between the two adjacent judgements	When compromise is needed
Reciprocals of above nonzero	If activity *i* has one of the above nonzero numbers assigned to it when compared with activity *j*, then *j* has the reciprocal value when compared with *i*	

Source Authors

Methodology and Estimation

The extensive literature review has helped this study to do find out the different attributes, criteria, and activities that may have an impact on generating higher learning outcomes by following the case study pedagogy within the marketing education domain that has been shown in Table 13.2.

After identifying the different variables which can address the current research we develop the questionnaire. After developing the questionnaire, we identified the premier B-Schools wherein case study is the main pedagogical methodology for imparting marketing sessions. Across India, we have identified 9 B-Schools that follow the case study method of teaching devotionally viz. IIMA, IIMB, IIMC, ISB, MDI Gurgaon, XLRI, IMT Ghaziabad, Great Lakes Chennai, SP Jain Mumbai. After

Table 13.2 Dimensions and attributes

Case study teaching pedagogy	Bhattacharya and Chattopadhyay (2019), Christensen and Carlile (2009), Dixit et al. (2005), Matthew et al. (2019), Mesny (2013); Matthews et al. (2011), Roy and Banerjee (2012), Tripathy (2008), Goebel and Humphreys (2014), Koh (2014), Shapiro et al. (2021), Sudhir and Unnithan (2018)
Decision-making skill	Neely and Tucker (2013), Novák et al. (2017), Peden and Eisenhart (2010)
Managerial efficiency	Christensen and Hansen (1987, Jain (2005), Shivakumar (2012)
Business foresight	Jain (2005), Gupta and Shah (2013), Kepner and Tregoe (1976)
analytical ability	Bridgman et al. (2018), Brownell and Daphne (2004), Hallinger and Lu (2011)
Self-efficacy	Bonney (2015), Mukherjee (2015), Mukherjee (2018), Tripathy (2008), Yoon et al. (2006)
Problem-solving ability	Rennick and McKay (2018), Warnock and Mohammadi-Aragh (2016), VanderZanden et al. (2008), Mukherjee (2018), Jain (2005), Gupta and Bharadwaj (2013), Jackson (2011)
Creativity	Selkrig and Keamy (2017), Xunyu (2017), Raya (2017), Bhattacharya and Chattopadhyay (2019),Mukherjee (2018)
Attitude building	Gupta and Bharadwaj (2013), Jackson (2011), Jain (2005), Matthew et al. (2019)
Industry readiness	Bhattacharya and Chattopadhyay (2019), Mukherjee (2018), Jackson (2011), Christensen and Carlile (2009), Corey (1998), Neely and Tucker (2013)

Adopted from the Literature Review

identifying these B-Schools we collected a sample of 117 responses mostly from the faculty members and students maintaining the ratio of 1:12 (faculty: students). It took more than three months to capture the data by following the survey implementing the AHP-based questionnaire related to the implication of case teaching pedagogy in marketing education. In our research, we have used the analytical hierarchy process in finding the impact of the case study method application in the domain of marketing. The questionnaire was designed in the fashion of the Analytical Hierarchy Process (AHP) as per the requirements of questionnaire execution. The empirical data were collected from different course instructors across top business schools and the students. After getting the data the geometric mean of the individual component was calculated to develop the AHP matrices. The entire methodology of AHP was then executed to assess the impact of the case study in the creation of marketing acumen. The findings of the present research have critically examined and established that there are three main dimensions of case teaching in marketing, viz. decision-making skill, managerial efficiency, and business foresight which are related to sharpening analytical ability, self-efficacy, problem-solving, creativity, attitude building, and industry readiness.

Likewise, we collected the judgments for the other variables like analytical ability, decision-making ability, problem-solving ability, creativity, attitude building, and industry readiness from the responders. Likewise, we collected the judgments for the other variables such as:

- Analytical ability,
- Self-efficacy,
- Problem-solving ability,
- Creativity,
- Attitude building, and
- Industry readiness.

The initial matrix was prepared by following the sample shown as below:

Research Model

As per the research hypothetical framework depicted in Fig. 13.1, we have

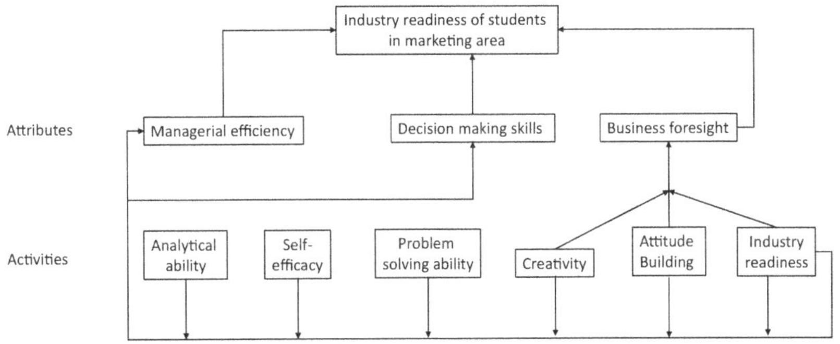

Fig. 13.1 Hypothetical framework (*Source* Authors)

Table 13.3 Paired correlation judgments

Decision-making skill	9	8	7	6	5	4	3	2	1	2	3	4	5	6	7	8	9	Managerial efficiency
Managerial efficiency	9	8	7	6	5	4	3	2	1	2	3	4	5	6	7	8	9	Business foresight
Business foresight	9	8	7	6	5	4	3	2	1	2	3	4	5	6	7	8	9	Decision-making skill

tried to see how the different learning activities performed by case study-based pedagogy to boost all the important kills like analytical ability, self-efficacy, problem-solving, creativity, attitude building, and industry readiness as specified by the scale used for this current research. And also, to see how the above-mentioned skills can jointly influence the three most important key domain abilities like decision-making skills, managerial efficiency, and business foresight for marketing students as to be more industry readiness. This model can also help to understand how the different skill sets can be followed by the different ranks on basis of responders' opinions too.

Data Analysis and Model Validation

The current research has followed some specific steps to gather and analyze the data that has been stated as follows.

Stage 1: in this stage, the responders' trade-off judgments related to different skill nurturing scope through case-study pedagogy were plotted in the paired correlation matrix. As depicted over, the questionnaire was floated (as in Tables 13.3 and 13.4). The shown cell values in the above

Table 13.4 Paired correlation matrix for Case study teaching pedagogy outcomes

Attributes	*Managerial efficiency*	*Decision-making skill*	*Business foresight*
Managerial efficiency	1		
Decision making skills	$1/\alpha_{12}$	1	
Business foresight	$1/\alpha_{13}$	$1/\alpha_{23}$	1

matrixes (as in Tables 13.3 and 13.4) where αij and βij speak of the responders' opinions and judgments. Similarly, residual cells shown in the paired correlation matrix represent the opposite opinions and judgments (indicated as 1/αij and 1/βij) (Table 13.5).

Stage 2: in this stage, the consistency of the model was tested based on the responders' opinions and judgments. This cake of consistency was done through consistency ratio (CR), consistency index (CI), and upon random index (RI) as prescribed by Thomas L. Saaty (1980) and Forman, E. H. (2001).

Consistency Ratio = Consistency Index /Random Index

CI is computed as ($\lambda_{max} - N$) upon ($N - 1$) where N stays for number of measurements and λ_{max} demonstrates the greatest eigenvalue:

$$CI = (\lambda_{max} - N)/(N - 1)$$

Eigenvalues are scalars associated with an immediate course of action of numerical values (or a network correlation):

$$\lambda_{max} = C_{JM1} \times R_{PM1} + C_{JM2} \times R_{PM2} + C_{JM3} \times R_{PM3}$$

wherein λ_{max}, the maximum eigenvalue of a matrix; C_{JM1}, indicates the sum total of the column total of the responders' opinions matrix of the first column; R_{PM1}, row average of priority matrix of the second row; C_{JM2}, column total of responders' opinions matrix of the second column;

Table 13.5 Paired correlation matrix for case study teaching pedagogy outcomes

Attributes	*Analytical Ability*	*Self-efficacy*	*Problem-solving ability*	*Creativity*	*Attitude Building*	*Industry readiness*
Analytical ability	1	β_{12}	β_{13}	β_{14}	β_{15}	β_{16}
Self-efficacy	$1/\beta_{12}$	1	β_{23}	β_{24}	β_{25}	β_{26}
Problem solving ability	$1/\beta_{13}$	$1/\beta_{23}$	1	β_{34}	β_{35}	β_{36}
Creativity	$1/\beta_{14}$	$1/\beta_{24}$	$1/\beta_{34}$	1	β_{45}	β_{46}
Attitude building	$1/\beta_{15}$	$1/\beta_{25}$	$1/\beta_{35}$	$1/\beta_{45}$	1	β_{56}
Industry readiness	$1/\beta_{16}$	$1/\beta_{26}$	$1/\beta_{36}$	$1/\beta_{46}$	$1/\beta_{56}$	1

Table 13.6 Random consistency (RI) indices

N	1	2	3	4	5	6	7	8	9	10
RI	0	0	0.58	0.9	1.12	1.24	1.32	1.41	1.45	1.49

R_{PM2} represents row mean of priority matrix of the second row; C_{JM3} indicates a total of the responders' opinions column total of responders' opinions matrix the third column, and R_{PM3} represents row mean of priority matrix of the second row. By following the same process other matrix values were calculated.

Then we have followed the method as prescribed by Saaty (1980) and square relatives of responders' opinions were calculated. Similarly, the random consistency index (RI) was checked from Table 13.6.

λ_{max}	6.029
CI	0.0145
N	6
CR	0.0117

Consider [$Ax = l_{max}x$] where A is the comparison matrix of size $n \times n$, for n criteria, also called the priority matrix. x is the Eigenvector of size $n \times 1$, also called the priority vector. l_{max} is the Eigenvalue, $l_{max} \in \Re > n$. To find the ranking of priorities, namely the Eigen Vector X.

In this model CR = CI/RI.

0.010/0.58 = 0.017 which is less than 0.10 that is signifying the robustness as prescribed by Thomas L. Saaty (1980).

From Table 13.7 this can be seen that on basis of responders' opinions related to the contribution of the case study-based pedagogy is significant in nurturing skills like analytical ability, self-efficacy, problem-solving, creativity, attitude building and industry readiness. This can also be identified by the rank wise contributing in strengthening the skills; industry readiness is ranked first, self-efficacy ranked second, problem-solving ability ranked third, the analytical ability is ranked fourth, attitude building ranked fifth, and creativity ranked sixth after the first level of data interpretation. At the end of the analysis (see Table 13.8) this was found that managerial efficiency, decision-making skill, business foresight are supported by case pedagogy in marketing education. The relative rank of the managerial efficiency, decision-making skill, business foresight was

Table 13.7 Normalized pared correlation matrix for the skill learned from case study pedagogy

	Analytical ability	*Self-efficacy*	*Problem-solving ability*	*Creativity*	*Attitude building*	*Industry readiness*	*Weight*	*Rank*
Analytical ability	0.113	0.154	0.042	0.156	0.293	0.098	0.143	4
Self-efficacy	0.144	0.196	0.376	0.329	0.100	0.138	0.214	2
Problem-solving ability	0.366	0.072	0.137	0.179	0.333	0.098	0.197	3
Creativity	0.065	0.054	0.069	0.091	0.053	0.250	0.097	6
Attitude Building	0.036	0.182	0.038	0.158	0.093	0.175	0.114	5
Industry readiness	0.277	0.342	0.338	0.087	0.128	0.241	0.235	1

found third, second, and first, respectively, in conjunction with analytical ability, self-efficacy, problem-solving, creativity, attitude building, and industry readiness.

Managerial Implication

This article has so many managerial implications; firstly our study has critically examined the different dimension of managerial abilities which are required to perform well in the domain of marketing management and classroom is the best place to make sure all those necessary skills were required for doubling managers. The classroom environment is very imperative to you to bring out the real-time situations with the help of diverse management cases studies. The replication of the facts and circumstances which are common in today's business and marketing ecosystem motivate the student to connect the theoretical concepts and understanding. The application of the theoretical understanding can blend very well with the case study based teaching pedagogy to imbibed the skills of a future manager like managerial efficiency, decision-making skill and business foresight. In an Indianized B-school learning environment the role of the faculty is also very important to select the very relevant cases

Table 13.8 Normalized paired correlation matrix for skill-led management abilities

	Analytical ability	*Decision-making ability*	*Problem-solving ability*	*Creativity*	*Attitude building*	*Industry readiness*	*Final score*	*Rank*
Managerial efficiency	0.223	0.496	0.143	0.193	0.508	0.481	0.355	3
Decision-making skill	0.078	0.318	0.44	0.069	0.332	0.32	0.285	2
Business foresight	0.699	0.186	0.417	0.738	0.16	0.199	0.358	1

in class discussion that would be very affirmative to increase the engagement label of the marketing management students that would inspire the student to use their analytical abilities, creativity, problem-solving abilities which would, in turn, help the future managers reducing the gap in between the practical environment and theoretical concepts. Thus, the motive of the case study-oriented teaching will be fulfilled in generating a sense of self-efficacy; creativity will be enhanced and Indian marketing management students will be more industry ready. This article creates the opportunity for the faculty members across the different B-schools in India, who put their effort to create the perspective of the students related to the different consequences and to reduce the biases of a false assumption. The faculty members need to be very particular in the selection of the management cases which would be much relevant and also blended with different exercises to nurture managerial efficiency, decision-making skill, and business forecasting.

Conclusion

The managers graduating from the B-Schools have to engage themselves in critical and crucial decisions hence their intellectual acumen as regards their spontaneity in decision-making and the prudence in the same is the need of the corporate management hierarchy. This tests the efficiency of the managers in the decision-making process and the foresight value of their thought process and the practical boldness of their decisions are judged when they are encompassing a Catch 22 situation. It is in this context the above three parameters, viz. decision-making skill, managerial efficiency, and business foresight is to be developed which is the outcome of the individual's ability to analyze the situations considering the pros and cons of every dimension of the same; the efficiency of handling complex situations, i.e., self-efficacy, how to overcome the hurdles that come in the way of business and self, i.e., problem-solving, the balance between the logic and emotions and nurturing the same sophisticatedly using the creative bent of mind, development of positive attitude and will power to come out winning the different situations. This all impacts the industry readiness to handle the different marketing situations by going into the core of the matter and easing out the complexities and the bottlenecks for a simple solution to the cumbersome real-life situations that a marketing professional is constantly exposed to either internally or externally.

References

Albert, S., & Grzeda, M. (2015). Reflection in strategic management education. *Journal of Management Education, 39*(5), 650–669.

Anderson, P. H., & Lawton, L. (2005). The effectiveness of simulation exercise for integrating problem-based learning in management education. *Developments in Business Simulation and Experiential Learning, 32*(1986), 10–18.

Bakhru, K. M. (2018). Aligning teaching methods for learning outcomes: A need for educational change in management education using quality function deployment approach. *International Journal of Learning and Change, 10*(1), 54–69.

Bandura, A. (1982). Self-efficacy mechanism in human agency. *American Psychologist., 37*(2), 122–147.

Bauer, C., Viola, K., & Strauss, C. (2011). Management skills for artists: "learning by doing"? *International Journal of Cultural Policy, 17*(5), 626–644.

Bhattacharya, S., & Chattopadhyay, S. (2019). Eliminating thought boundaries through fiction movies and books. *South Asian Journal of Business and Management Cases, 8*(3), 324–334.

Boet, S., Everett, T., Gale, M., Lai, A., Haligua, A., & Bould, D. (2013). Learning crisis management: Practicing versus an observational role in simulation training—A randomized controlled trial. *Anaesthesia Critical Care & Pain Medicine, 35*(4), 275–281.

Bonney, K. M. (2015). Case study teaching method improves student performance and perceptions of learning gains. *Journal of Microbiology & Biology Education, 16*(1), 21–28.

Borin, N., Metcalf, L. E., & Tietje, B. C. (2008). Implementing assessment in an outcome-based marketing curriculum. *Journal of Marketing Education, 30*(2), 150–159.

Bridgman, T., McLaughlin, C., & Cummings, S. (2018). Overcoming the problem with solving business problems: Using theory differently to rejuvenate the case method for turbulent times. *Journal of Management Education, 42*(4), 441–460.

Brownell, J., & Daphne, A. J. (2004). Problem-based learning in graduate management education: An integrative model and interdisciplinary application. *Journal of Management Education, 28*(5), 558–577.

Burkill, S., Dyer, S. R., & Stone, M. (2008). Lecturing in higher education in further education settings. *Journal of Further and Higher Education, 32*(4), 321–331.

Carriger, M. S. (2015). Problem-based learning and management development – Empirical and theoretical considerations. *International Journal of Management Education, 13*(3), 249–259.

Christensen, C. M., & Carlile, P. R. (2009). Course research: Using the case method to build and teach management theory. *Academy of Management Learning and Education, 8*, 240–251.

Christensen, C. R., & Hansen, A. J. (1987). *Teaching and the case method.* Harvard Business School.

Corey, R. (1998, November 6). Case method teaching. Review No. 9-581-058, Harvard Business School.

Davis, M. H. (2003). Outcome-Based Education. *Journal of Veterinary Medical Education, 30*, 258–263.

Ellis, R. B., & Waller, D. S. (2017). Marketing education at the University of Melbourne. *History of Education Review, 46*(1), 95–106.

Farrell, C. (2020). Do international marketing simulations provide an authentic assessment of learning? A student perspective. *International Journal of Management Education, 18*(1), 100362.

Fry, H. (2014). *A handbook for teaching and learning in higher education.* Routledge.

Gersel, J., & Thaning, M. S. (2020). The plight to choose: Cultivating practical deliberation in management learning and education. *Journal of Management Education, 44*(5), 663–676.

Gibbs, G. (1988). *Learning by doing: A guide to teaching and learning methods.* [EBook]. Reflective Gibbs – Study Skills – Upgrade Study Advice Service – Oxford Brookes University.

Goebel, D. J., & Humphreys, M. A. (2014). The relationships among student learning styles, course delivery method, and course outcomes: A quasi-experiment investigating the case method of course delivery. *Atlantic Marketing Journal, 3*(2), 33–48.

Greenberg, D. N., Deets, S., Erzurumlu, S., Hunt, J., Manwaring, M., Rodgers, V., & Swanson, E. (2017). Signing to living PRME: Learning from a journey towards responsible management education. *International Journal of Management Education, 15*(2), 205–218.

Griffin, R. W., & Cashin, W. E. (1989). The lecture and discussion method for management education: Pros and cons. *Journal of Management Development, 8*(2), 25–32.

Gundala, R., & Singh, M. (2016). Role of simulations in student learning: A case study using marketing simulation. *Journal of Educational Research and Innovation, 5*(2), 2.

Gupta, N., & Bharadwaj, S. S. (2013). Agility in business school education through richness and reach: A conceptual model. *Education and Training, 55*(4), 370–384.

Hallinger, P., & Lu, J. (2011). Implementing problem-based learning in higher education in Asia: Challenges, strategies and effect. *Journal of Higher Education Policy and Management, 33*(3), 267–285.

Harrison, D. E., & Ajjan, H. (2019). Customer relationship management technology: Bridging the gap between marketing education and practice. *Journal of Marketing Analytics, 7*(4), 205–219.

Horney, N., Pasmore, B., & O'Shea, T. (2010). Leadership agility: A business imperative for a VUCA world. *Human Resource Planning, 33*(4), 34.

https://www.gmac.com/-/media/files/gmac/research/curriculum-insight/2015-gmegs-survey-report-final-for-web.pdf

https://www.outlookindia.com/outlookmoney/fixed-assets/are-you-industry-ready-691

https://timesofindia.indiatimes.com/home/education/news/how-does-a-b-school-make-students-industry-ready/articleshow/68645586.cms

Jackson, G. (2011). Rethinking the case method. *Journal of Management Policy & Practice, 12*(5), 142–164.

Jain, A. K. (2005). Management education and case method as a pedagogy. *Vikalpa, 30*(1), 77–84.

Joyce, P. (2012). Learning as doing: Common goals and interests across management and education. *Journal of Nursing Management, 20*(1), 113–119.

Kaliannan, M., & Suseela, D. C. (2012). Empowering students through Outcome-Based Education (OBE). *Research in Education, 87*(1), 50–63.

Kayes, D. C. (2002). Experiential learning and its critics: Preserving the role of experience in management learning and education. *Academy of Management Learning & Education, 1*(2), 137–149.

Kepner, C. H., & Tregoe, B. B. (1976). *The rational manager: A systematic approach to problem solving and decision making* (2nd ed.). Kepner-Tregoe.

Koh, A. (2014). The "magic" of tutorial centres in Hong Kong: An analysis of media marketing and pedagogy in a tutorial centre. *International Review of Education, 60*(6), 803–819.

Kolb, A. Y., & Kolb, D. A. (2005). Learning styles and learning spaces: Enhancing experiential learning in higher education. *Academy of Management Learning and Education, 4*(2), 193–212.

Kolb, A. Y., & Kolb, D. A. (2009). *Experiential learning theory: A dynamic, holistic approach to management learning, education and development* (pp. 42–68). The SAGE Handbook of Management Learning, Education and Development. SAGE Publications Inc.

Konst (e. Penttilä), T. and Kairisto-Mertanen, L. (2020). Developing innovation pedagogy approach. *On the Horizon, 28*(1), 45–54.

Langendahl, P.-A., Cook, M., & Mark-Herbert, C. (2017). Exploring gamification in management education for sustainable development. *Creative Education, 08*(14), 2243–2257.

Levy, F., & Rodkin, J. (2015). The Bloomberg job skills report: What recruiters really want. *Bloomberg Business*. Retrieved from https://www.bloomberg.com/graphics/2015-job-skills-report/. (Accessed on 26th October 2020)

Madhavaram, S., & Laverie, D. A. (2010). Developing pedagogical competence: Issues and implications for marketing education. *Journal of Marketing Education, 32*(2), 197–213.

Matthews, R., Bexley, J., & Sullivan, L. (2011). Using case studies to prepare business students to perform: A practical application. *Academy of Entrepreneurship Journal, 17*(1), 1–6.

Matthew, J. S., Christina, B., Anna, B. H., & René, R. (2019). Five strategic foresight tools to enhance business model innovation teaching. *Journal of Business Models, 7*(3), 77–88.

Mesny, A. (2013). Taking stock of the century-long utilization of the case method in management education. *Canadian Journal of Administrative Sciences, 30*(1), 56–66.

Mukherjee, J. (2015). Case study based pedagogy for marketing education in India. *Management and Change, 19*(2), 9–24.

Mukherjee, J. (2018). Using new case studies for evaluation of marketing student's academic performance. *Vision, 22*(1), 1–7.

Neely, P., & Tucker, J. (2013, April). Case study: An examination of the decision making process for selecting simulations for an online MBA program. *Education and Training, 55*(2), 128–138.

Novák, P., Dvorský, J., Popesko, B., & Strouhal, J. (2017). Analysis of overhead cost behavior: Case study on decision-making approach. *Journal of International Studies, 10*(1), 74–91.

Omkarprasad, S. V., & Kumar, S. (2006). Analytic hierarchy process: An overview of applications. *European Journal of Operational Research, 16*(9), 1–29.

Peden, J. G., & Eisenhart, H. A. (2010). A case-study approach to managerial decision making. *SCHOLE: A Journal of Leisure Studies and Recreation Education, 25*, 104–199.

Perry, M., Foley, P., & Rumpf, P. (2011). Events management: An emerging challenge in Australian higher education. *Festival Management and Event Tourism, 4*(3), 85–93.

Popova, N., Kryvoruchko, O., Shynkarenko, V., & Zéman, Z. (2018). Enterprise management in VUCA conditions. *Economic Annals-XXI, 170*(3–4), 27–31.

Raya, M. J. (2017). La pedagogía de casos como estrategia catalizadora del cambio hacía la autonomía del alumno y del profesor en la formación inicial del profesorado de secundaria. *Educar Em Revista, 63*, 67–83.

Rennick, C., & McKay, K. (2018). Componential theories of creativity: A case study of teaching creative problem solving. In *Proceedings of the Canadian Engineering Education Association (CEEA)*. https://doi.org/10.24908/pceea.v0i0.12991.

Rivera, J., & Alarcón, V. (2018). Model for assessing the quality of marketing-management education. *Journal of Economics, Finance and Administrative Science, 25*(49), 5–25.

Roh, Y. S., & Kim, S. S. (2015). Integrating problem-based learning and simulation: Effects on student motivation and life skills. *CIN - Computers Informatics Nursing, 33*(7), 278–284.

Roy, S., & Banerjee, P. (2012). Understanding students' experience of transition from lecture mode to case-based teaching in a management school in India. *Journal of Educational Change, 13*(4), 487–509.

Saaty, T. L. (1980). *The analytic hierarchy process*. McGraw-Hill.

Saaty, T. L. (1990). How to make a decision: The analytic hierarchy process. *European Journal of Operational Research, 48*(3), 9–26.

Saiful, S. A., & Puteh, A. (2011). Outcome-based learning and modified problem-based learning for accounting education. *International Conference on Economics, Business and Management, 2*(2011), 120–124.

Sarkar, A. (2016). We live in a VUCA world: The importance of responsible leadership. *Development and Learning in Organizations, 30*(3), 9–12.

Schoemaker, P. J. H., Heaton, S., & Teece, D. (2018). Innovation, dynamic capabilities, and leadership. *California Management Review, 61*(1), 15–42.

Selkrig, M., & Keamy, R. (2017). Creative pedagogy: A case for teachers' creative learning being at the centre. *Teaching Education, 28*(3), 317–332.

Shapiro, S., Beninger, S., Domegan, C., Reppel, A., Stanton, J., & Watson, F. (2021). Macromarketing pedagogy: Empowering students to achieve a sustainable world. *Journal of Macromarketing, 41*(1), 104–115. https://doi.org/10.1177/0276146720949637.

Shivakumar, K. (2012). The case study method in training and management education. *IUP Journal of Soft Skills, 6*(2), 55–64.

Singh, A. K., Srivastava, S., & Singh, D. (2015). Student engagement as the predictor of direct and indirect learning outcomes in the management education context. *Metamorphosis: A Journal of Management Research, 14*(2), 20–29.

Sudhir, S., & Unnithan, A. (2018). The role of theoretical breadth and student engagement in the use of case methods in marketing pedagogy. *E-Journal of Business Education and Scholarship of Teaching, 12*(2), 78–91.

Sunley, R., Harding, L., & Jones, J. (2019). Realising creativity in management education: Putting student energy into action. *International Journal of Management Education, 17*(2), 172–181.

Teng, W. N., Su, B. C., & Cheng, H. W. (2019, August 1). *Innovation in sedation and analgesia training. Current Opinion in Anaesthesiology*. Lippincott Williams and Wilkins.

Tingley, C., & Vrooman, M. (2020). From education to employment: Using marketing simulation games to foster meta-skill. *BRC Journal of Advances in Education, 4*(1), 17–33.

Tripathy, M. R. (2008). Case methodology for adult learning: A critical review of theory and practice. *Asian Journal of Management Cases, 5*(1), 5–19.

Ungaretti, T., Thompson, K. R., Miller, A., & Peterson, T. O. (2015, June 1). *Problem-based learning: Lessons from medical education and challenges for management education*. Academy of Management Learning and Education. George Washington University.

VanderZanden, A. M., Sandrock, D., & Kopsell, D. (2008). Student attitudes and perceptions of an online problem-based learning case study in landscape management. *HortTechnology, 18*(3), 520–523.

Vos, L. (2014). Marketing simulation games: A review of issues in teaching and learning. *The Marketing Review, 14*(1), 67–96.

Vos, L. (2015). Simulation games in business and marketing education: How educators assess student learning from simulations. *International Journal of Management Education, 13*(1), 57–74.

Warnock, J. N., & Mohammadi-Aragh, M. J. (2016). Case study: Use of problem-based learning to develop students' technical and professional skills. *European Journal of Engineering Education, 41*(2), 142–153.

Xunyu, C. (2017). A mentoring approach for developing creativity in teaching. *Malaysian Journal of ELT Research, 14*(2), 23–61.

Yoon, S., Pedretti, E., Pedretti, L., Hewitt, J., Perris, K., & Van Oostveen, R. (2006). Exploring the use of cases and case methods in influencing elementary preservice science teachers' self-efficacy beliefs. *Journal of Science Teacher Education, 17*(1), 15–35.

Young, M. R. (2002). Experiential learning=hands-on+minds-on. *Marketing Education Review, 12*(1), 43–51.

Zhao, S., & Jiang, C. (2009). Learning by doing: Emerging paths of chinese management research. *Management and Organization Review, 5*(1), 107–119.

CHAPTER 14

The Effect of Consumer Values on Engagement and Behavioral Intent: Moderating Role of Age

Pradeep Kautish, Linda D. Hollebeek, Arpita Khare, and Raouf Ahmed Rather

Introduction

In environments characterized by rapidly rising competition, online brand-related platforms, including social media or virtual communities, are proven tools to engage consumers (Bowden et al., 2017; Brodie et al., 2013; Carlson et al., 2017). These environments offer myriad interactive tools, including through virtual reality-, digital content marketing-, or

P. Kautish (✉)
Department of Marketing, Institute of Management, Nirma University, Ahmedabad, India
e-mail: pradeep.kautish@nirmauni.ac.in

L. D. Hollebeek
Montpellier Business School, Montpellier, France
e-mail: l.hollebeek@montpellier-bs.com

Rajagopal and R. Behl (eds.), *Managing Disruptions in Business*, Palgrave Studies in Democracy, Innovation, and Entrepreneurship for Growth, https://doi.org/10.1007/978-3-030-79709-6_14

gamification-based applications, to name the substantial ones (e.g. Hollebeek et al., 2020; Leclercq et al., 2020), which let consumers to engage with brands, including by sharing brand-related ideas, posting brand-related content, or private messaging the company (Labrecque et al., 2013; Pookulangara & Koesler, 2011). These tools also afford personalized, typically opt-in-based interactivity that tends to be synonymous with high consumer-perceived relevance and value, thereby offering significant business opportunity (Füller, 2010; Hollebeek et al., 2017).

In this environment, interactive consumer engagement (CE) is a firm performance indicator of rising cachet (De Vries & Carlson, 2014; Kumar et al., 2010), warranting its growing research interest (Harmeling et al., 2017). CE is understood as consumer's attachment with his/her brand and the resources spent on building association with it (Brodie et al., 2011; Hollebeek et al., 2019). In the last decade, the CE literature has made significant strides, and studies have explored the various facets of the concept (e.g., involvement), and its influence on behavior and brand loyalty (Harrigan et al., 2018; Nyadzayo et al., 2020).

However, while a range of CE's nomological network-based associations have been examined (France et al., 2016; Junaid et al., 2020), the influence of consumer *values*, which reflect an individual's belief in or ascribed importance to particular issues (e.g. purchasing sustainable products), in shaping or affecting CE remains tenuous (Etgar, 2008), thus exposing an important research gap. While, in a study, Islam et al. (2018) examined the association of value congruity and CE, they did not differentiate terminal vs. instrumental values, as undertaken in this study that thus builds on and extends prior research. Though Marbach et al. (2019) deployed individualistic values as a moderator to understand the association between consumer personality dimensions and online brand engagement, the impact of personal values on CE remains obscure, thus warranting further research in this area.

A. Khare
University of Allahabad, Uttar Pradesh, India

R. A. Rather
Department of Management Studies (South Campus), University of Kashmir, Jammu and Kashmir, India

Consumer values have been argued to be crucial in the development of value-laden consumer/brand relationships. Specifically, the greater a brand's alignment or fit with a consumer's values, the higher the individual's expected brand engagement (Higgins & Scholer, 2009; Islam et al., 2018), as explored empirically in this paper. We offer the following main contribution. Our analyses offer novel acumen regarding the effect of consumer values in driving their engagement with fashion brands online (Loureiro et al., 2018), thus responding to the Marketing Science Institute's (2018) Research Priorities, which solicit further research on consumer/customer engagement. Empirical exploration of CE's theoretical interface with consumer values is important, given the identified key role of personal values in affecting a range of consumer behavior outcomes, including engagement, as explored in this paper. Our findings matter, because if personal values, which tend to be relatively stable and difficult to change (Roccas et al., 2002), affect CE, a wealth of recommended firm investments in activities aligning with (vs. diverging from) their target customers' predominant values would ensue.

The paper is structured as follows. The review of past literature on consumer values, engagement, and behavioral intent, is followed by development of research hypotheses. We then proceed by outlining the methodology adopted to explore the hypotheses, followed by explanation of the results. We complete the study by discussing the results and deriving key implications from the analyses.

Literature Review and Hypothesis Development

Consumer Values

Consumer values are important conscious and subconscious drivers of consumer behavior (Schiffman et al., 2003; Torelli et al., 2012), including the formation of attitudes and purchase (Rokeach, 1968, 1979). Debate however surrounds the conceptualization of values. Schwartz (1994) conceptualized values in terms of "desirable trans-situational goals that vary in importance, and serve as guiding principles in the life of a person or other social entity" (p. 21) while Rokeach (1973) views values in terms of "an enduring belief that a specific mode of conduct or end-state of existence is personally or socially preferable to an opposite or converse mode of conduct or end-state of existence" (p. 5). Overall, consumer values reflect consumers' deeply-held, relatively stable convictions and beliefs that are expected to impact their purchase-related behaviors (Lee et al., 2011; Novak & MacEvoy, 1990).

Values also see different operationalization. For example, the List of Values (LoV) addresses the individual's fulfilment of various roles through value. It includes nine values such as security, self-respect, self-fulfillment, warm relationships, being well-respected, and sense of accomplishment, sense of belonging, fun, enjoyment and excitement in life (Kahle et al., 1986). In the LoV method, participants are typically asked to rank their two most important values. Second, Values and Life Styles (VALS) classified people according to nine lifestyle groups. It segmented individuals as 'sustainers, survivors, belongers, emulators, I-am-me, achievers, societally conscious, experiential, and integrated' based on a proprietary scoring system (Kahle et al., 1986; Mitchell, 1983).

Third, Schwartz' (1992) Values Survey uses a quasi-circumplex structure to explain the associations between 10 near-universal values. The key values include openness to change (OC) vs. conservation (CO), and self-enhancement (SE) vs. self-transcendence (ST). The OC-CO facet is an internal conflict of "intellectual and emotional interests in unpredictable and uncertain directions" versus preservation of "the status quo and the certainty it provides in relationships with close others, institutions and traditions" (Schwartz, 1992, p. 43). The SE-ST facet is a conflict situation due desire to pursue success and dominance over others, versus a concern for others' welfare and interests (Lee et al., 2012; Munson & McQuarrie, 1988). Overall, our review shows that a range of conceptual approaches to consumer values already exist that have been successfully applied in the literature. We, further zoom in on consumers' terminal and instrumental values, which have been taken up in current research.

Terminal and Instrumental Values

Rokeach (1968) sees 'values' as operating together as a system in which different values hold differing importance levels for different individuals. Rokeach (1973) distinguishes *terminal values* were demarcated as beliefs about preferred end-states of life (i.e., a comfortable life-style), and *instrumental values*, which are beliefs about preferred modes of action to achieve one's desired end-states of life (e.g., ethical behavior). Rokeach's hierarchical system directs behavioral choices (instrumental values) that yield to particular end-states desired over other states, in line with one's terminal values. This model thus stresses the non-mutually exclusive nature of values, which can both be achieved simultaneously (Kautish et al., 2020a). However, in some situations, values may compete (e.g. for the individual's scarce resources, e.g. time), requiring the person to prioritize their perceived most important value (Sundström et al., 2019). Based on their prioritization of terminal (vs. instrumental) values, consumers are expected to behave differently. For example, Allen et al. (2002) report that individuals who favor instrumental (vs. terminal) values were predisposed to extracting functional, utilitarian meanings from their brands, while those favoring terminal values focused on attributing symbolic meaning to brands.

Consumer Engagement

The literature reveals a lack of consensus on consumer engagement's (CE's) definition (Groeger et al., 2016). For example, while Hollebeek et al. (2019, p. 166) state that CE can be described as a consumer's "motivationally driven, volitional investment of... operant resources (e.g. cognitive, emotional, behavioral, and social knowledge/skills), and operand resources (e.g. equipment) in brand interactions". Researchers like Kumar et al. (2019) and Brodie et al. (2011, p. 260) opine CE as "a psychological state that occurs by virtue of interactive, cocreative customer experiences with a focal agent/object (e.g. a brand) in focal service relationships." We deduce the following CE hallmarks from our review.

First, CE is an interactive concept that transpires within the consumer-brand interaction (Harrigan et al., 2018). Second, CE reflects consumers' investment in their brand interactions, with greater investments denoting higher engagement (Harmeling et al., 2017; Hollebeek, 2011). Third, it is understood as a multi-faceted conception which encompasses cognitive, emotional, and behavioral magnitudes (Hollebeek et al., 2014; Vivek et al., 2012). Some scholars have focused their research on engagement behaviors, including brand-related citizenship behaviors such as advocacy or blogging (e.g. Groeger et al., 2016). Fourth, common agreement among researchers is that CE is conducive to a number of firm performance improvements, including sales growth, enhanced referrals, etc. (Brodie et al., 2011).

While several studies have linked consumer values and CE (e.g. Marbach et al., 2019), insufficient acknowledged the role of consumers' terminal (vs. instrumental) values in driving their engagement with brands. First, consumers' instrumental values reflect an individual's desired mode of action, as discussed. Given CE's interactive nature (Clark et al., 2020), consumers' desired *modus operandi* will affect their resource investments and the route they take to achieve their goal, thus impacting CE (Aghekyan-Simonian et al., 2012; Gambetti & Graffigna, 2010). Second, terminal values are a consumer's beliefs about preferred end-states (e.g. owning their desired brands). Therefore, individuals' terminal values are likely to affect the way they go about in reaching their goal fulfillment, thus impacting the consumer's interactive resource investment. We posit:

H_{1a}: Terminal values positively affect consumer engagement.

H_{1b}: Instrumental values positively affect consumer engagement.

Interface of Values, Consumer Engagement, and Behavioral Intent

Prior research demonstrates the important role of consumer values in driving their ensuing behavioral intent (e.g. purchase intent) and actual behavior in a range of contexts or sectors (Kahle et al., 1986; Kim et al., 2002; Xiao & Kim, 2009). Hence, we posit that consumer values would exert a direct effect on consumers' behavioral intent:

H_{2a}: Terminal values positively affect consumers' behavioral (purchase) intent.

H_{2b}: Instrumental values positively affect consumers' behavioral (purchase) intent.

Prior studies also show CE's favorable effect on consumer purchase intent (e.g. Hollebeek et al., 2014; Islam et al., 2019; Rather et al., 2019). We propose:

H_3: CE positively affects consumers' behavioral (purchase) intent.

Moreover, given CE's nature as a consumer's resource investment within a brand interaction (Hollebeek and Chen, 2014; Kumar et al., 2019), repeated instances or episodes of CE reveal a CE trajectory or process (Brodie et al., 2011). Since CE is very much about the *interactive* process, we expect consumers' instrumental (vs. terminal) values to exert a particularly significant effect on CE. That is, with instrumental values addressing consumers' desired mode of action, they directly relate to the notion of consumer resource investments throughout these modes of action and interactions. For the same reason, we anticipate consumers' instrumental values, which describe their way of achieving their goals, to exert a greater effect on their behavioral intent than terminal values, which address consumers' desired end-states. We hypothesize:

H4: Instrumental (vs. terminal) values have a greater effect on CE.
H5: Instrumental (vs. terminal) values have a greater effect on consumers' behavioral intent.

Moderating Role of Consumer Age

Moderators systematically modify the strength or (form) of the relationship between a predictor and a criterion factor (Hair et al., 2010). Hence, we suggest a moderating role of consumer age in the relationship of CE and behavioral intent, as delineate. Our contention is rooted in the following basis: During the individual's life-span, which likely value other persons, services and objects differently (Loureiro & Roschk, 2014). Accordingly, consumer age has been considered as a key demographic variable in consumer-research (Khan et al., 2020; Schirmer et al., 2018). Thus, consumers with different age profiles are likely to reveal varying psychological-, cognitive-, and behavioral- facets toward specific offerings that impact their consequent customer behavior (Rather & Hollebeek, 2021). Extant works claims that customer desires and responses alter throughout the life cycle (Loureiro & Roschk, 2014; Ye et al., 2018). As a result, consumer age can influence the way consumers perceive brand cues and react to marketing messages (e.g., Hervé & Mullet, 2009), generating its moderating affect. Such as aged customers are most driven by schema or heuristic-based processing (e.g., Yoon, 1997), representing their decreased likelihood to look for novel information to make decisions (Rather & Hollebeek, 2021), that can be elucidated by these customers having superior maturity and emotional control.

Furthermore, older verses (younger) consumers likely reveal elevated brand-commitment and loyalty, generating distinctive behavioral and affective responses (Homburg & Giering, 2001). Thus, consume rage has been revealed to effect the relationship between consumer behavior-related factors (Homburg & Giering, 2001; Rather & Hollebeek, 2021). Although, the role of consumers' age on their consequent behavioral factors remains hazy, call for further investigation. Particularly, the effect of consumer age on the relationship between CE and behavioral intent remains nebulous (Khan et al., 2020; Rather & Hollebeek, 2021), as thus investigated in this research. That is to say, we presume consumers with different age profiles having different wants, preferences, or needs (Hervé & Mullet, 2009), therefore differentially effecting the path between CE and behavioral intent across age groups (Khan et al., 2020). On the basis of this justification, we suggest:

> H_6: Consumer age moderates the impact of CE on consumer's behavioral intent.

Research Methodology

Data Collection and Sampling

In the present study, we concentrated on the online fashion situation, where consumers purchase fashion or apparel though e-tailing websites or portals. We chose fashion, given the centrality of fashion brands to consumers' identity (Sprott et al., 2009) and their typical high engagement with their clothing choices, particularly in our chosen Indian context (Kautish et al., 2020b; Khare, 2014; NASSCOM, 2018). We selected younger respondents (aged 18–30), given their typical interest in fashion and their high usage of online purchase (e.g. e-commerce) channels (Ladhari et al., 2019; Pandey & Chawla, 2014). Table 14.1 outlines demographic characteristics of the study participants.

Prior to data collection, we used the a-priori sample size calculator for structural equation models (Iacobucci, 2010). For the model, which contains four latent, eighteen observed variables, and an estimated effect size of 0.3 ($p = 0.5$), the requisite sample size was 137 (Soper, 2020). The data was collected from students at three premier fashion schools in the metropolitan cities of New Delhi, Jaipur and Ahmedabad, in north India between November 2019 and February 2020. Each of the respondents made frequent online purchases. Before the main survey, screening

Table 14.1 Demographic respondent profile (*N* = 412)

Variables or criteria	*Frequency*	*Percent*
Gender		
Male	228	55.34
Female	184	44.66
Age (in years)		
16–18	55	13.35
19–21	135	32.77
22–24	222	53.88
Qualification		
Diploma	26	6.31
Graduate	92	22.33
Postgraduate	245	59.47
Professional	49	11.89
Household income (monthly)		
Below 50,000/- (Indian Rupees)	284	68.93
Above 50,000/- (Indian Rupees)	128	31.07

Source Authors

questions ensured all participants were in the required age range between 18 and 30 years and should have made at least one purchase in the last month via e-commerce-based fashion sites. After distributing 1,256 questionnaires, we obtained 412 complete responses, yielding a 32.8% response rate (Hair et al., 2006). Though our use of a convenience sample has its limitations, students have been shown to offer reliable responses in e-tailing research (Kinley et al., 2010; Kautish & Rai, 2018, 2019; Kautish & Sharma, 2018).

Common Method Variance Testing

We drew on Podsakoff et al.'s (2003) suggestions to minimize the occurrence of common method variance in our data. Firstly, at the research design phase, item priming effect, consent bias in the survey instrument (i.e., "yes or no argument"), and other possible issues were smoothed out in our survey instrument. Secondly, we formally verified for common method variance by adopting Harman's single-factor test. The results revealed that the variance explicated by the highest factor loading was 14% only; hence none of the factors exceeded the50% threshold (Malhotra et al., 2006). Consequently, common method variance was not an issue in the present research.

Measures

To establish our measures, we first generated relevant scale items from the extant literature, followed by item refinement procedures to ensure the items' suitability in our chosen context. We then pilot-tested our items with two Marketing/Fashion Professors to further test the items' face validity before administering the survey, which revealed no issues. We sourced the following measures from the literature. To measure terminal/instrumental values, we drew on Allen and Ng's (1999), Kamakura and Mazzon's (1991), and Kamakura and Novak's (1992) scales. To gauge consumer engagement, we used Baldus et al. (2015) and Hollebeek et al. (2014) instruments. Finally, we measured behavioral intent by drawing on Goldsmith et al. (2012) and Kim and Kim (2004).

All scale items were rated on a 7-point Likert-type measures (where 7: strongly agree and 1: strongly disagree). The mean and standard deviation for terminal values ranged from 4.15 to 5.33, and 1.05 to 1.27, respectively. Likewise, the mean and standard deviation for instrumental values ranged from 2.86 to 5.28, and 1.01 to 1.34, respectively. For consumer engagement, the mean and standard deviation ranged from 4.27 to 5.65, and 1.02 to 1.21, respectively. Similarly, for behavioral intent, the mean and standard deviation ranged from 4.83 to 5.65, and 1.13 to 1.27, respectively (see Table 14.2).

Results

Anderson and Gerbing's (1988) two-stage method for structural equation modeling (SEM) was applied (Bagozzi & Yi, 2012; Bollen and Long, 1993), which includes analysis of the measurement and the structural models (Byrne, 2010). While the measurement model is utilized to assess construct validity and model fit through confirmatory factor analysis (CFA), the structural model is utilized to evaluate the hypothesized relationships described in the conceptual model (Bollen and Long, 1993).

Measurement Model Testing Results

The measurement model with four-factors was subjected to confirmatory factor analysis by utilizing the maximum likelihood assessment (Hu & Bentler, 1998). The fit indices included: CFI = 0.95; NFI = 0.96; NNFI = 0.95; RMSEA = 0.053, revealing the acceptable model fit. While the

Table 14.2 Constructs, items, and descriptive statistics

Construct	*Scale items*	*Mean*	*SD*
Terminal value	I buy online branded fashion apparels so I could sense of worthiness for myself (TVQ1)	4.28	1.24
	Online branded fashion apparel purchase is convenient and easy for my style statement (TVQ2)	5.32	1.05
	Online branded fashion apparel is pleasant and satisfactory (TVQ3)	4.96	1.16
	Online branded fashion apparel purchases make me happy for myself (TVQ4)	4.15	1.24
	Though the cost of online branded fashion products is greater still I am willing to buy them (TVQ5)	5.33	1.27
Instrumental value	Online branded fashion apparels are convenient to shop (IVQ1)	5.28	1.01
	Online branded fashion apparel shopping is rational and practical to me (IVQ2)	4.74	1.15
	It is not a money wasting activity to purchase online branded fashion apparels (IVQ3)	2.86	1.34
	Online branded fashion apparels are suitable for me to wear and in fitting (IVQ4)	5.24	1.07
	Online branded fashion apparels quality is always very good (IVQ5)	4.92	1.14
Consumer engagement	Online branded fashion apparels get me to think about online shopping (CEQ1)	4.41	1.02
	I think about branded fashion a lot when I buy apparel online (CEQ2)	5.65	1.06
	Branded fashion apparels arouses my curiosity to learn more about online shopping (CEQ3)	5.30	1.21
	I feel very confident when I shop for online branded fashion apparels (CEQ4)	4.27	1.15
	Online branded fashion apparel shopping makes me happy (CEQ5)	5.25	1.09
	I feel good when I shop branded fashion apparel online (CEQ6)	4.80	1.17
	I'm proud to shop for branded fashion apparel online (CEQ7)	5.13	1.21
	I devote a lot of time buying online branded fashion apparel compared to any other shopping mode (CEQ8)	4.94	1.25

(continued)

Table 14.2 (continued)

Construct	*Scale items*	*Mean*	*SD*
	Whenever I shop for branded fashion apparels, I usually shop online (CEQ9)	4.89	1.37
	The X fashion portal is one of the online portal I usually shop branded fashion apparels (CEQ10)	4.05	1.38
Behavioral intent	I am willing to carry on purchasing online branded fashion apparels in the future also (BIQ1)	4.83	1.27
	I am willingto recommend the online branded fashion apparels to my relatives, friends and others (BIQ2)	5.65	1.13
	I am willing to increase purchase/use of online branded fashion apparels for me (BIQ3)	5.23	1.18

Source Authors' data analysis
SD, Standard Deviation

model's Chi-square was significant: $\chi^2 = 268.39$; $df = 96$ ($p < 0.001$). The attained χ^2/df was 2.79, which is within the tolerable range of 2–5 (Bagozzi & Yi, 2012).

However, two instrumental values items, and one terminal values item, did not fulfill the minimum threshold of 0.40 on their respective standardized factor loadings (Fornell & Larcker, 1981). These items were thus eliminated from further data analysis, thus improving the model's reliability and lowering the scale's measurement error (Nunnally & Bernstein, 1994). The residual 15 items were tested through confirmatory factor analysis, which led to an acceptable model fit: CFI = 0.97; NFI = 0.96; NNFI = 0.97, RMSEA = 0.055; and $\chi^2 = 216.85$; $df = 82$ ($p < 0.001$; Bagozzi & Yi, 2012). The measurement model results considerably improved, as the delta Chi-square estimates between the first and second CFA models estimate was significant: $\Delta\chi^2 = 51.54$; $\Delta df = 14$ ($p < 0.001$). All items exceeded the minimum threshold of 0.40 for their standardized factor loadings (Hu & Bentler, 1999).

Construct Reliability and Validity Testing Results

Our constructs' convergent validity was established by considering average variance extracted (AVE) and composite reliability (CR). Convergent validity testing indicated that all constructs' items correlated well with each other (Hair et al., 2006). Moreover, the AVE and CR were within the tolerable limits: AVE > 0.50; CR > 0.70 and CR > AVE (Fornell & Larcker, 1981; Hair et al., 2006). Our constructs' AVEs were calculated and matched with Fornell and Larcker's (1981) ratio, which yielded results exceeding.50 (see Table 14.3), supporting convergent validity of the constructs. Average shared squared variance (ASV), maximum shared squared variance (MSV), and AVE was employed to test for discriminant validity (Hair et al., 2006).

As per Fornell and Larcker (1981), higher AVE values (vs. the shared variance amongst the squared correlations for separately construct pair) establish discriminant validity. Since the ASV and MSV values were lower than the AVEs, the constructs were shown to not correlate highly, thereby confirming discriminant validity (Table 14.3). Further, to ascertain the internal consistency or reliability of the scale items, we used reliability coefficient (Cronbach's alpha). All Cronbach's alpha values bettered the minimum threshold of 0.70 (Nunnally & Bernstein, 1994), thus confirming the adequate reliability of the constructs (Jöreskog, 1993).

Structural Model

The structural model was examined by using maximum likelihood assessment. The structural model results are as follows: CFI = 0.98; NFI = 0.97; NNFI = 0.97, RMSEA = 0.056 and $\chi^2 = 220.84$; $df = 83$ ($p <$ 0.001, revealing acceptable model fit (Bagozzi & Yi, 2012; Byrne, 2010; also see Table 14.4). The model's structural relationships are shown in the Fig. 14.1. As presented in the Table 14.4 and Fig. 14.1, the association of terminal values and CE was significant, leading to the acceptance of H_{1a}. Likewise, the association of instrumental values and CE support H_{1b}. These outcomes show that both instrumental and terminal values are key drivers of CE. Moreover, as instrumental and terminal values were evident to exert a significant influence on behavioral intent, H_{2a} and H_{2b}were also accepted. As expected, CE emerged as a significant

Table 14.3 Measurement model

	Measure	*Terminal values*	*Instrumental values*	*Consumer engagement*	*Behavioral intention*	*MSV*	*AVE*	*ASV*	*CR*
1	Terminal values	1.00				0.373	0.618	0.274	0.762
2	Instrumental values	0.683 (0.469)	1.00			0.365	0.548	0.305	0.746
3	Consumer engagement	0.691 (0.482)	0.792 (0.613)	1.00		0.427	0.716	0.297	0.873
4	Behavioral intent	0.586 (0.368)	0.785 (0.641)	0.864 (0.753)	1.00	0.442	0.784	0.315	0.910

Source Authors' data analysis
Notes Measurement model fit: $\chi^2 = 220.84$; $df = 83$, $\chi^2/df = 2.66$; $p < 0.001$; RMSEA = 0.056; CFI = 0.98; NFI = 0.97; NNFI = 0.97; All correlations were significant at 0.05 level; AVE = average variance extracted; ASV = average shared squared variance; MSV = maximum shared squared variance; CR = composite reliability

Table 14.4 Structural model

Hypotheses	*Path model*	*Coefficient*	*SE*	*t-value*	*Result*
H_{1a}	Terminal value → Consumer engagement	0.33	0.053	3.65**	Supported
H_{1b}	Instrumental value → Consumer engagement	0.57	0.075	6.39**	Supported
H_{2a}	Terminal values → Behavioral intent	0.15	0.112	2.14*	Supported
H_{2b}	Instrumental values → Behavioral intent	0.25	0.071	3.25**	Supported
H_3	Consumer engagement → Behavioral intent	0.74	0.129	9.20**	Supported

Source Authors' data analysis
Notes Goodness-of-fit: $\chi^2 = 220.84$; $df = 83$; $\chi^2/df = 2.66$; CFI = 0.98; NFI = 0.97; NNFI = 0.97; RMSEA = 0.056; $p < 0.001$; R^2 (Consumer engagement) = 0.69; R^2 (Behavioral intention) = 0.76; * $p < 0.05$, ** $p < 0.01$

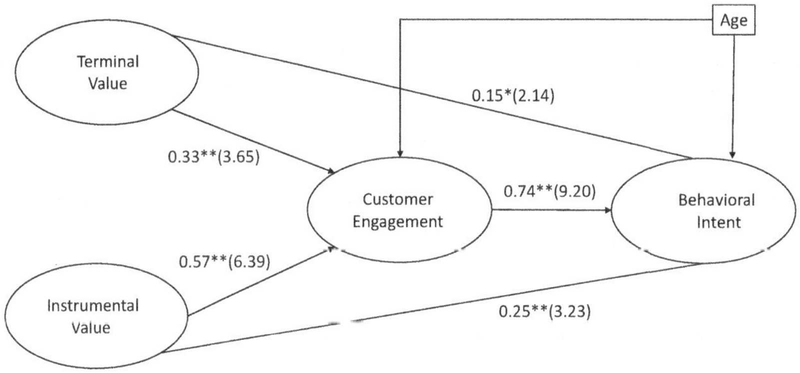

Fig. 14.1 Measures of structural equations (*Source* Authors' data analysis)

predictor of consumers' behavioral intent, thus support H_3.As the influence of instrumental values on CE exceeded that of terminal values, $H_4$was also accepted. Instrumental (vs. terminal) values also revealed a stronger effect on consumers' behavioral intent, thus accepting H_5.

Indirect/Mediating Effect Results

Mediation is used when one aims to understand how changes are transmitted from an independent variable via one or more mediators or intervening variables, which in turn affects the dependent variable (Kline, 2015; Little, 2013). Based on Fox (1985), CE's mediating effect was measured to further insight into our model. Because the data was normalized and the conceptual model was relatively straightforward, we used Sobel's (1982) test for indirect/mediating effects. Sobel offers a significance test that gauges the indirect influence of the independent variable on the dependent variable through the mediator for a single mediating model (MacKinnon, 2008), as is the case here. We thus employed the test to measure whether CE significantly affects the independent variables' (i.e. terminal/instrumental values) impact on the dependent variable (e.g., behavioral intent). The Sobel test results confirm that both instrumental and terminal values had a significant influence on consumers' behavioral intent through the mediating factor, CE (coefficient $_{\text{TV-CE-BI}}$ = 0.21; coefficient $_{\text{IV-CE-BI}}$ = 0.43) at an alpha value of 0.01. The indirect path specifies that t-value = mediating influence/standard deviation. Since the direct associations of terminal values and behavioral intent (coefficient = 0.15; t = 2.14; $p < 0.05$) and instrumental values and behavioral intent (coefficient = 0.25, t = 3.23, $p < 0.01$) were significant, respectively, CE emerges as a mediator (partial) in the association between instrumental and terminal values with behavioral intent (Hair et al., 2006).

We also measured mediation strength through Variance Accounted For (VAF) (Kline, 2015; MacKinnon et al., 2002). The attained VAF estimates exceeded the 40 percent effect for terminal values and the 60 percent effect for instrumental values, respectively, on behavioral intent, as explained by CE. In addition, as the VAF values ranged from 20–80%, these findings corroborate CE's partially mediating effect in the association of consumers' instrumental vs. terminal values for favorable behavioral intents. The total influence of instrumental values on behavioral intent (0.72) exceeded that of terminal values (0.37), revealing the significance of instrumental values in enhancing consumers' behavioral intent (Sobel, 1982).

Moderating Role of Age

Notable studies have reported that socio-cultural and demographic variables (Khan et al., 2020; Schirmer et al., 2018), i.e., age can potentially affect consumers' behavioral intent (Rather & Hollebeek, 2021). Therefore the current study operationalized age as moderator in the hypothesized model. The data analyses specified that consumer engagement was influenced by the demographic variable, viz., consumer age ($\beta = 0.13$, $p > 0.05$). Furthermore, consumer age ($\beta = 0.15$, $p > 0.05$) affect the behavioral intent for online fashion apparel purchase so H_6 have empirical results for supporting the relationship and the findings are in tandem with the previous studies on consumer engagement (Hervé & Mullet, 2009; Homburg & Giering, 2001).

Discussion, Implications, and Limitations

Theoretical Contributions

This study examined the relationship between consumers' terminal/instrumental values, engagement, and their ensuing behavioral intent in the e-commerce fashion context. Our structural equation modeling analyses confirm the proposed research hypotheses, thus suggesting the important role of consumers' values on their engagement, in particular their instrumental (vs. terminal) values. Instrumental values, which are the consumer's beliefs about desired modes of action in their goal fulfilment processes (Rokeach, 1973, 1979), while terminal values reflect one's views regarding desired end-states, as discussed. In line with consumer engagement concept's interactive and process-based characteristics (Brodie et al., 2011), our findings submit that engagement acts as an important vehicle, *through* which consumers' highly latent (e.g. instrumental) values become more observable or manifest. Put differently, consumers' core instrumental values influence their engagement with specific brands (e.g. by seeking out socially responsible brands), thus offering an important theoretical contribution (Kumar & Pansari, 2016).

We also found consumers' terminal and instrumental values to directly affect their behavioral (purchase intent) for particular brands, in addition to the mediated path via consumer engagement. The findings substantiate the strong role of consumers' values on consumer behavior. The indirect, mediated path via consumer engagement, in particular, suggests engagement's capacity as a strategic opportunity for managers. That is, by designing their marketing mix to fit with or appeal to consumers' key (e.g. instrumental) values, an important strategic opportunity exists to first capture and then capitalizes on consumer engagement. For example, brands aligned with consumers' instrumental values (e.g. purchasing a gym membership to achieve the terminal value of getting fit), are likely to favorably impact consumer engagement and sparking its positive (vs. negative) expressions (Clark et al., 2020). In turn, once consumers are engaged, their brand-related behavioral intent rises in parallel (Rather et al., 2018).

Managerial Contributions

The current study also provides important managerial strategies for managers. First, we uncovered that consumers' terminal and instrumental values directly affect consumers' behavioral intent, as well as via an indirect path mediated by consumer engagement. Our results therefore suggest that appealing to consumers' values represents a viable basis for marketing tactics and strategy (Hui et al., 2000). It is therefore critical to understand consumers' main driving values, distinguish their core (vs. peripheral) values, and design brand-related marketing mixes in line with particular customer segments' core (e.g. instrumental) values (Marbach et al., 2019). As marketers build their brands' unique personality or identity (Aaker, 1997), they are advised to align their brands' values with those of their key (prospective) customer segments, which based on our findings is expected to induce their respective engagement with particular brands. As differing values may dominate across segments, managers also need to understand their respective values-based differences to establish effective segment-specific strategies (Kautish & Rai, 2019). To incite or optimize values-based engagement, we recommend brands to offer consumers regular linking and reminders of the ways in which consumers' personal values align with and are reflected in those of the brand (e.g. through authentic, opt-in-based content marketing deploying high brand symbolism; Cooper et al., 2019; Hollebeek & Macky, 2019).

Second, we identified consumers' instrumental (vs. terminal) values to *asymmetrically* impact consumer engagement and behavioral intent, with instrumental values playing a more decisive role. To stimulate engagement's development by drawing on consumers' instrumental values, we recommend marketers to emphasize the nature of the customer's journey in their brand-related marketing mix. The rationale for this assertion is that the customer journey fits with instrumental values' process-based nature, including the brand's *modus operandi*, as outlined. The customer journey comprises a series of touchpoints or engagement episodes that collectively make up the journey (Lemon & Verhoef, 2016). Herein, each of touchpoint offers an opportunity to engage consumers by appealing to their instrumental values, which may be also be linked to the achievement of their desired end-states or terminal values. Ideally, marketing strategies should be designed to attain consumers' instrumental as well as terminal values.

Limitations and Further Research

Despite of its notable contribution to the scholarly exploration on consumer engagement, the present research has a few limitations, which should be identified for future studies. First, our data was sourced from a single country (India), by using convenience sampling, and therefore, the findings may not be generalized for other regions. Thus, further research may be conducted in different (e.g. cultural) settings, thus enhancing academic acumen with respect to the role of consumer values in shaping their engagement with brands, which is likely to vary across cultures or countries (Gupta et al., 2018; Hollebeek, 2018).

Second, though we explored the effect of consumers' terminal/instrumental values on their ensuing engagement, future studies may like to extend our model (i.e., by incorporating additional constructs, such as consumer involvement, brand love, brand attachment, and so so). The specific constructs contained in future models should be guided by the particular perspective deployed (e.g. by adopting differing or potentially competing values paradigms, such as List of Values or Values and Life Styles, as discussed).

Third, since consumer engagement is a state-based variable that may fluctuate over time (Brodie et al., 2011; Calder et al., 2009), the model should ideally be examined in a longitudinal research design, which - unlike our cross-sectional data-affords a better ability to capture this variability (Viswanathan et al., 2017). For example, the attained results may reveal varying perceived importance levels of particular values throughout the consumer's life-cycle, with particular values differentially affecting their engagement and behavioral intent over time.

References

Aaker, J. L. (1997). Dimensions of brand personality. *Journal of Marketing Research, 34*(3), 347–356.

Aghekyan-Simonian, M., Forsythe, S., Kwon, W. S., & Chattaraman, V. (2012). The role of product brand image and online store image on perceived risks and online purchase intentions for apparel. *Journal of Retailing and Consumer Services, 19*(3), 325–331.

Allen, M. W., & Ng, S. H. (1999). The direct and indirect influences of human values on product ownership. *Journal of Economic Psychology, 20*(1), 5–39.

Allen, M. W., Ng, S. H., & Wilson, M. (2002). A functional approach to instrumental and terminal values and the value-attitude-behavior system of consumer choice. *European Journal of Marketing, 36*(1/2), 111–135.

Anderson, J. C., & Gerbing, D. W. (1988). Structural equation modeling in practice: a review and recommended two-step approach. *Psychological Bulletin, 103*(3), 411–423.

Bagozzi, R. P., & Yi, Y. (2012). Specification, evaluation, and interpretation of structural equation models. *Journal of the Academy of Marketing Science, 40*(1), 8–34.

Baldus, B. J., Voorhees, C., & Calantone, R. (2015). Online brand community engagement: Scale development and validation. *Journal of Business Research, 68*(5), 978–985.

Bollen, K. A., & Long, S. J. (1993). *Testing structural equation models*. Sage.

Bowden, J. L.-H., Conduit, J., Hollebeek, L. D., Luoma-aho, V., & Solem, B. A. (2017). Engagement valence duality and spillover effects in online brand communities. *Journal of Service Theory and Practice, 27*(4), 877 897.

Brodie, R. J., Hollebeek, L. D., Jurić, B., & Ilić, A. (2011). Customer engagement: Conceptual domain, fundamental propositions, and implications for research. *Journal of Service Research, 14*(3), 252–271.

Brodie, R. J., Ilić, A., Jurić, B., & Hollebeek, L. D. (2013). Consumer engagement in a virtual brand community: An exploratory analysis. *Journal of Business Research, 66*(1), 105–114.

Byrne, B. (2010). *Structural equation modelling with AMOS: Basic concept, applications and programming* (2nd ed.). Routledge.

Calder, B. J., Malthouse, E. C., & Schaedel, U. (2009). An experimental study of the relationship between online engagement and advertising effectiveness. *Journal of Interactive Marketing, 23*(4), 321–331.

Carlson, J., deVries, N. J., Rahman, M. M., & Taylor, A. (2017). Go with the flow: Engineering flow experiences for customer engagement value creation in branded social media environments. *Journal of Brand Management, 24*(4), 334–348.

Clark, M., Lages, C., & Hollebeek, L. D. (2020). Friend or Foe? Customer engagement's value-based effects on fellow customers and the firm. *Journal of Business Research, 121*, 549–556.
Cooper, T., Stavros, C., & Dobele, A. R. (2019). The levers of engagement: An exploration of governance in an online brand community. *Journal of Brand Management, 26*(3), 240–254.
De Vries, N. J., & Carlson, J. (2014). Examining the drivers and brand performance implications of customer engagement with brands in the social media environment. *Journal of Brand Management, 21*(6), 495–515.
Etgar, M. (2008). A descriptive model of the consumer co-production process. *Journal of the Academy of Marketing Science, 36*(1), 97–108.
Fornell, C., & Larcker, D. F. (1981). Evaluating structural equation models with unobservable variables and measurement error. *Journal of Marketing Research, 18*(1), 39–50.
Fox, J. (1985). Effect analysis in structural equation models II: Calculation of specific indirect effects. *Sociological Methods and Research, 14*(1), 81–95.
France, C., Merrilees, B., & Miller, D. (2016). An integrated model of customer-brand engagement: Drivers and consequences. *Journal of Brand Management, 23*(2), 119–136.
Füller, J. (2010). Refining virtual co-creation from a consumer perspective. *California Management Review, 52*(2), 98–122.
Gambetti, R. C., & Graffigna, G. (2010). The concept of engagement: a systematic analysis of the ongoing marketing debate. *International Journal of Market Research, 52*(6), 801–826.
Goldsmith, R. E., Flynn, L. R., & Clark, R. A. (2012). Materialistic, brand engaged and status consuming consumers and clothing behaviours. *Journal of Fashion Marketing and Management, 16*(1), 102–119.
Groeger, L., Moroko, L., & Hollebeek, L. D. (2016). Capturing value from non-paying consumers' engagement behaviours: Field evidence and development of a theoretical model. *Journal of Strategic Marketing, 24*(3/4), 190–209.
Gupta, S., Pansari, A., & Kumar, V. (2018). Global customer engagement. *Journal of International Marketing, 26*(1), 4–29.
Hair, J. F., Anderson, R. E., Babin, B. J., & Black, W. C. (2010). *Multivariate data analysis: A global perspective* (7th ed.). Pearson.
Hair, J. F. Jr, Black, W. C., Babin, B. J., Anderson, R. E., & Tatham, R. L. (2006). *Multivariate data analysis* (6th ed.). New Delhi: Pearson Education.
Harmeling, C. M., Moffett, J. W., Arnold, M. J., & Carlson, B. D. (2017). Toward a theory of customer engagement marketing. *Journal of the Academy of Marketing Science, 45*(3), 312–335.
Harrigan, P., Evers, U., Miles, M. P., & Daly, T. (2018). Customer engagement and the relationship between involvement, engagement, self-brand connection and brand usage intent. *Journal of Business Research, 88*, 388–396.

Hervé, C., & Mullet, E. (2009). Age and factors influencing consumer behaviour. *International Journal of Consumer Studies, 33*, 302–308.

Higgins, E. T., & Scholer, A. A. (2009). Engaging the consumer: The science and art of the value-creation process. *Journal of Consumer Psychology, 19*(2), 100–114.

Hollebeek, L. D. (2011). Demystifying customer brand engagement: Exploring the loyalty nexus. *Journal of Marketing Management, 27*(7/8), 785–807.

Hollebeek, L. D. (2018). Individual-level cultural consumer engagement styles: Conceptualization, propositions and implications. *International Marketing Review, 35*(1), 42–71.

Hollebeek, L. D., & Chen, T. (2014). Exploring positively-versus negatively-valenced brand engagement: A conceptual model. *Journal of Product & Brand Management, 23*(1), 62–74.

Hollebeek, L. D., Glynn, M., & Brodie, R. J. (2014). Consumer brand engagement in social media: Conceptualization, scale development and validation. *Journal of Interactive Marketing, 28*(2), 149–165.

Hollebeek, L. D., Juric, B., & Tang, W. (2017). Virtual brand community engagement practices: A refined typology and model. *Journal of Services Marketing, 31*(3), 204–217.

Hollebeek, L. D., Kumar, V., & Srivastava, R. K. (2020). From customer-, to actor-, to stakeholder engagement: Taking stock, conceptualization, and future directions. *Journal of Service Research*. https://doi.org/10.1177/1094670520977680 (in press).

Hollebeek, L. D., & Macky, K. (2019). Digital content marketing's role in fostering consumer engagement, trust, and value: Framework, fundamental propositions, and implications. *Journal of Interactive Marketing, 45*(1), 27–41.

Hollebeek, L. D., Srivastava, R. K., & Chen, T. (2019). S-D logic-informed customer engagement: Integrative framework, revised fundamental propositions, and application to CRM. *Journal of the Academy of Marketing Science, 47*(1), 161–185.

Homburg, C., & Giering, A. (2001). Personal characteristics as moderators of the relationship between customer satisfaction and loyalty-an empirical analysis. *Psychology & Marketing, 18*(1), 43–66.

Hu, L.-T., & Bentler, P. M. (1998). Fit indices in covariance structure modeling: Sensitivity to underparameterized model misspecification. *Psychological Methods, 3*(4), 424–453.

Hu, L.-T., & Bentler, P. M. (1999). Cutoff criteria for fit indexes in covariance structure analysis: Conventional criteria versus new alternatives. *Structural Equation Modeling: A Multidisciplinary Journal, 6*(1), 1–55.

Hui, C., Lam, S. S. K., & Law, K. K. S. (2000). Instrumental values of organizational citizenship behavior for promotion: A field quasi-experiment. *Journal of Applied Psychology, 85*(5), 822–828.

Iacobucci, D. (2010). Structural equations modeling: Fit indices, sample size, and advanced topics. *Journal of Consumer Psychology, 20*(1), 90–98.

Islam, J., Hollebeek, L. D., Rasool, A., Khan, I., & Rahman, Z. (2019). Customer engagement in the service context: An empirical investigation of the construct, its antecedents and consequences. *Journal of Retailing & Consumer Services, 50*, 277–285.

Islam, J., Rahman, Z., & Hollebeek, L. D. (2018). Consumer engagement in online brand communities: A solicitation of congruity theory, *Internet Research, 28*(1), 23–45.

Jöreskog, K. G. (1993). Testing *Structural Equation Models*. In K. A. Bollen (Ed.), *Testing Structural Equation Models* (pp. 294–316). Sage.

Junaid, M., Hussain, K., Basit, A., & Hou, F. (2020). Nature of brand love: Examining its variable effect on engagement and well-being. *Journal of Brand Management, 27*(3), 284–299.

Kahle, L. R., Beatty, S. E., & Homer, P. (1986). Alternative measurement approaches to consumer values: The list of values (LOV) and values and life style (VALS). *Journal of Consumer Research, 13*(3), 405–409.

Kamakura, W. A., & Mazzon, J. A. (1991). Value segmentation: A model for the measurement of values and value systems. *Journal of Consumer Research, 18*(2), 208–218.

Kamakura, W. A., & Novak, T. P. (1992). Value-system segmentation: Exploring the meaning of LOV. *Journal of Consumer Research, 18*(1), 208–218.

Kautish, P., Khare, A., & Sharma, R. (2020a). Influence of values, brand consciousness and behavioral intentions in predicting luxury fashion consumption. *Journal of Product & Brand Management, 30*(4), 513–531.

Kautish, P., & Rai, S. K. (2018). Fashion portals and generation Y consumers in India: An exploratory study. In S. Soni & V. Sharma (Eds.), *Marketing Magic for Millennials: Rise of Gen YO!* (pp. 125–150). Bloomsbury.

Kautish, P., & Rai, S. K. (2019). Fashion portals and Indian consumers: An exploratory study on online apparel retail marketing. *International Journal of Electronic Marketing and Retailing, 10*(3), 309–331.

Kautish, P., & Sharma, R. (2018). Consumer values, fashion consciousness and behavioral intentions in the online fashion retail sector. *International Journal of Retail & Distribution Management, 46*(10), 894–914.

Kautish, P., Sharma, R., & Khare, A. (2020b). Multi-Item scale development for online consumption emotion construct and psychometric evaluation for relationship marketing. *Journal of Relationship Marketing, 20*(2), 91–134.

Khan, I., Hollebeek, L., Fatma, M., Islam, J., & Riivits-Arkonsuo, L. (2020). Customer experience and commitment in retailing: Does customer age matter? *Journal of Retailing and Consumer Services, 57*, 102219.

Khare, A. (2014). How cosmopolitan are Indian consumers? A study on fashion clothing involvement. *Journal of Fashion Marketing and Management, 18*(4), 431–451.

Kim, E. Y., & Kim, Y. K. (2004). Predicting online purchase intentions for clothing products. *European Journal of Marketing, 38*(7), 883–897.

Kim, J., Forsythe, S., Gu, Q., & Jae Moon, S. (2002). Cross-cultural consumer values, needs and purchase behavior. *Journal of Consumer Marketing, 19*(6), 481–502.

Kinley, T. R., Josiam, B. M., & Lockett, F. (2010). Shopping behavior and the involvement construct. *Journal of Fashion Marketing and Management, 14*(4), 562–575.

Kline, R. B. (2015). The mediation myth, basic and applied. *Social Psychology, 37*(4), 202–213.

Kumar, V. (2008). *Managing customers for profit*. Wharton School Publishing.

Kumar, V., Aksoy, L., Donkers, B., Venkatesan, R., Wiesel, T., & Tillmans, S. (2010). Undervalued or overvalued customers: Capturing total customer engagement value. *Journal of Service Research, 13*(3), 297–310.

Kumar, V., & Pansari, A. (2016). Competitive advantage through engagement. *Journal of Marketing Research, 53*(4), 497–514.

Kumar, V., Rajan, B., Gupta, S., & DallaPozza, I. (2019). Customer engagement in service. *Journal of the Academy of Marketing Science, 47*(1), 138–160.

Labrecque, L. I., vordem Esche, J., Mathwick, C., Novak, T. P, & Hofacker, C. F. (2013). Consumer power: Evolution in the digital age. *Journal of Interactive Marketing, 27*(4), 257–269.

Ladhari, R., Gonthier, J., & Lajante, M. (2019). Generation Y and online fashion shopping: Orientations and profiles. *Journal of Retailing and Consumer Services, 48*, 113–121.

Leclercq, T., Hammedi, W., Poncin, I., Kullak, A., & Hollebeek, L. D. (2020). When gamification backfires: The impact of perceived justice on online community contributions. *Journal of Marketing Management, 36*(5/6), 550–577.

Lee, J. A., Soutar, G. N., Daly, T. M., & Louviere, J. J. (2011). Schwartz values clusters in the United States and China. *Journal of Cross-Cultural Psychology, 42*(2), 234–252.

Lee, Y-K., Park, J-H., Chung, N., & Blakeney, A. (2012). A unified perspective on the factors influencing usage intention toward mobile financial services. *Journal of Business Research, 65*(11), 1590–1599.

Lemon, K. N., & Verhoef, P. C. (2016). Understanding customer experience throughout the customer journey. *Journal of Marketing, 80*(6), 69–96.

Little, T. D. (2013). *Longitudinal structural equation modeling*. Guilford Press.

Loureiro, S. M. C., & Roschk, H. (2014). Differential effects of atmospheric cues on emotions and loyalty intention with respect to age under online/offline environment. *Journal of Retailing and Consumer Services, 21*(2), 211–219.

Loureiro, S. M. C., Cavallero, L., & Miranda, F. J. (2018). Fashion brands on retail websites: Customer performance expectancy and e-word-of-mouth. *Journal of Retailing and Consumer Services, 41*, 131–141.

MacKinnon, D. P. (2008). *Introduction to statistical mediation analysis*. Mahwah.

MacKinnon, D. P., Lockwood, C. M., Hoffman, J. M., West, S. G., & Sheets, V. A. (2002). A comparison of methods to test mediation and other intervening variable effects. *Psychological Methods, 7*(1), 83–104.

Malhotra, N. K., Kim, S. S., & Patil, A. (2006). Common method variance in IS research: A comparison of alternative approaches and a reanalysis of past research. *Management Science, 52*(12), 1865–1883.

Marbach, J., Lages, C., Nunan, D., & Ekinci, Y. (2019). Consumer engagement in online brand communities: The moderating role of personal values. *European Journal of Marketing, 53*(9), 1671–1700.

Marketing Science Institute. (2018). Research Priorities 2018–2020. Marketing Science Institute. Retrieved on August 21, 2021. http://www.msi.org/uploads/articles/MSI_RP16-20.pdf.

Mitchell, A. (1983). *The Nine American Life Styles*. Warner.

Munson, J. M., & McQuarrie, E. (1988). Shortening the Rokeach value survey for use in consumer research. In M. J. Houston (Eds.), *Advances in Consumer Research* (Vol. 15, pp. 381–386).Association for Consumer Research.

NASSCOM. (2018). #India Trends 2018: Trends Shaping Digital India, https://www.nasscom.in/knowledge-center/publications/india-trends-2018-trends-shaping-digital-india. Accessed 21 Dec 2021.

Novak, T. P., & MacEvoy, B. (1990). On comparing alternative segmentation schemes: The list of values (LOV) and values and life styles (VALS). *Journal of Consumer Research, 17*(1), 105–109.

Nunnally, J. C., & Bernstein, I. H. (1994). *Psychometric theory* (3rd ed.). McGraw Hill.

Nyadzayo, M. W., Leckie, C., & Johnson, L. W. (2020). The impact of relational drivers on customer brand engagement and brand outcomes. *Journal of Brand Management, 27*(5), 561–578.

Pandey, S., & Chawla, D. (2014). E-lifestyles of Indian online shoppers: A scale validation. *Journal of Retailing and Consumer Services, 21*(6), 1068–1074.

Podsakoff, P. M., MacKenzie, S. B., Lee, J. Y., & Podsakoff, N. P. (2003). Common method biases in behavioral research: a critical review of the literature and recommended remedies. *Journal of Applied Psychology, 88*(5), 879–903.

Pookulangara, S., & Koesler, K. (2011). Cultural influence on consumers' usage of social networks and its' impact on online purchase intentions. *Journal of Retailing and Consumer Services, 18*(4), 348–354.

Rather, R., Hollebeek, L. D., & Islam, J. (2019). Tourism-based customer engagement: The construct, antecedents, and consequences. *Service Industries Journal, 39*(7/8), 519–540.

Rather, R. A., & Hollebeek, L. D. (2021). Customers' service-related engagement, experience, and behavioral intent: Moderating role of age. *Journal of Retailing and Consumer Services, 60*, 102453.

Rather, R., Tehseen, S., & Parrey, S. (2018). Promoting customer brand engagement and brand loyalty through customer brand identification and value congruity. *Spanish Journal of Marketing, 22*(3), 319–337.

Roccas, S., Sagiv, L., Schwartz, S. H., & Knafo, A. (2002). The big five personality factors and personal values. *Personality and Social Psychology Bulletin, 28*(6), 789–801.

Rokeach, M. (1968). *Beliefs*. Jossey-Bass.

Rokeach, M. (1973). *The nature of human values*. Free Press.

Rokeach, M. (1979). *Understanding human values*. Free Press.

Schiffman, L. G., & Sherman, E., Long, M. M. (2003). Toward a better understanding of the interplay of personal values and the internet. *Psychology & Marketing, 20*(2), 169–186.

Schirmer, N., Ringle, C., Gudergan, S., & Feistel, M. (2018). The link between customer satisfaction and loyalty: The moderating role of customer characteristics. *Journal of Strategic Marketing, 26*(4), 298–317.

Schwartz, S. H. (1992). Universals in the content and structure of values: Theoretical advances and empirical tests in 20 countries. In M. P. Zanna (Ed.), *Advances in experimental social psychology* (Vol. 24). NY: Academic Press.

Schwartz, S. H. (1994). Are there universal aspects in the structure and contents of human values? *Journal of Social Issues, 50*(4), 19-45.

Sobel, M. E. (1982). Asymptotic confidence intervals for indirect effects in structural equation models. In S. Leinhardt (Ed.), *Sociological methodology* (pp. 290–312). American Sociological Association.

Soper, D. S. (2020). A-priori sample size calculator for structural equation models [software]. Retrieved on August 21, 2021. http://www.danielsoper.com/statcalc.

Sprott, D., Czeller, S., & Spangenberg, E. (2009). The importance of a general measure of brand engagement on market behavior: Development and validation of a scale. *Journal of Marketing Research, 46*(1), 92–104.

Sundström, M., Hjelm-Lidholm, S., & Radon, A. (2019). Clicking the boredom away – Exploring impulse fashion buying behavior online. *Journal of Retailing and Consumer Services, 47*, 150–156.

Torelli, C. J., Özsomer, A., Carvalho, S. W., Keh, H. T., & Maehle, N. (2012). Brand concepts as representations of human values: Do cultural congruity and compatibility between values matter? *Journal of Marketing, 76*(4), 92–108.

Vivek, S. D., Beatty, S. E., & Morgan, R. M. (2012). Customer engagement: Exploring customer relationships beyond purchase. *Journal of Marketing Theory and Practice, 20*(2), 127–145.

Xiao, G., & Kim, J. (2009). The investigation of Chinese consumer values, consumption values, life satisfaction, and consumption behaviors. *Psychology & Marketing, 26*(7), 610–624.

Ye, B. H., Barreda, A. A., Okumus, F., & Nusair, K. (2018). Website interactivity and brand development of online travel agencies in China: The moderating role of age. *Journal of Business Research, 99*, 382–389.

Yoon, C. (1997). Age differences in consumers' processing strategies: An investigation of moderating influences. *Journal of Consumer Research, 24*(3), 329–342.

PART IV

Organizational Behavior and Human Resources

CHAPTER 15

Theoretical Model to Gauge the Organization's Readiness of Flexible Work Arrangements (Work-From-Home)

Munmun Goswami

Introduction

Since early January 2020, the world is battling the biggest health scare of the century, due to the spread of covid19, creating a pandemic situation. Infection rates are high with no known cure in sight yet. The World Health Organization (WHO) declared it "A Global Pandemic" on 11 March 2020 and had outlined detailed guidelines for the world to follow. With neither a cure nor a prevention (vaccine) is yet developed, the only known way to restrict its spread is through social distancing, isolating the sick from the healthy. Thus, most countries were placed under lockdown (mid-March onwards). This has led to huge hampering of business. The way of functioning, in every aspect of life, has changed,

M. Goswami (✉)
XLRI School of Management, Jamshedpur, India
e-mail: fh18002@astra.xlri.ac.in

Rajagopal and R. Behl (eds.), *Managing Disruptions in Business*, Palgrave Studies in Democracy, Innovation, and Entrepreneurship for Growth, https://doi.org/10.1007/978-3-030-79709-6_15

some drastically, most permanently. In this context, it becomes imperative to understand how an organization is changing/how to control the change/how to successfully navigate the change, so that the organization sustains. One glaring change in work-life which has happened is the way work is being conducted. For instance, in the days of social isolation and movement restrictions, most companies have mandatory work-from-home policies implemented for their employees, whichever role possible. Thus, the importance of work-from-home mandates has become more pronounced in the pandemic situation the world is currently facing. While manufacturing, production, operations, supply chains, tourism, travel, hospitality, etc. requiring physical presence have been adversely affected, with many coming to a standstill, others who could, shifted to work-from-home for its employees in the lockdown period. Initially, there were external compulsions to do so, but then many organizations are waking up to the possibility of having continued work-from-home options for its employees, even in the post-pandemic situation. This is changing the very facet of organization as we understand, right from strategic, structural, functional as well as process implications.

Study Motivation

Though flexible work arrangements including work-from-home have been in existence in organizations since long time as a family-supportive policy/family-friendly work culture ('showing we care'), opting for this was voluntary or on consideration grounds, and hence, the impact at the organizational level (structure, functioning) have never been that significant to be explored much by prior researchers at the macro-level. The reason for choosing to inspect work-from-home is twofold—one, covid19 pandemic has made organizations opt for work-from-home, whichever role possible, thus impacting the functioning/design of the organization as a whole, and two, prior studies have not really analyzed much at the macro-level, i.e., the organizational level. I have also chosen to specifically look at the interventions required through the HRM lens, as the role of HR is also transforming with the transforming organizations, and this requires further deliberation, both for the academicians as well as the practitioners.

Scope

Since most firms are still grappling with the unprecedented situation the world is forced into, and are responding and reacting accordingly, the scope of research is vast. It is not possible to categorize nor explore them all within the limited purview of this paper. Hence, I am looking at only one such strategic change, that is, implementing work-from-home mandates, and present a theoretical model to gauge the organization's readiness to implement work-from-home policies/mandates so as derive maximum benefit for the organization.

Literature Review

Flexible Work Arrangements

Flexible work arrangements are defined as "*employer provided benefits that permit employees some level of control over when and where they work outside of the standard workday*" (Lambert et al., 2008, p. 107). While there are multitudes of flexible arrangements, researchers have broadly demarcated them under "flex-time" and "flex-place", the former meaning having flexibility in the time of work, whereas the latter meant flexibility in the location where work is done. Flex-place includes work-from-home, telecommuting, work-from-anywhere options. Flex-time arrangements include reduced workload, compressed work weeks, variable shifts, job sharing, work sharing, phased retirement, and partial retirement.

First introduced to the world by Christel Kammerer in the 1960s (Stanley, 1995), research on flexible work arrangements has come a long way since. Researchers have long established the beneficial effects of flexible work arrangements aiding employees' work-life balance (Lee et al., 2002), along with increased well-being (Rudolph & Baltes, 2017; Shockley & Allen, 2007), greater satisfaction (Baltes et al., 1999; Chen et al., 2018) and higher productivity (Baltes et al., 1999; Bloom, 2014). However, I have observed that barring a few papers, researchers focused more on examining the individual-level antecedents and outcomes. Among the studies which have addressed the macro-level of analyses, researchers explored the influence of organization's size (Kotey & Koomson, 2019), financial constraints, and workforce characteristics to managing flexible work arrangements (in small NFP firms) (Townsend et al., 2017). In another study, researchers examined data from employers and observed that industry sector, labor market conditions, and organizational cultural support of flexibility are predictive of wide-scale availability of flexible work arrangements (Sweet et al., 2014). Other researchers examined the role of flexible work arrangements toward sustainable development (Čiarnienė et al., 2018) analyzed at individual, company, and societal levels, as well as network perspective for opting for this, based on the concept of exploration and exploitation in organizational learning (Litrico & Lee, 2008). I came across only one study which looked at how flexible work arrangements are designed, implemented, work processes affected, and how structural and cultural factors shaped them (Fisher, 2010). Interestingly, there was only one cross-cultural study which I came across, comparing findings from twenty-one countries on the mediating role of national culture and organization characteristics on organizational outcomes of flexible work arrangements (Peretz et al., 2018). It can be seen from the above that none of these above studies really looked into how to gauge the readiness of the organization for implementing flexible work arrangements. This is not surprising, as the choice of working under flexible arrangements has always been driven by few selected groups (working mothers, especially with small children, dependant/ill family member(s), etc.), that is to say, some constraints the individual employee had in his/ her personal domain, which made him/her opt for a flexible work arrangement. The numbers have not been high in the pre-covid19 situations, on a regular basis. But this scenario has changed with the pandemic situation, and hence, importance as well as inclination toward such flexible work arrangements is something which is of growing interest for researchers and practitioners alike.

Flex-Place Arrangement—Work-From-Home (WFH)

Work-from-home is a type of flexible work arrangement, where the concerned person can carry on his/her work from any space/anywhere. This has been possible due to the advent of digitization, change in work profiles (jobs which can be done online/virtually/remotely), and family-supportive organization policies and practices.

Prior studies have shown that flex-place kind of work arrangements are less effective in spillover of roles, i.e., interferences created by work on family and vice-versa (Byron, 2005; Mesmer-Magnus & Viswesvaran, 2006; Shockley & Allen, 2007). Thus, the probability of occurring of conflict due to blurring of boundaries (Kossek et al., 2006; Lapierre &

Allen, 2006) is higher in flex-place arrangements like work-from home. Flexible work arrangements are associated with a variety of attitudes and outcomes like productivity, performance, and job satisfaction (Baltes et al., 1999; Chen et al., 2018), this holds true even after controlling for gender, age, marital status, education, number of children, and hours worked (Mcnall et al., 2009). On the flipside, flex-place arrangements like WFH also increases the probability of work-to-family due to blurring of boundaries in conflict situations (Kossek et al., 2006; Lapierre & Allen, 2006). Benefits to the employees include greater work-life-balance, lesser commute time, lower stress, thus increased well-being (Mcnall et al., 2009; Hayman, 2009; Rudolph & Baltes, 2017; Shockley & Allen, 2007) and work-family enrichment (Baral & Bhargava, 2011; Jain & Nair, 2017; Wadsworth & Owens, 2007; Zhang et al., 2015). However, there are added issues of monitoring, maintaining ethics, and the challenge of retaining and developing the organization's culture, which makes this challenging for the organization.

Discussion

This section describes the current scenario, that is the Covid19 pandemic, and how it is impacting the organization, through the external factors which are created. While decoding the impact on the organization, the design challenges mentioned by Kates and Galbraith (2007) for the STAR Model of organization designing—strategy, structure, processes, rewards, and people have been used.

Decoding the Pandemic Scenario (COVID-19)

When we look at the kind of uncertain environment faced by everyone across the world, be it nations, organizations, global groups (like GVCs), inter-organizational networks, intra-organizational groups, and individuals, everyone is in a flux, forced to go the backfoot (at least initially). For organizations, the focus is forced into building resilience, sustainability, and revisiting their processes, rather than growth and expandability. External environmental changes act as a catalyst, forcing firms to change internally, to adapt, and sustain. This is coming from the Open System perspective, which defines organization as "*congeries of interdependent flows and activities linking shifting coalitions of participants embedded in wider material-resource and institutional environments*" (Scott & Davis,

2007, p. 32). Thus, the focus is more on the process than on the structure, valuing the interdependencies with the environment. In a crisis situation, like the covid19 pandemic, organizational performance is hampered due to both external and internal challenges and restructuring to adapt to such challenges require not only an in-depth understanding of the external environment, but also organization designing to address the same (Lin et al., 2006).

There is little doubt on this unprecedented situation being a Black Swan event. As per Taleb (2007), an event is called a Black Swan Event when (a) it is high-profile, hard-to-predict, rare beyond normal expectation, (b) probability of its occurrence is non-computable, and (c) psychological biases are present due to uncertainty and rarity of the event as also its huge role in history. Apart from numerous blogs claiming the Black Swan event leading to a global economic crisis (worse than the Great Depression in America), multiple researchers have already published articles substantiating this claim with support and evidence (Balsa-Barreiro et al., 2020; Mazzoleni et al., 2020; Platje et al., 2020; Wind et al., 2020). This background is essential to investigate the far-reaching impact the pandemic situation has already created and is expected to be furthered in the future. The uncertainty situation in which the whole world is pushed into has changed the way organizations are functioning, some drastically, some not so much. Among the numerous impacts of this pandemic situation at various levels (world, nation, firm, group, individual), the external macro-factors, which, are the ones needing immediate attention of the organization have been listed.

External Factors Impacting the Organization

Economic Recession

Countries across the globe have been plunged into recession due to the global pandemic. IMF has warned that we are into a global recession, worse than the 2008 Financial crisis. The global growth rate was pegged at –3% in April 2020, and revised to a grimmer –4.9% in June 2020.[1] During the lockdown period (March–July/August 2020), countries across the world had gone into recession, and experts predict little

[1] Retrieved on 4 October 2020 at 00:03 hrs from https://www.imf.org/en/Publications/WEO/Issues/2020/06/24/WEOUpdateJune2020.

chance of a V-shaped recovery. Admittedly, though the impact of the pandemic has been adverse for all, the intensity has been different for different industries, with the most hard-hit ones being manufacturing, aviation, tourism, and hospitality services. Growth has been dealt yet another blow with global value chains, supply chains et al. shocked into exposing their weakest points, and firms and multi-national companies (MNCs) and trans-national companies (TNCs), from startup to e-commerce giants, have all had to think on their feet, be agile, shifting focus on building resilience and sustainability, in place of the aggressive vision of exponential growth of the last decade.

Deglobalization

Some researchers have opined that the third wave of deglobalization has already started (Tang, 2020). Along with already present geopolitical tensions (U.S–China trade wars, sanctions imposed by the U.S. on various countries, Brexit, etc.), the pandemic has triggered risk-aversion among organizations as well as individuals. Global trade has become, and is destined to become more fragmented, with the rise in AI, digitization, and other technological progresses. China, from being the biggest supplier to the world, has lost credibility, and many nations are cutting/decreasing their dependencies on the country from whose labs the covid19 virus has been alleged to be generated. Most countries had sealed their borders, and the aviation, tourism, and hospitality industry being severely hit due to the movement restrictions imposed by the pandemic. World travel, business or pleasure, has been hit tremendously under this very eminent scare, with countries worldwide imposing travel restrictions, quarantines, and curfews, quite a few still remaining. Even the role of global value chains (GVCs) is getting redefined, with new equations being formed (China's role lessening and other developing nations of Asia gaining prominence, including India). Disruptions to global value chains, however, pose additional risk of amplifying the shocks of the pandemic on the trade, production, as well as the financial markets.

Accelerated Digitization

Due to social movement restrictions, online platforms came to the rescue for the socially isolated human beings. Forced to stay at home, unable to venture out, people turned to online avenues for business, education, entertainment, and social interactions. Schools and colleges and offices, whoever can, shifted to working from home, and continue to do so. Digitization has been accelerated. While progresses in machine learning, artificial intelligence, IoT had ushered in Industry 4.0, with the pandemic situation, the focus has shifted to furtherance of digitization, especially to the masses. For example, in the education sector, digitization had been sporadic till now (reference point here is India). Prior to the pandemic, only some schools, colleges, and universities of urban India boasted of being at par with contemporaries worldwide. Post covid19 lockdown was imposed, education institutions, right from pre-schoolers to doctoral students, were forced to relook, revamp, and retrain to use digital as a medium for teaching, and thus online classes were started full-swing. Though a lot still remains to be done, especially for the rural students, stop gap arrangements have been made, and fast. For organizations, work-from-home mandates for employees has furthered the requirement of digitization. Firms have rushed to implement work-from-home directives, however well-prepared or ill-prepared they were to do so. This has created new challenges and opportunities for all the parties involved. Right from internet connectivity issues to security problems, the challenges thrown up are many, let alone the concerns of well-being of the employee.

Cybersecurity Concerns

Cybersecurity is defined as "*the organization and collection of resources, processes, and structures used to protect cyberspace and cyberspace-enabled systems from occurrences that misalign de jure from* de facto *property rights*" (Craigen et al., 2014). With accelerated digitization came the concerns of security and safety. Cybercrime had risen manifold since the onset of the pandemic, due to the vulnerabilities in the cyber landscape. Security flaws in tools used, malware and ransomware attacks, hacking, attack on digital payment systems—all point toward the risk of data breaches and frauds (phishing, scamming). This holds especially true for rural and semi-urban population of India. Additionally, with the rise in the levels of online activities, confidentiality, integrity, and network traffic (bandwidth) are of significant concern, more so for remote-working arrangements.